Humans and Other Animals

Anthropology, Culture and Society

Series Editors:

Professor Vered Amit, Concordia University
and
Dr Jon P. Mitchell, University of Sussex

Recent titles:

HUMANS AND OTHER ANIMALS

Cross-Cultural Perspectives on Human–Animal Interactions

Samantha Hurn

PlutoPress
www.plutobooks.com

First published 2012 by Pluto Press
345 Archway Road, London N6 5AA
www.plutobooks.com

Distributed in the United States of America exclusively by
Palgrave Macmillan, a division of St. Martin's Press LLC,
175 Fifth Avenue, New York, NY 10010

A catalogue record for this book is available from the British Library

ISBN   9780745331201   Hardback
ISBN   9780745331195   Paperback

Library of Congress Cataloging in Publication Data applied for

This book is printed on paper suitable for recycling and made from fully managed
and sustained forest sources. Logging, pulping and manufacturing processes are
expected to conform to the environmental standards of the country of origin.

10   9   8   7   6   5   4   3   2   1

Designed and produced for Pluto Press by Chase Publishing Services Ltd
Typeset from disk by Stanford DTP Services, Northampton, England
Simultaneously printed digitally by CPI Antony Rowe, Chippenham, UK and
Edwards Bros in the United States of America

Contents

Series Preface

Anthropology is a discipline based upon in-depth ethnographic works that deal with wider theoretical issues in the context of particular, local conditions – to paraphrase an important volume from the series: *large issues* explored in *small places*. This series has a particular mission: to publish work that moves away from an old-style descriptive ethnography that is strongly area-studies oriented, and offer genuine theoretical arguments that are of interest to a much wider readership, but which are nevertheless located and grounded in solid ethnographic research. If anthropology is to argue itself a place in the contemporary intellectual world, then it must surely be through such research.

We start from the question: 'What can this ethnographic material tell us about the bigger theoretical issues that concern the social sciences?' rather than 'What can these theoretical ideas tell us about the ethnographic context?' Put this way round, such work becomes *about* large issues, *set in* a (relatively) small place, rather than detailed description of a small place for its own sake. As Clifford Geertz once said, 'Anthropologists don't study villages; they study *in* villages.'

By place, we mean not only geographical locale, but also other types of 'place' – within political, economic, religious or other social systems. We therefore publish work based on ethnography within political and religious movements, occupational or class groups, among youth, development agencies, and nationalist movements; but also work that is more thematically based – on kinship, landscape, the state, violence, corruption, the self. The series publishes four kinds of volume: ethnographic monographs; comparative texts; edited collections; and shorter, polemical essays.

We publish work from all traditions of anthropology, and all parts of the world, which combines theoretical debate with empirical evidence to demonstrate anthropology's unique position in contemporary scholarship and the contemporary world.

Professor Vered Amit
Dr Jon P. Mitchell

1
Why Look at Human–Animal Interactions?

The merits of studying human interactions with other nonhuman or other-than-human animals (henceforth animals) have been recognized for some time by scholars from across the social sciences and humanities. While social and cultural anthropologists (henceforth anthropologists) have certainly had a hand in furthering our understanding of human–animal interactions, especially in recent years, it has been scholars from cognate disciplines such as philosophy, sociology, social history and cultural geography who have taken the lead. There are some noteworthy anthropological examples from the discipline's early years, such as Evans-Pritchard's study of the Sudanese Nuer's 'bovine idiom' (1940), or Rappaport's (1967, 1968) observations of Tsembaga Maring 'pig love', but these forays into the realms of human interactions with other animals were exceptions that proved the rule.

It is perhaps unsurprising that anthropologists have traditionally been disinclined towards the study of the human–animal bond, or at least less inclined than colleagues in cognate subject areas. Indeed, it might be argued that their disinclination is largely a result of the perceived semantic and ideological boundaries of their discipline (see also chapters 3 and 16). Anthropology, more so than any other social science or humanities subject, is premised, as the etymology of the name suggests – it loosely translates as 'knowledge of man' – on the primacy of the human. This in turn suggests the presence of fundamental and immutable differences between humans and other animals. As a result, as far as most anthropologists have been concerned, animals are of peripheral interest at best, constituting mere objects to be utilized by the human subjects of ethnographic inquiry.

While it has been perfectly acceptable for *biological* or *physical* anthropologists to consider the relationships between humans and other nonhuman primates within an evolutionary framework, *social* or *cultural* anthropologists have been constrained by the limits set by their species. Yet such a distinction is, like all systems

1

of classification, not only arbitrary but also a cultural construct, and one which is not necessarily shared by many of the human cultures and societies which have themselves been the focus of anthropological attention.

Over time, as anthropologists have become intimately familiar with a diverse range of world views, systems of classification and cultural practices, they have also come to scrutinize what it is they are doing and why. In the process, the 'animal question' has become increasingly pressing. Indeed, the burgeoning interest in human–animal interactions in contemporary anthropology can be regarded as an inevitable consequence of the so-called reflexive turn, of the introspection and critical analysis of anthropology as an academic discipline and professional practice which emerged in response to a series of disciplinary 'crises' in the 1960s. First, there was the recognition that anthropologists and their ethnographic data often played decisive roles in colonial activities; second, the recognition that anthropology was at times an ethnocentric and androcentric discipline whose (predominantly male, predominantly white Euro-American) practitioners had presented a male-biased view of the male realms of indigenous societies; and, third, the recognition that objectivity in ethnographic research was an unattainable goal.

Each of these 'crises' will be discussed in more detail in subsequent chapters, but it is worth dwelling on the third a little longer here. It is an unfortunate irony that Bronislaw Malinowski, the so-called 'founding father' of British social anthropology, who established ethnographic fieldwork as a methodological paradigm, was also inadvertently responsible for the ideological shift which led to 'objectivity' being dispelled as a methodological myth. While his published academic work advocated grasping 'the native's point of view' (1922: 25) the posthumous publication of Malinowski's personal diary revealed that the fieldworker can never completely discard his or her cultural baggage. This point is perfectly illustrated, coincidentally enough, in relation to 'the natives', animals and their collective 'irrelevance' (as far as Malinowski was concerned) to the anthropological endeavour: 'I see the life of the native as utterly devoid of interest or importance, something as remote from me as the life of a dog ...' (1967: 167).

THE COMPARATIVE APPROACH

Anthropologists study what it means to be human, and while the purported aim of anthropologists since the days of Malinowski has been to study humanity 'through its diverse manifestations' (Lévi-Strauss, 1985 [1983]: 49), in reality anthropologists have traditionally been concerned with the comparative study of 'otherness'. In the colonial past, indigenous peoples were the 'others' against whom proto-anthropologists, the so-called armchair theorists such as J.G. Frazer (1922) and E.B. Tylor (1968 [1871]) measured their own 'civilization'.

In the contemporary postcolonial world, anthropological attitudes towards human subjects have radically changed, and the tenets of social evolutionism, which were so influential for the early anthropologists, are no longer regarded as appropriate when it comes to thinking about variation within the human species. Yet it is perfectly acceptable to think about animals within an evolutionary framework. As will be revealed in the coming chapters, some anthropologists have instead turned their attentions to nonhuman 'others' who fill the void created by the reflexive turn.

As Eugenia Shanklin noted in her own review of anthropological interest in animals up until the mid 1980s 'the investigation of human and animal interaction may well be one of the most fruitful endeavours of anthropology' (1985: 380). The reasons given by Shanklin include the diverse ways in which 'animals are used, how they function in various societies, and how their many meanings are derived' (1985: 379–80). To use (and adapt) the words of philosopher Donna Haraway: 'we [as anthropologists] polish an animal mirror to look for ourselves [and what it means to be human]' (1991: 21). This has also been true of human anthropological subjects over the years. As a comparative discipline, anthropology can only operate when there are 'others' against whom one's own ideas and customs (or those of one's 'home' society) can be measured and judged.

Ingold's (1994a [1988]) edited volume entitled *What is an animal?* brought together scholars from across the social sciences who were tasked with addressing the book's title from their respective disciplinary perspectives. Perhaps unsurprisingly, there was no general consensus in response to what is a rather loaded and contentious question, but overall the contributors did agree on two points: 'First, that there is a strong emotional undercurrent to our ideas about animality; and, second, that to subject these ideas to critical scrutiny is to expose highly sensitive and largely unexplored aspects of the understanding of our own humanity' (1994a [1988]: 1). In other words, when asked 'what is an animal?' contributors were forced to tackle the corollary 'what does it mean to be human?'

For several years now I have run courses on human interactions with other animals, and one of my opening gambits is to ask students how they personally would define the term 'animal'. More often than not definitions exclude mention of the human animal, and some students even go so far as to explicitly state that an animal is a living entity 'other than a human'. Indeed, regardless of our own individual perspectives on the issue there persists, for many, especially those who hail from within a mainstream Euro-American 'scientific' tradition, the assumption that nature stands in binary opposition to culture, something 'other' and 'out there', awaiting human action in order to acquire meaning. At the core of this premise lies the human–animal dualism. Animals are the antithesis of humans. 'Culture', we are often led to believe, elevates humans above other animals and the natural world. Such polarized thought becomes unsettled however, when confronted with the increasingly widespread recognition that, in addition to biological continuity between humans and animals, many of the defining characteristics of 'being human' (such as the possession of 'culture', language, conscious thought and so on) are also found, in varying degrees, outside the human species.

That anthropologists have tended to view the nonhuman members of the societies they study in an objectified manner – as 'things' in relation to human subjects, as opposed to active social agents in their own right – reveals a great deal about the world views of the anthropologists in question. So, while Haraway has a point, many scholars who comment on the use of animals in human societies do not necessarily polish the animal mirror in a conscious fashion. While they may think through, and write about, human interactions with animals, it does not automatically follow that they are reflexively aware of what it is that their thoughts and writing reveal about themselves, as individuals who have been shaped by their own personal experiences, broader cultural expectations and professional perceptions of what animals are (see chapter 16).

WHAT'S IN A NAME?

Scholars who choose to study human relationships with other animals (or who end up doing so by chance) find themselves faced with several terms of reference. I have opted to refer to my own research, and that conducted by the vast majority of like-minded anthropologists, as 'anthrozoology' because anthropologists, by dint of their disciplinary training, prioritize the 'human'. Scholars who align themselves more closely with what has been termed 'human–animal studies' on the other hand (a) tend to come from academic subject areas where the 'them/us' distinction is not so strong, and as a result (b) are more inclined to level the playing field and 'bring in' the animal, to consider the interactions under investigation from the perspectives of both the humans and nonhumans concerned (see Hurn, 2010).

Another frequently applied label is 'animal studies' which, like 'gender studies' or 'queer studies' before it, is driven by a much more political agenda. 'Animal studies' seeks to prioritize the perspectives of animals themselves. However, such categorization fails to take into account the plethora of additional specializations from within anthropology itself (some emergent, some well-established) which deal with humans and other animals. These include, for example, ethnoornithology, ethnoprimatology, ethnoentomology and ethnoichthyology whose practitioners also contribute to our knowledge and understanding of human interactions with other members of the animal kingdom.

Unfortunately it is necessary here for the sake of clarity and because of constraints of space to focus the following discussion primarily on human interactions with other mammals. This raises an important issue worthy of further consideration because in prioritizing the class *mammalia* I am guilty of promoting those 'others' who are most 'like us' at the expense of those with whom it is more difficult to engage. So, while what follows will be to all intents and purposes, mammal-centric, the implications of this editorial decision will be revisited and discussed in relation to many of the themes covered in the book.

WHY ANIMALS?

Many social scientists have documented the multifarious relationships which exist between humans and other animals across geographical, historical and cultural divides (for example, Bekoff, 2007; Franklin, 1999; Sanders and Arluke, 1993; Serpell, 1996 [1986]), and while there are a few comprehensive syntheses of anthropological contributions available in addition to Shanklin's (for example, Mullin, 1999, 2002; Noske, 1997), the comparative explosion of interest in the issues presented by human–animal interactions over the last decade or so means that there is now a much broader base of scholarship to collate, and an extremely wide range of theoretical ideas to consider. Indeed, while Shanklin was referring to the 'functions' of animals in human societies, recent anthropological attitudes towards the subject matter have also started to incorporate animals as social actors in their own right; such studies therefore, as noted above, fall more under the rubric of animal studies.

The effects of such a paradigm shift in thinking about humans and *other* animals are still being played out. Consequently, the current volume is an attempt at consolidating existing anthropological and ethnographic work which has been undertaken in relation to anthrozoology or human–animal studies or, more recently, 'multi-species ethnography' (see chapter 16) and considering the ways in which anthropological ideas about humans vis-a-vis animals have changed and are continuing to do so. However, as the field is growing all the time, this volume cannot possibly be exhaustive in its coverage. Rather, what follows is a consideration of a range of anthropological and related works and, in particular, theoretical ideas about humans and other animals in relation to key thematic areas, which, it is hoped, will encourage interested readers to consult primary texts for themselves. As anthropologists do not operate in a vacuum, influential works and ideas from cognate disciplines will also be thrown into the mix.

While there has been some anthropological debate over whether or not anthropologists should concern themselves with animal behaviour and cognition (Ingold, 2000; Tapper, 1994), aspects of ethology will also feature in the discussions. Indeed, without such input from beyond the confines of the social sciences, post-humanists would lack the necessary substance to justify their clarion call to 'bring in' the animal. The 'cross-cultural perspectives' of the book therefore also refer to the frequently contrasting and conflicting cultures within academia as well as within the ethnographic record.

A great deal of variation and inconsistency occurs in relation to the ways in which humans think about and interact with animals. Given their comparative approach to the study of human culture and society, anthropologists are particularly well positioned to be able to scrutinize these human–animal relationships. Some humans eat animals, but only certain animals, and the animals which are deemed edible vary to such an extent both within and between cultures that dietary preferences and taboos have been referred to as riddles of culture (Harris, 1974: 35; see also chapter 7).

Some humans keep certain animals as pets and these animals are more often than not regarded as members of the human family with whom they reside. Yet many humans may also eat animals who belong to the same species as the pets they keep. On the basis of such apparently inexplicable inconsistency alone, anthrozoology would be eminently worthy of anthropological attention. But there's more! For some humans, animals can be physical manifestations of gods or ancestors. For others they are servants or slaves who can be put to work, or even tortured and killed to satisfy human wants and needs. In addition to the sheer scale of the diversity of attitudes and actions which humans experience and exhibit towards animals, the historical longevity of such interactions also makes anthrozoology an immensely interesting emergent sub-field within anthropology.

ANIMALS AND HUMAN HISTORIES

Animals have always been of interest to humans. The oldest cave paintings which depict humans interacting with animals are some 35,000 years old (Clottes, 2003a, 2003b). Some scholars argue that, in addition to depicting the obvious functional relationship between hunter and prey, these paintings also represent spiritual connections which have united humans and animals in the context of a hunter-gatherer mode of subsistence since the Paleolithic (see chapter 4). The animals are depicted in great detail, in stark contrast to the accompanying matchstick-style human hunters, and such contrast is suggestive of the reverence with which humans once regarded the animals on whose lives and deaths their own survival depended. Such a reverence is still encountered by anthropologists in various fields, but this way of viewing animals sits in stark contrast to most contemporary engagements in what Bulliet (2005) has termed 'post-domestic' societies. Post-domesticity sees the separation of producers from consumers and of humans from the 'natural' world. That's not to say that post-domestic humans no longer rely on animals for their survival (or indeed that all individuals within 'domestic' or post-domestic societies share commensurate views about animals – see chapter 4). In fact, the converse is true.

Almost every aspect of human existence in the post-domestic world requires input from animals at some stage in the proceedings, from the food we eat and clothes we wear to the medicines upon which our lives often depend. It is often assumed that in contemporary post-domestic societies humans are more 'removed' from 'nature' and 'animals' (a premise which subsequent chapters will investigate and challenge), while in many of the 'domestic' (or pre-domestic) societies which have traditionally been the focus of anthropological attention, humans and animals live in much closer proximity. A consideration of such subsistence arrangements is just one of numerous ways in which anthropologists try to shed light on conflicting attitudes and relationships between humans and animals.

Take the relationships between humans and pigs. Many post-domestic societies consume vast quantities of pork products, but it is highly unusual for post-domestic individuals to kill the animals they consume themselves. In much of Europe and the United States for example, the process of hog production is undertaken in factory conditions, which places the pigs themselves out of sight and out of mind (Thu and Durrenberger, 1998). Even in rural post-domestic contexts where individuals may keep pigs for their own consumption, they are legally bound to send their animals away for slaughter at an authorized establishment. In many rural, domestic Melanesian contexts on the other hand, some humans still live in very close proximity to their porcine charges, in a state of 'total community' (Harris, 1974: 39).

THE CASE OF THE SUCKLING PIG

There is plenty of evidence, both ethnographic and photographic, for the practice employed by some Melanesian women of suckling piglets at their own breasts (for example, Bulmer, 1967: 20; Dwyer and Minnegal, 2005: 37). Care and attention will be lavished on these piglets, who may also be given names and referred to by their human carers as their 'children'. Such a striking representation of the level of attachment which can be formed with a domestic animal, an animal which will eventually be killed and eaten by its human 'mother', is quite unsettling to most post-domestic sensibilities.

There are several interesting questions which arise from this complex situation, but they do not relate exclusively to the relationship between the woman with the piglet at her breast. Nor are they exclusively concerned with the features of some Melanesian societies which allow for such seemingly contradictory interactions to happen. While these are of significant anthropological interest, of equal import are the questions concerning the reactions of post-domestic audiences, which typically take the form of shock, horror, disgust or a combination of the three. What is it about the practice that makes it so objectionable to 'outsiders'?

The idea of breastfeeding a piglet might be shocking to many for any number of reasons. First, perhaps, because of the appalling conditions in which most pigs in the post-domestic world are kept (see Serpell, 1996). The fact that in other (predominantly 'domestic') contexts people can treat pigs as quasi-humans is thus unsettling for those who don't because it forces a reconsideration of what is 'normal' (and conversely why such a 'transgression' is not; see also chapters 15 and 16).

Second, perhaps because in a specifically European context breastfeeding has a rather long and convoluted social history attached to it. Wet nurses have commonly been used in many parts of the world where women experience high rates of mortality in childbirth. In European history, there has been a tradition of working-class women acting as wet nurses for babies of higher rank, thereby freeing their mothers from the constraints of caring for young dependent children. It is interesting to note (as Mullin, 1999: 213 also does) that the Swedish biologist Carl von Linné (Linnaeus), who was responsible for devising the taxonomic system which is a common scientific system for classifying animals (see chapter 6), was also influential in turning public opinion against the use of wet nurses. Linnaeus named the class *mammalia* which included humans, as a result of the child-rearing practices of warm-blooded animals. In other words he recognized the importance of breast milk (from the *mammary* gland) in the survival of all mammals.

Despite the 'naturalness' of breastfeeding, there are still many cultural taboos surrounding the exposure of female breasts in public – largely because, in many cultural contexts, these organs are sexualized and the legacy of religious doctrine (which persists even within largely secular societies) casts the exposure of naked flesh as potentially sinful. So the act of breastfeeding tends to be a private affair between a mother and her child. The mother–child bond is widely regarded by anthropologists as one of the basic building blocks of society (Holy, 1996), and therefore breastfeeding is not only beneficial to the health, nutrition and development of the newborn baby, it also has significant implications for societal health and development.

Finally, as noted above, there is a very clear divide between humans and animals for many members of post-domestic societies. Humans are 'special', separated from other animals by their intelligence, their language, their rationality, their sentience, their immortal soul … the list is endless (see chapters 2, 3 and 10). Anthropologist Edmund Leach's treatise on the use of animal terms of abuse (1964) reveals that we reserve animal nomenclature for particularly bad human behaviours; 'They live like pigs' or 'Stop eating like a pig' are common phrases in the English language. Pigs are 'filthy animals' in the eyes of many because, to quote one of the gangsters in Quentin

Tarantino's *Pulp Fiction*, a pig 'ain't got sense enough to disregard its own faeces'.

So does any of this help us to think about why the act of breastfeeding a *pig* in particular seems so shocking? Well, pigs are 'filthy animals', and should therefore be kept at arm's length, on the far side of the human–animal divide. But this act also deprives a *human* baby of sustenance (and humans are, to many minds, infinitely more deserving than any other animal). If breastfeeding is concerned with ensuring the health and well-being of the human child, developing the mother–child bond, and leading to a stable society, how can we even begin to rationalize allowing an animal, a lesser being, an 'object' (as in 'livestock') which may also constitute a potential food source, to intrude in such a manner?

As anthropologists know only too well, it is easy to judge the beliefs and practices of others and find them lacking. A reflexive anthropological approach to the study of other cultures attempts to counter this danger of ethnocentricity through a reflexive consideration of the societal norms and individual perceptions not just of the people and practices being studied, but of the anthropologist as well. Yes, a woman suckling a piglet might be 'weird' by some standards, but is it any 'weirder' than the practice common throughout much of the post-domestic world of shooting newborn calves in the head and plugging their mothers' udders to industrial suction pumps to provide milk for human children? Which is an equally 'shocking' practice when presented in such stark terms. What is so beneficial about an anthropological approach to anthrozoology is that, in the process of looking at the ways in which others interact with animals, we are provided with a lens through which we can evaluate our own taken-for-granted assumptions and maybe, in the process, change the way we think about other humans *and* other animals.

SUGGESTIONS FOR FURTHER READING

The items listed at the end of each chapter are suggestions *in addition* to the sources cited in the main text.

Arluke, A.B. 2002. A sociology of sociological animal studies. *Society & Animals* 10(4): 369–374.

Arluke, A.B. and Sanders, C. 1996. *Regarding animals*. Philadelphia, PA: Temple University Press.

Bekoff, M. 2007. *Encyclopedia of human–animal relationships: a global exploration of our connections with animals*. London: Greenwood Press.

DeMello, M. 2010. *Teaching the animal: human–animal studies across the disciplines*. Herndon, VA: Lantern Books.

Flynn, C. 2008. *Social creatures: a human and animal studies reader*. Herndon, VA: Lantern Books.

Freeman, C., Leane, E. and Watt, Y. 2011. *Considering animals: contemporary studies in human–animal relations*. London: Ashgate.

Johnson, J. 1988. Mixing humans and nonhumans together: the sociology of a door-closer. *Social Problems* 35(3): 298–310.

Manning, A. and Serpell, J. (eds). 1994. *Animals and human society*. London: Routledge.

Noske, B. 1993. The animal question in anthropology. *Society & Animals* 1(2). Available at: http://www.psyeta.org/sa/sa1.2/noske.html

Philo, C. and Wilbert, C. 2000. *Animal spaces, beastly places: new geographies of human–animal relations*. London: Routledge.

Serpell, J. 2009. Having our dogs and eating them too: why animals are a social issue. *Journal of Social Issues* 65(3): 633–644.

2
Animality

While humans are free agents in making their own sociocultural history, animals are unfree in that their (natural) history is made *for* them. (Noske, 1997: 76)

Men confidently assert that Negroes have no history. (Du Bois, 2005 [1915]: 61)

THINKING ABOUT ANIMALS

The value of the anthropological study of human interactions with other animals becomes particularly salient when considered in relation to historical conceptions of 'animality' or the essence of 'animalness', and the use of this definitional tool to distinguish between humans and other nonhuman species. Perhaps more significant from an anthropological perspective however, is the recognition that notions of animality have also been used (and in many contexts still are), to categorize groups of humans themselves on the often dubious grounds of 'difference' (see for example, Marks, 2003; Mullin, 1999; Noske, 1997).

The ways in which humans perceive and organize the world around them (including other humans and animals) are often thought to be shaped by the specific cultural and historical circumstances within which they are socialized; fixed, culturally constructed meanings are attached to things and these become taken-for-granted assumptions which enable individuals to 'construct' a world view. The limitations of a strictly 'constructivist' model have been revealed by comparatively recent theoretical developments in anthropology such as the phenomenological emphasis on the fluidity of perspectives as a result of experiential immersion within the world (see chapter 10).

It is now widely recognized that individual experiences in the world, and the ways in which our physical bodies respond to these, are also fundamental in shaping perceptions, which can then come to be at odds with dominant 'cultural' norms (Ingold, 2000; Milton, 2002). For example, in contemporary upland Japan, where there is a long history of bear hunting and where bears are widely perceived as 'criminals' and threats to human safety, hunters sometimes experience bears in ways that cause them to rethink their perceptions of, and actions towards, these animals:

> Fujiwara Chôtarô tells of how, when on a culling mission to dispatch problem bears, through his binoculars he caught sight of a family of bears on a facing mountainside. 'When I saw this innocent scene of the parents and cubs together, even I, who has made a living by killing bears, lost my hunting desire. My heart was attacked by this all too wonderful scene, which I just stood watching, forgetting myself'. (Knight, 2000b: 158–9)

Knight does not reveal how this story ends, but such experiences, which can lead individuals to go against their 'cultural' conditioning and rethink their own values and actions, are common throughout the ethnographic record and in daily social life. They can also, on occasion, result in individuals permanently changing their lifestyle, livelihood or ideology.

While a constructivist position may at times allow individual experience to be overlooked, there is still much to be gained from considering the role of 'culture' in shaping attitudes towards and perceptions of 'others' because, while we are all individuals, we nonetheless use 'cultural norms' to ground our experiences. These experiences may then confirm or lead us to reject what we have been 'taught' to think (for example, that bears are pests and need to be culled), but in every socio-cultural context there will be a certain 'dominant' world view. Even if individuals don't subscribe to it fully, they will be acutely aware of this and it will guide their own thoughts and actions to some extent. In relation to animals, ideas pertaining to what constitutes 'animality' at a societal or cultural level vary according to context. This variation provides valuable insight into how dominant ideologies have informed both collective and individual attitudes towards 'others', human and nonhuman alike.

DEFINITIONS

The most obvious point to make at the outset is that humans are themselves animals. However, most dictionary definitions of 'animal' skirt around the issue, implying that humans are elevated beyond their animal origins by virtue of their spiritual and cognitive capabilities. For example, the *Oxford English Dictionary* defines 'animal' as:

1. *Zool.* Any living organism characterised by voluntary movement, the possession of rapid response to stimuli, and the ingestion of complex organic substances. 2. any mammal, esp. except man. 3. a brutish person. 4. *Facetious.* A person or thing ... 5. of, relating to, or derived from animals. 6. of, or relating to physical needs or desires; carnal; sensual.

The situation becomes even more confusing when the term 'animality' is considered and we are told that humans are, at least in part, animals; '1. the animal side of man, as opposed to the intellectual or spiritual. 2. the characteristics of an animal.'

So 'man' has an animal side, the side which needs to be kept in check and overcome. As the philosopher Mary Midgley notes (1994b: 192), human behaviours which are regarded as socially undesirable are labelled animalistic and this label can be applied to achieve both moral and political ends:

> when human beings behave really badly, they are said to behave 'like animals', however unlike their acts may be to those that any other species could perform. This is a way of disowning the motives concerned and distancing them from the rest of us.

This goes some way towards explaining why human characteristics and actions such as rape and murder at one end of the spectrum, and sexual promiscuity or bad table manners at the other, are often labelled as animalistic. By using 'animal categories and verbal abuse' (Leach, 1964) humans chastise and censure those others who are thought incapable of controlling that which 'society' deems inappropriate or unacceptable. Conversely this 'animal side of man [sic]' can also be a fallback position, to exonerate minor transgressions which might occur when we let our 'cultural' guard down (under the influence of alcohol or drugs for example).

Anthropologist Tim Ingold suggests that humans (*Homo sapiens sapiens*) are a species of animal, but humanity exists in 'a state of transcendence over animality' (1994b: xxi). In many contexts animality is constructed in opposition to humanity. Again, Ingold puts it well, stating, in relation to dominant post-domestic ideologies: 'every attribute that it is claimed we [humans] uniquely have, the animal is consequently supposed to lack; thus the generic concept of "animal" is negatively constituted by the sum of these deficiencies' (1994b: 3).

HISTORICAL LEGACIES

European thought on the human–animal divide owes much to the thinking of 17th-century philosopher René Descartes. Descartes (2007 [1649]) argued that consciousness was an exclusively human preserve, and most accounts dealing with historical attitudes towards animals frequently start here. For Descartes, animals lacked consciousness and, as a result, were nothing more than animated machines – their cries as he dissected them alive were involuntary and reminiscent of the springs and cogs in, say, a clock. This mechanistic approach to nonhuman life has been hugely influential in the development of 'scientific' ideas about animals vis-a-vis humans. Yet Descartes' arguments did not go unchallenged and 18th-century responses from, for example, Voltaire and Hume demonstrate further that, as a result of their individual experiences or ways of being in the world, many of Descartes' near contemporaries found his arguments unconvincing:

> Next to the ridicule of denying an evident truth, is taking such pains to defend it; and no truth appears to me more evident than that beasts are endowed with thought and reason as well as man. (Hume, 1826: 232)

and:

> Is it because I speak to you, that you judge that I have feeling, memory, ideas? Well, I do not speak to you; you see me going home looking disconsolate, seeking a paper anxiously, opening the desk where I remember having shut it, finding it, reading it joyfully. You judge that I have experienced the feeling of distress and that of pleasure, that I have memory and understanding. Bring the same judgement to bear on this dog which has lost its master, which has sought him on every road with sorrowful cries, which enters the house agitated, uneasy, which goes down the stairs, up the stairs, from room to room, which at last finds in his study the master it loves, and which shows him its joy by its cries of delight, by its leaps, by its caresses. Barbarians seize this dog, which in friendship surpasses man so prodigiously; they nail it on a table, and they dissect it alive in order to show the mesenteric veins. You discover in it all the same organs of feeling that are in yourself. Answer me, machinist, has nature arranged all the means of feeling in this animal, so that it may not feel? Has it

nerves in order to be impassable? Do not suppose this impertinent contradiction in nature. (Voltaire, 2010 [1764]: 'Animals')

So, for mechanists such as Descartes, animals were machines, while others who experienced animals in a different manner were able to recognize in them behaviours and emotions which they too shared. Such opposing perceptions of other animals can be found much further back in the historical record, in the philosophical writings of the Ancient Greeks such as Pythagoras and Aristotle.

ANCIENT DISAGREEMENTS

Pre-Socratic philosopher Pythagoras (570–500 BCE) was, so it is commonly thought, a vegetarian at a time when daily blood sacrifice and the conspicuous consumption of animal flesh was the cultural norm (Burkert, 1983). As Cartledge notes 'If there was one religious ritual that made a Greek conventionally and normatively "Greek", it was eligibility to participate in a bloody animal sacrifice, which constituted an act of communion in the strict sense' (1997: 177). Pythagoras' followers boycotted such sacrifices and philosophized on the moral and health benefits of a vegetarian diet. Plutarch, writing some 500 years after Pythagoras' death commented:

Can you really ask what reason Pythagoras had for abstaining from flesh? For my part I rather wonder both by what accident and in what state of soul or mind the first man did so, touched his mouth to gore and brought his lips to the flesh of a dead creature, he who set forth tables of dead, stale bodies and ventured to call food and nourishment the parts that had a little before bellowed and cried, moved and lived. How could his eyes endure the slaughter when throats were slit and hides flayed and limbs torn from limb? How could his nose endure the stench? How was it that the pollution did not turn away his taste, which made contact with the sores of others and sucked juices and serums from mortal wounds? (Plutarch, 2004: 385).

Aristotle (384–322 BCE) openly accepted that humans were *zoön* (animals), but animals of a particular kind. It could be argued that 'Western' 'speciesism' began with Aristotle (Ryder, 2000) and his continuum of living things, which saw humans at one end of a spectrum, the 'perfection' which for all other animals was unattainable. Yet not all humans were accorded the same standing for Aristotle and many of his contemporaries. It was Greeks, or, more specifically, free, Greek, adult men, who represented the ideal. This category of perfect individuals was defined in relation to the 'others' on the spectrum by way of a series of binary oppositions. So, for example, Greek men were associated with light, intelligence, culture, rationality and good, while their converse, women, non-Greeks, slaves, animals were dark, ignorant, uncultured (thus 'natural'), irrational and 'bad' (see Cartledge, 1997). It was on the basis of such polarized thought that Aristotle constructed the argument for one of his most controversial (from a contemporary perspective at least) treatise – his 'justification' for slavery.

Because only free Greek men possessed the capacity for reason it was thus 'natural' for those privileged few to be served by lower beings who were 'naturally' subservient; women, non-Greeks ('barbarians') and, of course, animals: 'Now if nature makes nothing incomplete, and nothing in vain, the inference must be that she has made all animals for the sake of man' (Aristotle, 2005, Book I, ll. 3–13: 7). However, while Aristotle talked of dualisms and hierarchy, and his treatise on the 'naturalness' of slavery was unreflexive (as a privileged citizen of one of the ancient world's slave-based societies, he understandably had a particular axe to grind), elsewhere he discussed difference by degree. For example, in his *History of animals*:

In most of the other animals, there are traces of the qualities of soul that are more evidently differentiated in human beings. For there are both gentleness and savagery, mildness and harshness, courage and timidity, fear and confidence, spiritedness and trickery, and, with respect to intelligence [*dianoia*], something like judgment [*sunesis*], similar in many ways, just as we have spoken of the parts of the body. For some of these qualities differ only more or less with reference to human beings, and so is man in reference to many things of animals. Some of these qualities are greater in man, others are greater in other animals, but in others they differ by analogy. (2004: 588a, 18–31)

ARISTOTLE'S LEGACY

Some of Aristotle's teachings retained currency long after his death and the decline of the Greek world. Indeed, some of the defining characteristics of a contemporary Euro-American way of life can be traced to the influence of Aristotle and other prominent Greek thinkers. As the poet Shelley remarked: 'We are all Greeks. Our laws, our literature, our religion, our arts have their root in Greece' (2008: 336). So, while Aristotle's perspectives have formed the basis of many of the dualistic positions, both theoretical and spiritual, which followed, he was not a mechanist. The following passage from *The Politics* reveals that, unlike his later followers, he did not advocate 'abuse' of 'lower' beings:

> The abuse of [the master's] authority is injurious to both [master and slave]; for the interests of part and whole, of body and soul, are the same, and the slave is a part of the master, a living but separated part of his bodily frame. Hence, where the relation of master and slave between them is natural they are friends and have a common interest, but where it rests merely on law and force the reverse is true. (2005, I.6: 1255b, 12–15)

Later scholars were selective in their adoption of Aristotle's ideas, accepting the notion of 'natural slavery' but ignoring difference by degree. Indeed, many aspects of Aristotle's teachings were expanded upon by the 13th-century theologian Thomas Aquinas, for whom animals were purely instinctual beings and, as Christianity spread, so the place of animals as resources for humans to utilize became firmly entrenched. While there are, and always have been, individuals who perceive animals as sentient beings, the widespread failure (or refusal?) to perceive the sentience of other animals provided powerful justifications for their treatment at human hands: 'So far as animals are concerned we have no duties. Animals are not self-conscious, and are there merely as a means to an end. That end is man' (Kant, 1930: 239). Given the innumerable ways in which humans are reliant upon the exploitation of other animals, it is perhaps unsurprising that these views have become so widely accepted.

MONSTROUS OTHERS

Another ancient writer, Herodotus, is important in considering the history of 'animality' in 'Western' thought. Herodotus is considered by many to have been one of the first anthropologists (for example, Eriksen, 2001), as in his book *The Histories* he provides detailed accounts of the socio-cultural institutions of different human societies based, allegedly, on his own observations. Herodotus was a Carian by birth (from Halicarnassus on what is now the coast

of modern Turkey), although by his time, in the 5th century BC
Halicarnassus was a Greek city subject to Persian rule. The Persians
and Greeks had been enemies for generations and their hostilities
culminated in the Persian Wars (480–479 BC) which saw the Persians
defeated by an alliance of Greek city states.

Herodotus went into exile, first to the Greek island of Samos and
then to Athens, where he began to write a history of Greece and the
other known countries and peoples surrounding the Greek world.
At that time Greece was not a unified country and the individual
states (*poleis*) were constantly at war with each other. In spite of
this, the Greeks as a people had a certain number of characteristics in common which differentiated them from, and united them
against, non-Greeks – what Herodotus refers to as '*to Hellenikon*' or
'the Greek thing'. These included shared culture, language, history,
religious belief and ancestry.

Herodotus' *Histories* are regarded by some Classicists (for
example, Hartog, 1988) as his attempt to show allegiance to Greece,
his adopted homeland. By revealing the animalistic characteristics
of non-Greeks or 'barbarians' Herodotus was demonstrating the
superiority of the Greek peoples. Herodotus gives the following
account of Scythian sacrifices for example:

> the victim has its front feet tied together, and the person who is
> performing the ceremony gives a pull on the rope from behind and
> throws the animal down, calling, as he does so, upon the name
> of the appropriate god; then he slips a noose round the victim's
> neck, pushes a short stick under the cord and twists it until the
> creature is choked. *No fire is lighted; there is no offering of first
> fruits, and no libation.* (2003: Book 4, 60–61, emphasis added)

Such omissions were clear markers of an 'uncivilized' people.

What is particularly noteworthy about Herodotus' *Histories*
for the current purpose, however, are his numerous accounts of
what later (under the Linnaean system of classification) came to
be referred to as *Homo monstrosus,* in other words, monstrous
humans or human–animal hybrids. For example:

> eastern Libya is low-lying and sandy as far as the river Triton,
> whereas the agricultural region to the west is very hilly, and
> abounds with forest and animal life. It is here that the huge snakes
> are found – and lions, elephants, bears, asps, and horned asses,
> not to mention dog-headed men, headless men with eyes in their

chests … wild men and wild women, and a great many other creatures by no means of a fabulous kind. (2003: Book 4, 191–2)

Later, other writers also reported the existence of animalistic, monstrous humans reminiscent of those thought to surround the Greek world. In the 4th century BC, Ktesias, a former doctor from the Persian royal court, described the many wondrous tribes living in India, including the Sciapods, who used their one foot as an umbrella or sunshade and who could hop faster than normal men could run, and the Blemmyae, who were headless but had a face in between their shoulders (de Malefijt, 1968: 112). Rather than being feared, these animalistic humans were supposed to represent important Christian virtues (for example, dog-headed people were meek).

EXPLORATION AND ENCOUNTER

The belief that the strange peoples encountered in the east were benevolent tied in with the economic links that European merchants had established to bring spices, tea, silk and other precious commodities into Europe from the Orient. Given the Socratic legacy of polarity in 'Western' thought (Aristotle was not the only ancient philosopher to use oppositions – it was a device common to the pre-Socratic and Socratic thinkers, and Aristotle belonged to the latter school), it stood to reason that if evidence of God was to be found in the east in the form of fabulous devout beings and rich benign kings with whom to engage in trade, then in the other direction, to the west of Europe, lay the dark and sinister lands which were to become the 'New World' of the Americas. Indeed, the binary distinction between 'them and us' assumed greater significance as the reaches of the 'Western' world extended rapidly during the overseas exploration and conquest of the medieval period and beyond.

In 1493 Christopher Columbus ventured west and 'discovered' first the Bahamas, and later the Americas. On his return to Spain, Columbus entertained the Spanish royal court with tales of demonic peoples who practised Satanism (Adams, 1892). The Castilian monarchy eventually provided Columbus with the funding he needed to make further voyages of discovery. However, the accounts given by Columbus and the belief that the Americas were populated by barbaric savages who were 'animals', not humans, served purposes other than the affirmation of the dominant cosmology of medieval Europe. At the time of Columbus' voyages, Spain was over-populated by nobles and there was also great competition between European mercantile nations to secure nautical trade routes with the east.

South America presented a solution to many domestic problems in Spain, such as over-population, providing prime land for colonization. Indeed, as Pieterse notes, 'the formation of images of non-Europeans [was and] is conditioned by internal European concerns' (1992: 31). More to the point, if the continent was inhabited by 'savages' then the conquistadors could take their land by force and without remorse, which they did, declaring war on the indigenous inhabitants. The following declaration, read by Rodrigo de Bastidas on landing on the coast of Sierra Nevada de Santa Marta in 1514, home of the indigenous Tairona, reveals the strength of European opinion:

> I assure you that with the help of God I will enter powerfully against you, and I will make war on you in every place and in every way that I can, and I will subject you to the yoke and obedience of the church and their highnesses, and I will take your persons and your women and your children, and I will make them slaves, and as such I will sell them, and dispose of them as their highnesses command: I will take your goods, and I will do you all the evils and harms which I can, just as to vassals who do not obey and do not want to receive their lord, resist him and contradict him. And I declare that the deaths and harms which arise from this will be your fault, and not that of their highnesses, nor mine, nor of the gentlemen who have come with me here.

HUMAN ANIMALS

Over time, and as more Europeans came into contact with the indigenous inhabitants of what became the colonies, stories of animalistic behaviours began to take the place of dog-headed men and one-eyed giants. The Tairona were accused of institutional-ized homosexuality for example, because of their gendered living arrangements (separate communal houses for men and women); this was sufficient to warrant their annihilation. Yet the most 'animalistic' behaviour of all as far as Europeans at the time were concerned, and one which has subsequently attracted considerable anthropological interest and debate, was cannibalism. Indeed, if they were cannibals indigenous peoples could legitimately be captured and sold as slaves by Europeans, their land colonized and its natural resources (for example, gold) exploited for European gain. As Midgley points out, these:

> human outsiders were ruled not to be really human at all. They could thus be placed, along with the animals, outside the species-barrier, at a distance which – it was hoped – would prevent their troubling anybody's conscience ever again. And in this way unnumbered atrocities have been justified. (1994b: 193)

This is not to say that all Europeans at the time regarded the actions of the conquistadors as appropriate or justifiable (for example, Pagden, 1982), but dominant ideology, informed by religious cosmology and a history of binary thought made colonial expansion politic, rational and acceptable as far as those in power were concerned.

Like the native peoples of South America before them (see Arens, 1979: 22–40), the indigenous inhabitants of Africa, the Caribbean, Polynesia and Melanesia were also regarded by Europeans as cannibals. Missionaries, colonists and slave traders who came into contact with these 'savage' indigenous populations sent horrific reports back to Europe of bizarre rituals involving sacrifices, human body parts, and feasts where the main course was human flesh. By regarding indigenous populations as cannibals, their European masters could deny their humanity – in the eyes of Europeans, only animals would eat their own kind. Such a view was not necessarily shared by those indigenous peoples who have themselves identified with a cannibalistic past however.

CANNIBALISM

In her review of accounts of cannibalism in what was the Belgian Congo, Ekholm-Friedman (1991) provides an insightful counter-argument to the perceived immorality of eating human flesh. Ekholm-Friedman comments on the 'ethnocentricity' of the 'Western' view that cannibalism is revolting, reprehensible and degrading. One of the reasons cannibalism was and is so troubling to many outsiders is that it reduces humans to mere foodstuffs (see also chapters 7 and 8), an act which flies in the face of human exceptionalism (see also chapter 16). Ekholm-Friedman demonstrates that this is an oversimplification and misunderstanding of what cannibalism means to those people for whom it is or rather was a cultural tradition.

In many of the areas documented by Ekholm-Friedman human meat was desirable because of similar (if inverted) beliefs in the primacy of humans; human meat was 'special' because humans had names, were intelligent and so on. To consume the flesh of, for example, a vanquished foe, was an act of incorporation which superseded the ingestion of mere 'meat' (see also chapter 7). While these differences of opinion are interesting, of particular relevance in relation to the current chapter is the apparent double standards of the 'Europeans' and the colonialists in particular. As Ekholm-Friedman asserts, viewing cannibalism as barbaric 'is, to be sure, a remarkable opinion in a culture that has been capable of the most extreme cruelty and destructive behaviour, both at home and in other parts of the world' (1991: 220).

Many of the people whose land was 'appropriated' by colonizers were also captured and sold into slavery. Turner's famous painting *The Slave Ship/Slavers Throwing Overboard the Dead and Dying – Typhoon Coming On* was first exhibited in 1840 and depicts the fate of slaves aboard an 18th-century slave ship called the *Zong*. As Warner recounts (1994: 65–79), the *Zong*'s captain decided to take advantage of an impending storm and throw overboard 122 dead and dying slaves who had been taken ill during the voyage. His motivation was purely financial, as the ship's insurance policy did not provide cover for death from illness. The slave owners and the ship's captain were eventually found guilty of fraud when they made a claim for the death of the slaves by drowning. However, Warner notes that no further criminal charges were brought against them, which highlights the way that slaves were regarded at that time; they were chattels or livestock, to be bought, sold and used without regard for their rights or welfare.

The painting itself depicts pink fish and sea monsters, representative of the European merchants who made their fortunes buying and selling African slaves. They are moving in to consume the human bodies in the water, and the image raises the question: who is the more barbaric? The alleged cannibalistic savages, who at least waited until their victims were dead before they cooked and ate them? Or the European slave traders who thrived on live meat, that is, the exploitation of these human 'animals'?

THE NOBLE SAVAGE AND THE MISSING LINK

While the land-hungry colonizers found animalistic savages in the colonies, in the wake of the Industrial Revolution the European bourgeoisie saw in the native people of newly discovered natural paradises an attractive metaphor and comparison for all that was wrong with industrial Europe – the 'noble savage' who lived in harmony with the environment (see also chapter 4). However, this positive imagery was both condescending (in the sense that it was influenced by an evolutionary perspective) and short-lived. With the advent of Victorian colonialism, the idea of the 'noble savage' was once again usurped by derogatory representations of, and attitudes towards native peoples, as described above; imperialist expansion, missionary activity and the cultural 'improvement' of the 'primitives', predominantly against their will, constituted the 'white man's burden' (Kipling, 1899).

During the height of late 19th- and early 20th-century European colonization some indigenous peoples were explicitly likened to animals. Because of the economic and political importance of Africa as a source of labour and vast reserves of natural commodities, the continent's indigenous peoples were targeted in particular (Pieterse, 1992: 36; see also Mullin, 1999: 203). Africans were incorrectly viewed by European colonialists as having no history or culture (like animals). Because they had 'nature in abundance' they were thought to be more akin to animals than the 'civilized', 'cultured' Europeans. Indeed, in accordance with the contemporaneous dominance of socio-cultural evolution as a way of accounting for 'difference', and advocating 'progress' as human societies 'evolved' from the most 'basic' or 'primitive' states through various stages of social and technological development to the most 'complex' or 'civilized' (epitomized by 19th-century Europeans), these 'primitive' people were regarded as the 'contemporary ancestors' of Europeans. Along with other 'less evolved' animals, they were thought to function largely on instinct, lacking the capacity for rational thought; they possessed what came to be referred to by anthropologists such as Lévy-Bruhl (1923) as a 'primitive mentality'.

These comparisons were 'justified' in scientific terms, as for some evolutionists African peoples such as the !Kung San represented the 'missing link' between apes and humans. Africans were therefore discussed and depicted in animal terms, with comparative photographs and portraits of African children and young nonhuman primates presented as 'proof' (see Pieterse, 1992). As Weiner's observations of Malinowski illustrate, the attitudes of anthropologists towards their subjects of study at this time resembled conventional 'Western' attitudes towards animals; 'Malinowski's strongest arguments were levelled against those who drew a picture of "primitives" as mechanical beings without individual personalities, who, as a group, merely followed the same customs without change' (Weiner, 1988: 7).

REFLEXIVITY

While this chapter has focused almost exclusively on the thoughts and actions of 'Europeans' through history, it is important to acknowledge that accusations of inhuman acts and the mistreatment of captives have also been common features of human social relations in many other parts of the world. However, the Occidental focus here is important for two reasons. First, anthropology has had a not altogether unjust reputation as the 'handmaiden of colonialism'. The link between anthropology and colonialism has undeniably played a role in shaping the ways in which practitioners of the discipline think (or thought) about their ethnographic subjects. Prior to the reflexive turn, non-Western others were 'primitives', but in the postcolonial period, when anthropologists are at pains to distance themselves from the abuses of (some of) their disciplinary ancestors, many have shied away from thinking about animal 'others' and human–animal continuity for fear of re-opening old wounds.

Thinking about animality has traditionally meant thinking about both differences between humans and similarities between 'some' humans and animals. While the reflexive turn awoke anthropologists to the fact that dominant ideologies resulted in the perpetuation of certain biases, to the extent that formerly 'muted groups' (Ardener, 1975) – women, children and the elderly for example – were largely excluded from the ethnographic record, animals have remained on the periphery. The second reason for the focus on the history of dominant European thought is to aid understanding of why, when the perspectives of 'other' peoples are discussed in subsequent chapters, they appear to be so at odds with mainstream Euro-American world views.

One final point to consider is how all of this comes together to make anthropologists particularly well placed to investigate human relationships with other animals. Humans habitually engage in 'othering' in their day-to-day interactions. This process of objectifying fellow humans in instances of war, genocide, rape, slave labour or violence and abuse of any kind is still regularly observed by anthropologists in a wide range of ethnographic situations. In the process, these 'others' are relegated to the status of lesser beings, typified in many contexts by animals. Thus the objectification of 'others' – human or nonhuman – in the past and in the contemporary world, justifies their treatment in the eyes and minds of the 'abusers'. The reason that 'animality' has been such a useful definitional tool for many boils down to a 'chicken and egg' conundrum; we might draw on the longevity of dualistic thought, which allows for objectification and the exploitation of others based on perceived 'difference', but it might also be the case that human exploitation of 'others' leads to the development of a system of dualistic thought based on difference. Through an exploration of different ways of being in the world experienced by members of particular cultures at particular points in history, anthropologists can attempt to shed light on contradictory and seemingly incompatible practices and the processes which led to them. Such an approach can in turn reveal important information about what it means to be human, or indeed animal at any given point in space and time.

SUGGESTIONS FOR FURTHER READING

Baker, S. 2001. *Picturing the beast: animals, identity, and representation*. Champaign: University of Illinois Press.
Corbey, R. 2005. *The metaphysics of apes: negotiating the animal–human boundary*. Cambridge: Cambridge University Press.
Elder, G., Wolch, J. and Emel, J. 1998. Race, place and the bounds of humanity. *Society & Animals* 6(2): 183–202.
Ellen, R. 1999. Categories of animality and canine abuse: exploring contradictions in Nuaulu social relationships with dogs. *Anthropos* 94: 57–68.
Fuentes, A. 2006. The humanity of animals and the animality of humans: a view from biological anthropology inspired by J.M. Coetzee's *Elizabeth Costello*. *American Anthropologist* 108(1): 124–132.
Fuentes, A., Marks, J., Ingold, T., Sussman, R., Kirch, P. V., Brumfiel, E.M. et al. 2010. On nature and the human. *American Anthropologist* 12(4): 512–521.
Kalof, L. 2007. *Looking at animals in human history*. London: Reaktion.
Osborne, C. 2007. *Dumb beasts and dead philosophers: humanity and the humane in ancient philosophy and literature*. Oxford: Oxford University Press.
Ritvo, H. 1987. *The animal estate: the English and other creatures in the Victorian age*. Cambridge, MA: Harvard University Press.
Rothfels, N. (ed.) 2002. *Representing animals*. Bloomington: Indiana University Press.
Sorabji, R. 1993. *Animal minds and human morals: the origins of the western debate*. London: Duckworth.

3
Continuity

Of all animals man alone can learn to make equal use of both hands. (Aristotle, 2004: 35)

We define ourselves as the only cultured species, and we generally believe that culture has permitted us to break away from nature. We are wont to say that culture is what makes us human. (de Waal, 2001: 6)

DEFINING CULTURE

Culture is a key area of interest for anthropologists. In fact, it would be fair to say that culture is a *defining* interest of social and cultural anthropologists. In addition to defining a whole branch of anthropology and its practitioners, culture is also a defining feature of anthropological subjects. Humans have long been regarded as uniquely cultural beings; while cultural practices differentiate one human group from another, culture has also often been seen as one of the ways in which humans are different from other animals. Anthropologists study *anthropos*, 'man' [sic] in 'his' most diverse manifestations. These manifestations are, in essence, 'culture'. Take for example Tylor's classic definition: 'Culture or Civilization, taken in its widest ethnographic sense, is that complex whole which includes knowledge, belief, art, morals, custom, and any other capabilities acquired by man as a member of society' (1968 [1871]: 1).

This Tylorean conception of culture is interesting on two counts. First, because it forms the basis of most subsequent anthropological definitions of culture and, second, because it rests upon the implicit assumption that culture is a uniquely human preserve. The latter point is explicitly made in the following quote from anthropologist Alfred Kroeber: 'We can appreciate what culture is by saying it is that which the human species has and other social species lack' (1948 [1923]: 253). However, culture is not the only characteristic deemed exclusive to humans. As Mullin (1999: 206) among others has noted, the general or rather dominant post-domestic view holds that while we may be animals, humans alone have language, are self-conscious, think rationally and experience emotions. Yet there is a growing body of evidence, largely generated by researchers in ethology and cognate fields, which challenges the premise that humans are 'unique' in relation to all of the counts mentioned by Mullin and many more besides (see also chapters 9, 10, 11 and 16). Some of this evidence will be presented in the following discussion, but the primary focus will be on 'culture' because of its centrality to anthropology.

As a simplified (but potentially more inclusive) version of Tylor's definition, Eriksen suggests that 'culture' consists of certain traits or behaviours which develop in a social context: 'those abilities, notions and forms of behaviour persons have acquired as members of society' (2001: 9). The wording is significant here. While Tylor specified 'man', by replacing this with 'persons' Eriksen opens up at least the possibility of extension beyond the species barrier, as in many cultural contexts nonhuman beings can indeed be persons (see chapters 4, 10, 15 and 16). So while the implication is that 'culture' applies to humans, other animals might be included if (a) they are accorded personhood, (b) their social organization is regarded as a form of society and (c) they exhibit the requisite 'abilities, notions and forms of behaviour' which constitute culture. And therein lies the difficulty. The ambiguity over issues such as: 'Are other animals persons?', 'Do their social groups constitute societies?' and 'Just what abilities, notions and behaviours are "cultural"?' allows external commentators from a wealth of disciplinary backgrounds to draw opposing conclusions on numerous grounds.

The necessarily subjective nature of interpretation means that even within disciplines where researchers share methodological approaches and theoretical orientations, there may be disagreement over whether animals other than humans are accorded 'personhood' and discrepancies with regard to interpretation of behaviours which 'could' be classified as cultural. The aim here isn't to convince readers one way or the other, but to raise for consideration the implications of all this for anthropology.

Traditionally anthropologists have not speculated on the question of whether or not animals other than humans have 'culture' – it has been taken for granted for the most part that they do not. As practitioners of a discipline which has, in the postcolonial world, undergone a series of reinventions to move away from the previous assumption that 'cultures' could be ordered hierarchically on the basis of their respective levels of 'sophistication', it is surprising that anthropologists accept such a position in an uncritical manner.

This lack of anthropological engagement with the question of culture in animals has not gone unnoticed in cognate disciplines, such as primatology. De Waal for instance sees this as 'curious', stating; 'anthropologists have hardly contested the idea of culture in animals even though culture used to be the central concept of their discipline' (2001: 214; cf. Sapolsky, 2006: 641). He continues: 'This lack of territoriality is due to their own ferocious internal battles combined with postmodernist nihilism: culture has become a politically loaded, relativistic, messy concept that anthropologists have turned away from' (2001: 214).

While the second half of de Waal's quote suggests a rather limited understanding of contemporary socio-cultural anthropological debates and concerns (an issue also taken up by Ingold, 2007, in response to a rather defamatory article published by Mesoudi et al., 2006, in the journal *Behavioural and Brain Sciences*), overall de Waal has a valid point.

The value of the 'culture concept' has indeed been widely debated by anthropologists in recent years (for example, Abu-Lughod, 1991; Brumann, 1999), and anthropologists recognize that culture is particularly difficult to define (Kuper, 1999). Yet, the belief persists that however it is defined or however useful it is, culture is uniquely human. This led de Waal to conclude 'with views such as these dominating one discipline, sparks should have flown when another [primatology] claimed culture in animals. Yet ... cultural anthropologists are nowhere in sight in this debate' (2001: 215).

The lack of anthropological participation is largely because, for many anthropologists, the matter simply isn't worth debating. It either goes without saying that culture is synonymous with humans, or conversely, if other animals are also cultural beings, this is perceived as of no real concern to the endeavour of social or cultural anthropology, whose practitioners are only interested in the human animal (see also chapters 11 and 16). Yet such positions seem to miss the key point here. The question of whether or not other animals are cultural beings matters a great deal, for a whole host of reasons.

In terms specific to the discipline of socio-cultural anthropology, if other animals do possess culture, no matter how rudimentary, this not only calls into question the classificatory framework within which disciplinary identities are constructed, but also reveals that, for all the progress that has been made since the reflexive turn, we still have a long way to go before anthropology can claim to be a truly reflexive discipline.

PERSONHOOD

'Culture' in animals has not been tackled by socio-cultural anthropologists, but nonhuman personhood is one issue which researchers
often have to face in the field, and as a result it has received
considerable attention. While in some cultural contexts, as Ingold
notes, 'personhood as a state of being is not open to nonhuman
animal kinds' (2000: 48) this position stands in stark contrast to
that found in many other contexts where humans have no such
qualms about recognizing animals as persons (see chapters 4, 10
and 16 for example). But what constitutes personhood?

Definitions vary enormously; however, there appears to be
a general consensus across cultural divides that a 'person' is an
individual, animate, self-conscious being who becomes a person in
a social context in which their individuality and intentionality is
recognized and acknowledged by another (de Castro, 1998: 476;
Kohn, 2008; see also Fortis, 2010). Again, de Waal makes a pertinent
observation in relation to differences in approach between Japanese
and European or North American primatologists, where the former
happily recognize the personhood of their research subjects:

> Being the product of a culture that doesn't set the human species
> apart as the only one with a soul, Imanishi [Japanese primatologist
> and founder of the sub-discipline 'cultural or ethno-primatology']
> had trouble with neither the idea of evolution nor that of humans
> as descendents of apes. To the Buddhist … mind, both ideas are
> eminently plausible, even likely, and there is nothing insulting
> about them. The smooth reception of this part of evolutionary
> theory – the continuity among all life forms – meant that questions
> about animal behaviour were from the start uncontaminated by
> feelings of superiority and aversion to the attribution of emotions
> and intentions that paralyzed Western science. (2001: 116)

Among peoples who have not been raised in the Cartesian
tradition, the binary distinction between human and nonhuman
and the exclusive synonymy between 'human' and 'person' does
not necessarily exist. As Rane Willerslev notes, Siberian 'Yukaghirs
… along with other hunter-gatherers, hold that animals and other
nonhumans possess qualities paralleling those of human selves
or persons, *qualities that come into view in the context of close
mutual engagement*' (2007: 19, emphasis added). This raises some
interesting philosophical questions of significant anthropological

import; which of these conflicting perspectives is 'right'? Or rather, can other animals be persons? And how might we 'know'?

Anthropologists have long believed that 'culture' provides the structure by which human thought is organized (see chapter 6). It is through this process of cultural construction that the personhood of others is either *attributed* or denied. So, for example, if we are raised within a cultural context where 'person' equals 'human' we will expect, or rather be expected, to see humans and only humans as persons, regardless of whether or not our *experience* of nonhuman others leads us to doubt this premise. In a post-Enlightenment 'scientific' context, to challenge the axiom of human exceptionalism is to indulge in anthropomorphism, because while we might think we see manifestations of personhood in animal others, what we are really doing is attributing human characteristics to animals (see for example, Carruthers, 1989 and chapters 10 and 16). This is because only humans can be persons.

Such a circuitous spelling out of the situation is obviously an over-simplification, but this simplistic rendering of cultural constructivism allows us to recognize its limitations and flaws. Many anthropologists have been 'forced' to re-think constructivism as a result of their contact with other peoples who do not *attribute* personhood, but rather *perceive* it, because in their interactions with animals the personhood of these nonhuman others is revealed in no uncertain terms (Milton, 2005; Willerslev, 2007: 20). So in cases where humans are free from the constraints imposed by a particular world view which sets humans apart from animals or where they make a decision – consciously or otherwise – to reject it, the behaviours of other animals can be observed and interpreted in much the same way that humans observe and interpret the behaviours of members of their own species (see also chapters 9, 10 and 16). Admittedly this is also a constructivism of sorts, as within certain cultures the recognition of personhood is part of the dominant world view!

Anthropologists usually discuss personhood in the context of animism (see chapter 4), but what is particularly noteworthy, given the current endeavour, is the fact that even when acknowledging the ways in which their human informants experience other animals (as animate beings or persons), many anthropologists working within a constructivist tradition still feel the need to account for these perceptions in familiar terms, as metaphorical for example (see chapter 6) which, by extension, undermines the validity of the 'indigenous' view (see also chapters 4 and 6). When employing a phenomenological orientation, however, personhood is acknowledged through interactions. So an animal becomes a person as a result of the hunter's (or indeed an anthropologist's) practical experience of that particular individual during a hunt.

The ways in which the animal behaves in relation to the hunter influence whether or not that individual is accorded personhood. Indeed, Willerslev makes a point of fundamental import when he acknowledges that in animistic thought not all animals are accorded personhood at all times (2007: 21). Neither, for that matter, are all humans. De Castro for example observes that for many Amerindian peoples, strangers are not necessarily persons (1998: 475). Nor are children (Fortis, 2010). Personhood follows from embodied interactions, and the ways in which individual humans experience individual 'others' will inform whether or not they perceive in those 'others' the requisite characteristics of personhood. Personhood will also be specific to the individual (so a human will have a particular kind of personhood, a dog will have a different but comparable kind and so on).

SOCIETY

Anthropological definitions of culture stipulate that, in order to qualify, particular abilities, notions and forms of behaviour are learnt in a social context – society. Eriksen differentiates between culture and society as follows: 'Culture refers to the acquired, cognitive and symbolic aspects of existence, whereas society refers to the social organisation of human life, patterns of interaction and power relationships' (2001: 4). Again the assumption here is that 'society' is something which humans have and other animals do not. However, even the most cursory of glances through high-ranking journals relating to primatology reveals that terms such as 'chimpanzee society' and 'baboon society' are habitually used to refer to the social and political organization of nonhuman primates (for example, Sapolsky, 2006). De Waal comments that the study on which his ground-breaking book *Chimpanzee politics* is based 'demonstrates something we had already suspected on the grounds of the close connection between apes and humans: that the social organization of chimpanzees is almost too human to be true' (2009: 4).

ACQUIRED BEHAVIOURS

So if some other animals can be persons and live in societies, all that remains is to consider the acquired cognitive and symbolic aspects of existence, the particular abilities, notions and forms of behaviour which are learnt and then exhibited by nonhuman persons in these social contexts. Anthropologists Roger Keesing and Andrew Strathern present the following example to illustrate just this in relation to human culture from a constructivist perspective:

> Consider a wink and an involuntary eye twitch. As physical events, they may be identical – measuring them will not distinguish the two. One is a signal, in a code of meanings Americans [among others] share (but which presumably would be unintelligible to Inuits or Australian Aborigines [sic]); the other is not. Only in a universe of shared meanings do physical [actions] and events become intelligible and convey information. (1998: 18)

It would be difficult to ascertain whether or not animals could differentiate between a wink and an involuntary eye-twitch and understand the symbolism of the former. There is, however, plenty of evidence which suggests that many animals are actually much better at reading such body language than humans. The infamous 'Clever Hans' (Pfungst, 1911) is a case in point. Hans was a horse who, so his trainer claimed, could understand quite complex mathematical sums. Hans' trainer would write the sums on a board and Hans would reveal the correct answer by tapping his front hoof the requisite number of times. Hans' mental arithmetic was called into question, however, when his trainer was positioned behind a screen. It transpired that rather than counting, Hans was actually reading what, to human observers, were the imperceptible (and allegedly unconscious) cues given by his trainer. As a result, Hans became widely known as the horse who confirmed rather than challenged the limitations of nonhuman cognitive abilities. But such an interpretation is misguided. While mental arithmetic is a useful skill, I imagine many anthropologists and psychologists would like to posses Hans' acute perceptual awareness of human body language! But what is additionally instructive about the example of Hans is that he 'learnt' to read the involuntary cues as a result of interacting with his trainer in a social context (see also chapters 9 and 10).

There are countless examples of individual animals who, when socialized with humans, can be taught all manner of complex behaviours. Koko, a female Lowland Gorilla (*Gorilla gorilla*) has been part of such a research programme for over 30 years. Koko, along with other gorillas at the Gorilla Foundation, has been taught American Sign Language (ASL). Not only do they use ASL to communicate with their human carers, but the gorillas also use ASL to communicate with each other (Patterson and Cohn, 1990). Moreover, as a result of her long association with humans, Koko appears to have 'learnt' how to communicate in detail her thoughts and emotions on issues ranging from death and her grief at losing mate, Michael, her subsequent fear of her own mortality and her wish to have a baby, in addition to detailed information about her particular likes and dislikes.

Koko, along with other captive Great Apes, has also demonstrated artistic flair, and what researchers perceive to be an ability to symbolically represent not just observable 'things' (such as a pet dog or flowers) but also abstract emotions such as love. I have deliberately used the term 'potential' here because, while the achievements of Koko and the other ASL apes are impressive, there remains some scepticism over just how much is being 'read into' their actions, and whether operant conditioning might be a factor (for example, Blackmore, 2000). Indeed, what is referred to as the 'Clever Hans effect' (de Waal et al., 2008) is an issue among researchers concerned with understanding the cultural and cognitive abilities of animals.

CULTURAL VARIATION

Such behaviours and abilities in captive animals, while impressive, do not necessarily convince sceptics that animals are 'cultured' because they are initiated by humans in an artificial environment. Nonetheless, McGrew has noted that 'teaching in captive apes can sometimes be directly compared with that shown by their wild counterparts' (2007: 171; see also chapter 11).

Primatologists and ethologists often refer to cultural variation in wild populations of animals, but just how their findings would stand up to anthropological scrutiny remains to be seen. To begin with, the definitions of culture given by ethologists tend to be less complex, having fewer criteria to be satisfied, and with a slightly different emphasis to those employed by anthropologists. They cover the same ground nonetheless. For example, primatologist and neuroscientist Robert Sapolsky's definition sees culture as 'regional variation in behavior that is not rooted in genetics or ecology and is transmitted beyond its originators' (2006: 641).

'Regional variation' is the ethological equivalent of an anthropologist's focus on the societal context within which behaviours are learned. As the diversity of human cultural practices documented in the ethnographic record clearly demonstrates, human 'culture' also shows 'regional variation'. The fact that the behaviours of other animals also vary across 'cultural' (or at least regional) boundaries suggests these behaviours arise and develop within particular social contexts too. If these behaviours are not rooted in genetics or ecology because animals sharing the same territories may exhibit different behaviours, the implication is that they are neither instinctive nor adaptive responses to external stimuli, but cognitive.

TRANSMISSION AND LEARNING

The final emphasis in the ethological definition is on learning and inter-generational transmission. Although absent from the anthropological definitions, it almost goes without saying in a human context that cultural behaviours must be shared and passed from one generation to the next. One of the most famous ethological examples of 'culture' in wild populations of nonhuman primates is the practice of potato washing among provisioned Japanese Macaques (*Macaca fuscata*) on Koshima Island.

The troop was initially provisioned by researchers for two reasons. First, to encourage them to accept human intrusion into their territory, thus making observation easier (much like the colonial practice of providing tobacco in return for information, as per Evans-Pritchard, [1940]), and, second, because of the commonplace Shintoist practice of feeding wild animals. The researchers provided sweet potatoes and wheat and one individual, a young female named Imo initiated a behaviour which was to become a cultural practice within the whole troop. Imo found her potato was dirty, so took it to the sea and washed it. The result was that the potato was clean, but also, so it was assumed, tasted much better (Kawai, 1965). This behaviour then spread 'horizontally' through Imo's peers, then to her mother and eventually to other females, then the whole troop (with the exception of the high-ranking older males). Imo initiated another behaviour, which also spread rapidly through the troop – taking handfuls of wheat which were also provided by researchers to the sea to separate the nutritional grains from the sand which clung to them. Imo threw the sandy wheat into the water and then skimmed off the clean wheat which floated on the surface. According to de Waal 'this sluicing technique ... was eventually adopted by most monkeys on the island' (2001: 202).

There is also a wide range of extensively documented behaviours commonly described by primatologists as 'cultural' which concern the manipulation and use of objects for both utilitarian and recreational ends. These examples constitute what anthropologists refer to as 'material culture', in other words the physical manifestations or products of culture. Again, the ability to produce material culture has also been thought to differentiate humans from animals. According to sociologist Tim Dant for example:

> Humans stand apart from other animal species ... because of the way they create, use and live with a wide variety of material objects. This world of man-made things modifies the natural world to provide a material environment as the context in which social interaction takes place. Things, both natural and man-made, are appropriated into human culture in such a way that they re-present the social relations of culture, standing in for other human beings, carrying values, ideas and emotions. (1999: 1)

This reveals a hierarchical way of thinking about culture which, as already noted, is commonplace within the social sciences. However, as with 'culture' more generally, there is ample evidence for animals appropriating 'natural' and manipulated things into their cultures. Stone-handling, also observed in Japanese Macaques (Huffman and Quiatt, 1986; Leca et al., 2007) involves individual animals collecting stones and either rubbing them together (in a manner reminiscent of the human use of worry beads) or scattering them on the floor before collecting them up and repeating the process again. This behaviour is one of the first to be learnt by infants during socialization (Nahallage and Huffman, 2007). Nut cracking is another example of a cultural behaviour, requiring the animals in question to locate and manipulate specific stone tools. It is typically observed in troops of chimpanzees (Pan troglodytes), and demands considerable skill not only in finding the right tools for the job, but in wielding them effectively (Boesch and Boesch, 1982: Matsuzawa, 1994).

The fact that other primates exhibit 'culture' is often 'explained' in evolutionary terms – because of shared ancestry, continuity is accepted to the extent that contemporary primates present useful models for helping physical anthropologists to try and recreate early human societies (McGrew, 1992). However, as Perry notes, despite the huge body of material which deals with culture in other animals, it is work focused on chimpanzee culture and cultural variation which has attracted most attention and been regarded as most credible. Perry claims this is 'because anthropologists found it more plausible to accept the notion of culture in the closest living relative to humans' (2006: 173). Yet primates are not the only animals to exhibit complex behaviours which ethologists define as cultural.

Many mammal, bird, insect and even crustacean species have been convincingly shown to manipulate and utilize a range of tools with varying levels of sophistication and success, without human intervention. Dolphins (*Tursiops truncatus*) use marine sponges to protect their snouts when foraging on the sea bed (Krutzen et al., 2005: 8939), Galapagos finches use thorns or twigs to extract larvae from crevices in rotting wood, and some varieties of assassin bugs cover themselves in sand from the entrance to a termite nest, then use the dead bodies of earlier victims to lure others out into the open (McMahan, 1983).

The following particularly innovative example shows birds utilizing both humans and human material culture:

> Carrion crows in the city of Sendai in Japan have discovered an ingenious way of cracking walnuts. They take the nuts and wait beside the road until the light turns red. Then they descend, place the nuts in front of the wheel of a car, and fly off. When the light turns green, they return and eat the pieces of the nuts that a vehicle has crushed. (Sax, 2003: 20; see also Nihei and Higuchi, 2001)

SYMBOLIC THOUGHT

But what about Dant's (1999: 1) assertion that 'things' are 'appropriated into human culture in such a way that they re-present the social relations of culture, standing in for other human beings, carrying values, ideas and emotions'? Renowned cognitive ethologist, the late Donald Griffin (whose pioneering work challenged the ways in which many scientists viewed animals), provided a wealth of evidence for symbolic thought in a wide range of species (Griffin, 2001), such as the waggle-dance of honey bees where the bees communicate information to each other about things which are not physically present (such as the location of food sources). Perhaps the most convincing evidence of this sort of symbolism in animals, where 'inanimate' objects are imbued with value and emotional significance is revealed in the practice of bone handling among African elephants (Douglas-Hamilton et al., 2006).

Elephants have been repeatedly observed interacting with the remains of dead conspecifics, and there is some evidence for elephants being particularly drawn to the bones and tusks of relatives (Douglas-Hamilton and Douglas-Hamilton, 1975; Moss, 1988; Spinage, 1994; cf. Douglas-Hamilton et al., 2006; McComb et al., 2006). The bones are examined carefully, smelt, picked up, pushed and caressed with trunks and feet. These remains are revisited on numerous occasions in the days, weeks, months and years following a death. The tentative conclusion drawn by some ethologists who have studied these behaviours is that the animals make some symbolic association with the remains of their deceased family members. These behaviours do not appear to have any evolutionary advantage and on occasion actually put the bereaved in danger of attack from scavengers who are feeding on the remains (Douglas-Hamilton et al., 2006: 98).

The particular attention paid to tusks and skulls suggest that the 'mourners' are confirming the identity of the deceased, as tusks and faces are frequently touched during social interactions between herd members when they are alive. This behaviour is suggestive of symbolic thought, as objects replace other persons, but, perhaps more pertinently, there is an emotional symbolism not observed in, say, 'symbolic' honey bee behaviour.

Another example of the ability of animals to make symbolic or abstract connections comes from experiments with dolphins where, for example, 'mothers responded preferentially to playbacks of their offspring's signature whistles and vice versa. Thus, dolphins appear to recognize the signature whistles of close associates' (Janik et al., 2006). This is referred to by ethnologists as 'symbolic referential communication'.

What becomes increasingly apparent as more is learnt about the cognitive abilities and socio-cultural lives of other animals is, as Aristotle himself noted, that differences are more of degree than kind. Admittedly other animals haven't 'created the industrial revolution, unravelled the secrets of their own genome [or] developed the concept of universal rights' (Malik, 2002: 2). They have nonetheless made significant cultural achievements which, when viewed in culturally (or 'species') relative terms, can be regarded as 'their *own* culture rather than a superficially imposed human version' (de Waal, 2001: 6; see also Cavalieri and Singer, 1996; Stamp Dawkins, 1998; Griffin, 2001; Lycett et al., 2007;

Whiten et al., 1999). Indeed, as McGrew notes, 'the fact that, for example, human digestion differs from gorillas' does not stop us from considering it to be a largely comparable process, so why should culture be different?' (1998: 304).

The examples provided above do not really do justice to the vast body of material relating to the presence of culture (and its attributes) in some animals which ethologists, zoologists, behavioural psychologists and primatologists have compiled in recent years (for more comprehensive overviews see Griffin, 2001; Sapolsky, 2006; Bentley-Condit and Smith, 2010). What they do provide, however, is grounds to reconsider some entrenched anthropological assumptions, namely that humans are uniquely cultural beings. Admittedly, the cultural practices of most animals are rather uninspiring when compared to even the most basic of human achievements, but that is not the point.

As noted at the outset, there is nothing to be gained from the hierarchical ordering of cultural practices (in relation to differences between humans or differences between humans and other animals) other than a rationale for exploitation. As Abu-Lughod has noted, 'it could be argued that culture is important to anthropology because the anthropological distinction between self and other rests on it' (1991: 137–8). This statement gains additional significance in relation to questions of human–animal continuity, and specifically in relation to culture in nonhuman *persons*. A considerable number of anthropological subjects see other animals as persons, yet many anthropologists find it difficult to accept either the possibility of nonhuman personhood, or the possibility that non-Western world views which are not rooted in such binary distinctions might offer a credible and *reflexive* insight into the place of humans and other animals along a linear as opposed to hierarchical evolutionary continuum.

SUGGESTIONS FOR FURTHER READING

Bekoff, M. 2007. Wild justice and fair play: cooperation, forgiveness, and morality in animals. In: L. Kalof and A. Fitzgerald (eds) *The animals reader: the essential classic and contemporary writings*. Oxford: Berg.

Caro, T.M. and Hauser, M.D. 1992. Is there teaching in nonhuman animals? *Quarterly Review of Biology* 67(2): 151–174.

Darwin, C. 1990. *The expression of the emotions in man and animals*. London: Folio Society.

Davidson, I. and McGrew, W.C. 2005. Stone tools and the uniqueness of human culture. *Journal of the Royal Anthropological Institute* 11: 793–817.

Galef, B.G. 1992. The question of animal culture. *Human Nature* 3: 157–178.

Grandin, T. 2006. *Animals in translation: the woman who thinks like a cow*. London: Bloomsbury Publishing.

Savage-Rumbaugh, S. 1998. *Apes, language, and the human mind*. Oxford: Oxford University Press.

Van Schaik, C.P., Ancrenaz, M., Borgen, G., Galdikas, B., Knott, C.D., Singleton, I. et al. 2007. Orangutan cultures and the evolution of material culture. In: L. Kalof and A. Fitzgerald (eds) *The animals reader: the essential classic and contemporary writings*. Oxford: Berg.

Wrangham, R.W., McGrew, W.C., de Waal, F.B.M. and Heltne, P.G. (eds) *Chimpanzee cultures*. Cambridge, MA: Harvard University Press.

4
The West and the Rest

[D]ifferent animals ... attend to the world in different ways. (Ingold, 2000: 51)

Money is to the West what kinship is to the rest. (Sahlins, 1976: 216)

It is a commonly held assumption in the 'Western' world that there is a human realm, usually associated with 'culture', which is diametrically opposed to the nonhuman or animal realm, the realm of 'nature'. This has been referred to as the 'modernist' perspective (or 'Western paradigm' [Pálsson, 1996]) because it has been shaped by many of the defining features of modernity which include, for example, the hegemonic influence of Judaeo-Christian doctrine, the legacy of Cartesian metaphysical thought and widespread participation (or rather inculcation) in a global capitalist system (Bird-David, 1999; Franklin, 1999: 37).

THERE IS NO SUCH THING AS THE 'WEST'

The 'West' is placed here in inverted commas to highlight the problematic nature of a category which is, to all intents and purposes, meaningless. The product of European colonial classification, the use of the term 'Western' makes essentialist assumptions about a region whose inhabitants are, in reality, often disparate and heterogeneous (see for example, Goddard et al., 1994; Macdonald, 1997). However, when used with caution the 'West' retains some currency as a referent to institutionalized modes of thought prevalent within industrial Europe and the United States and other post-domestic societies, where the dominance of a modernist 'progressive' perspective prevails.

Moreover, as James Carrier notes, for anthropologists the 'Occident' has important connotations; it is the known quantity against which many anthropological ideas of the 'Orient' (i.e. non-Western others) have been measured (1992; see also Said, 1978). So, while treating the West as an ethnographic region is problematic, it may still be useful to recognize that *mainstream* attitudes towards animals in much of Europe and North America do stand in opposition to those held by, for example, traditional hunter-gatherer peoples such as the !Kung San of Southern Africa (Lee, 1979), the BaMbuti of Zaire (Turnbull, 1965) and Guajá of eastern Amazonia (Cormier, 2003).

HUNTER-GATHERERS?

In a similar vein, there is no such thing as 'hunter-gatherers'. While there are many people the world over whose primary mode of subsistence involves hunting and gathering, and while it is certainly true to say that (as with 'Westerners') there are some additional unifying characteristics which serve to identify particular people through this ethnographic label, hunter-gatherers are by no means culturally homogeneous. Moreover, as Nurit Bird-David has noted (1990, 1992), defining a people by their mode of subsistence is unsatisfactory because most of those classified as 'hunter-gatherers' actually live by a wide range of procurement strategies (including waged labour). As such, the validity of employing 'hunter-gatherer' as a discrete category is called into question (Milton, 1996: 117). This point needs to be made at the outset, as, while the terms 'West' and 'hunter-gatherer' are still widely used by anthropologists when it is appropriate or convenient to do so, when making a point about generally held ideals and practices this needs to be underwritten by an awareness of often extensive variability in subsistence strategies and ideologies which can, on occasion, blur the boundaries between such seemingly distinct ways of life and world view.

The 'West' versus the 'Rest' opposition has been subjected to considerable anthropological scrutiny following the reflexive turn of the 1960s. In relation to 'hunter-gatherers' in particular, generally held assumptions about their mode of subsistence – which were arguably informed by the hierarchical perspectives of social evolutionism and the perception of industrialization and a capitalist economy as the epitome of progress – were challenged in the wake of Marshall Sahlins' controversial paper at the 1966 'Man the Hunter' symposium and his subsequent treatise *Stone age economics* published in 1972 (see for example, Barnard, 2007).

Sahlins presented a substantivist critique of the hegemony of formalist understandings of economics, which saw humans as essentially profit-driven, maximizing individuals. In his critique Sahlins argued that hunter-gatherer peoples did not fit such a model. Rather, they represented 'the original affluent society' because their mode of subsistence allowed them to live a comparatively leisured existence, affording the luxury of time and the associated benefits of increased interactions with family and friends. In addition, hunter-gatherers were described as essentially egalitarian; there were no clear gender divisions or social hierarchies (among, for example, the Matses of the Peruvian Amazon [Romanoff, 1983]; and Agta of the Philippines [Goodman et al., 1985], women hunt both alongside men and independently; see also Noss and Hewlett [2001] for a review of the success of female hunters in central Africa) and no notion of property or ownership. These aspects of human sociality were reflected in the ways hunter-gatherers thought about other animals and the environments in which they collectively lived (Willis, 1994: 6).

While these views of 'hunter-gatherers' have been refined over subsequent years, it is widely accepted by anthropologists that 'hunter-gatherer ontology' is such that it promotes an equality of sorts between humans and other animals, recognizing 'personhood' beyond the human species. As Bird-David (1992: 38) has observed, despite 'economic' variation, hunter-gatherer interactions with their environments validate the use of the term. Their essentially animistic way of relating to the 'natural' world sits in stark contrast to many other dominant beliefs and practices around the world. A consideration of some animistic beliefs, which might be held by many peoples who are mostly (but not always) hunter-gatherers, might call into question some commonly held occidental assumptions about humans and other animals.

ANIMISM

According to Bird-David in her 1999 paper '"Animism" revisited', animism – the belief that what outsiders would regard as inanimate objects and so-called 'natural' phenomena (including animals) possess some sort of animating force or spiritual essence – has been a source of anthropological debate since Edmund B. Tylor first developed the categorical concept of animism in 1871. For Tylor and other early anthropologists, the presence of animistic thought could be explained from an evolutionary perspective; animists were hampered by a pre-logical mind, beset by collective representations and, as a result, the 'primitive' (to use the politically incorrect terminology of the time) 'endow[ed] all things, even inanimate ones, with a nature analogous to his own' (Durkheim, 1976 [1915]: 53; see also chapter 6).

Animism as a practice has tended to be associated with indigenous peoples, hunter-gatherers in particular, and while it is now accepted that variations of animism exist beyond these narrow confines (among contemporary European neo-pagans for example; Lindquist, 2000), it is also true to state that animism is (or at least was) more commonly found among subsistence hunter-gatherers. This state of affairs is due, in no small part, to the fact that the beliefs and practices associated with animism do not sit entirely comfortably with other modes of subsistence. In traditional hunter-gatherer societies however, where humans are directly dependent on their relationships with animals and the surrounding environment for their immediate and ongoing survival, lived experience situates individuals in an animated world, a world where they must coexist and interact with other beings, human and nonhuman alike. The following account of a 'persistence hunt' enacted by contemporary !San in Botswana provides a very clear insight into such an ontology in practice:

> Tracking involves intense concentration resulting in a subjective experience of projecting oneself into the animal. The tracks indicate when the animal is starting to get tired; its stride becomes shorter, it kicks up more sand, and the distances between consecutive resting places become shorter.
>
> When tracking an animal, one attempts to think like an animal in order to predict where it is going. Looking at its tracks, one visualizes the motion of the animal and feels that motion in one's own body. Karoha explained: 'When the kudu becomes tired you become strong. You take its energy. Your legs become free and you can run fast like yesterday; you feel just as strong at the end of the hunt as in the beginning.' When the hunter finally runs the animal to exhaustion, it loses its will to flee and either drops to the ground or just stands looking at the approaching hunter with glazed eyes. Karoha explained that when the kudu's eyes glaze over, it is a sign that it feels that there is nothing it can do any more: 'What you will see is that you are now controlling its mind. You are getting its mind. The eyes are no longer wild. You have taken the kudu into your own mind.' The hunter will then finish off the animal with a spear. (Liebenberg, 2006: 1024)

It is hardly surprising that the most significant contributions to discussions of animism come from scholars working in Amazonia and Siberia, regions where an animistic world view prevails.

However, as Brian Morris (2000) observed during his fieldwork in rural Malawi, fraternal attitudes towards animals are also found in other contexts; across Africa, for example, among peoples such as the Maravi, Yao, Lomwe and Tumbuka who do not necessarily fulfil all the criteria necessary to be termed hunter-gatherers, but whose belief systems share many key aspects with a 'hunter-gatherer ontology'.

As has already been noted (see chapter 2), the dominant post-Enlightenment concept of 'humanity' is based on the assumption that humans are unique among animals (if, indeed, they are animals at all). This assumption is made in part because humans are capable of controlling the environments within which they live, they are self-conscious, able to think in a rational manner and, according to most Abrahamic religions, have a soul to grant them spiritual immortality. Consequently humans are accorded subjectivity and 'agency', whereas animals are widely thought merely to exhibit instinctive behavioural responses to certain external environmental stimuli, rendering them objects that humans can utilize. In many other contexts however, and particularly in most traditional hunter-gatherer societies, animals are recognized as independent actors. Actions taken by both humans and animals are therefore understood as having highly meaningful consequences, as part of the complex interactions which play out between hunter and hunted. Take, for example, the opening paragraph from Rane Willerslev's ethnography *Soul hunters*:

Watching Old Spiridon rocking his body back and forth, I was puzzled whether the figure I saw before me was man or elk. The elk-hide coat worn with its hair outward, the headgear with its characteristic protruding ears, and the skis covered with an elk's smooth leg skins, so as to sound like an animal when moving in snow, made him an elk; yet the lower part of his face below the hat, with its human eyes, nose, and mouth, along with the loaded rifle in his hands, made him a man. Thus, it was not that Spiridon had stopped being human. Rather, he had a liminal quality: he was not an elk, and yet he was not *not* an elk. He was occupying a strange place in between human and nonhuman identities.

A female elk appeared from among the willow bushes with her offspring. At first the animals stood still, the mother lifting and lowering her huge head in bewilderment, unable to solve the puzzle in front of her. But as Spiridon moved closer, she was captured by his mimetic performance, suspended her disbelief, and started walking straight toward him with the calf trotting behind her. At that point he lifted his gun and shot them both dead. Later he explained the incident: 'I saw two persons dancing toward me. The mother was a beautiful young woman and while singing she said: "Honored friend. Come and I'll take you by the arm and lead you to our home." At that point I killed them both. Had I gone with her, I myself would have died. She would have killed me.' (2007: 1)

This passage demonstrates the agency accorded to the nonhumans involved in the hunt. The Yukaghir hunter, dressed in the skins of former quarry, must engage in a mimetic performance to woo the elk, but such activity is not to be undertaken lightly. Indeed, for individuals within many traditional hunter-gatherer societies, the kill at the end of a hunt poses serious risks to hunter and hunted alike. For example, as an Inuit hunter explains:

The greatest peril in life lies in the fact that human food consists entirely of souls. All the creatures that we have to kill and eat, all those that we have to strike down and destroy to make clothes for ourselves, have souls like we have, souls that do not perish with the body, and which must therefore be propitiated lest they should avenge themselves on us for taking away their bodies. (in Serpell and Paul, 1994: 131)

Thus subsistence hunting is heavily ritualized, involves mimesis and is founded on the hunter's ability to 'think like' the animal who has become the focus of his or her attention (Serpell, 1996 [1986]). Provided the appropriate ritual steps and avoidances have been taken, a successful kill is celebrated as an indication of the harmonious and mutually beneficial relationships which obtain between humans and animals. This may appear to be a paradoxical statement, especially when, from a postcolonial, Euro-American perspective hunting widely signifies human control and 'superiority', as the animal is duped by the hunter's cunning or is overpowered by the hunter's superior skills or technology (Donald, 2006; see also chapter 14). When considered in terms of hunter-gatherer ontology, however, the notion that the hunt represents positive human–animal interactions becomes entirely credible.

As Tim Ingold has discussed in his accounts of fieldwork with Skolt Lapps in Finnish Lapland, reindeer are comparatively easy for human hunters to kill (1980: 53, 67). This is largely because when they realize they are being pursued they stop and turn to face whoever is pursuing them. This behaviour has been explained by 'scientists' as an evolutionary adaptation. If the hunter is not a human but a wolf, when the reindeer halts so does the wolf, enabling both to catch their breath. By stopping first, the reindeer gives itself a head start when the chase resumes and thus a greater chance of outrunning the wolf (Ingold, 2000: 13). When the hunter is a human, equipped with weapons to extend the reach and scope of his or her body however, this behaviour has fatal consequences.

This is also noted by indigenous hunters elsewhere in the ethnographic record, for example among many of the First Nations people in Canada, such as the Cree (Brightman, 1993, 2007; Tanner, 1979) and the Kluane (Nadasdy, 2003, 2005, 2007). For these indigenous peoples the reindeer appears to be sacrificing him or herself for the good of the hunter (who needs to eat) and, as a result, hunting becomes a reciprocal act between the animal 'gift' and the humans who share his or her environment. Reciprocity becomes necessary because the reindeer are perceived as (a) persons and (b) acting with intent. The 'personhood' of hunted animals is thus part of a cosmology in which the killing of these generous, life-giving animals is justifiable.

ANIMAL SPIRITS AND THE GIFT

While for hunter-gatherers every animal is thought to have a spiritual essence which animates them, individual members of particular species are widely believed to be under the stewardship of a spiritual guardian. These 'supreme beings' are ultimately responsible for the fate of their charges, and decide whether they are to live or die at the hands of human hunters. Consequently, it is these spirits with whom the human hunters relate on equal terms. While the individual animals are representatives of the supreme spirits, they are, as Ingold notes, 'manifestations of an essential type [the species], and it is the type rather than its manifestations that is personified' (1987: 247). Nonetheless, because all individual animals are perceived as animate beings, human hunters must take steps to propitiate both the hunted animal and its spiritual guardian, thereby demonstrating their respect and gratitude and protecting themselves from retribution (see also chapter 14).

These propitiations account for the ritualized nature of much 'traditional' (subsistence) hunting. In many cases hunters will adhere to strict dietary and behavioural restrictions before, during and after the hunt. These include fasting, abstaining from sexual activity and certain 'taboo' foods, and offering prayers and sacrifices to the victim. Once the quarry is caught, the hunter(s) treat it with the utmost respect and apologize to it for their actions. Every effort is made to ensure that as much of the animal's body as possible is utilized and anything which cannot be eaten or put to use is disposed of ritually, so as to avoid offending the animal's spirit. Spiritual retribution is thought to take the form of the subsequent illness or even the death of the hunter and/or the hunter's family, or in unsuccessful future hunting expeditions (see for example, Ingold, 1994a [1988]: 15; Serpell, 1999b).

Another central premise of hunter-gatherer ontology is that in hunting animals, humans are actually playing an essential role in helping the individual animal to fulfil its destiny; there is a widespread belief that every animal who dies a 'noble' death will be re-born to strengthen the herd. An example of this concept at work can be found in Marcel Mauss's classic description of the Maori *hau*. For many years the *hau* was approached from a purely economic perspective in terms of the obligatory return of reciprocal ceremonial exchange. However, it has significance for understanding hunter-gatherer ontology within a holistic system of relationships both between humans and between humans, animals, the environment and the spirit world:

I will speak to you about the hau ... Let us suppose that you possess a certain article (taonga) and that you give me this article. You give it me without setting a price on it. We strike no bargain about it. Now, I give this article to a third person who, after a certain lapse of time, decides to give me something as payment in return (utu). He makes a present to me of something (taonga). Now this taonga that he gives me is the spirit (hau) of the taonga that I had received from you and that I had given to him. The taonga that I received for these taonga which came from you must be returned to you. It would not be fair (tika) on my part to keep these taonga for myself, whether they were desirable or undesirable. I must give them to you because they are a hau of the taonga that you gave me. If I kept this other taonga for myself, serious harm might befall me, even death. This is the nature of the hau, the hau of personal property, the hau of the taonga, the hau of the forest. (Maori informant Tamati Ranaipiri quoted in Mauss, 2001 [1954]: 14)

The meaning of the *hau* becomes much clearer when it is considered as a manifestation of the egalitarian relationship between hunter-gatherers, animals and the environment. The *hau* is an expression of respect for the natural world, and indeed all forms of life, which is central to hunter-gatherer prosperity. It also symbolizes the retribution that may be inflicted if the natural order of things is disrespected. Maori priests are perceived as having a relationship with the birds and animals of the forest similar to that between hunters and their prey, but additionally between humans more generally in their day-to-day social activities – they are bound to each other by ties of mutual obligation. The priest is therefore the steward of the forest 'game' and engages with the spirits of the forest to ensure that the hunters are successful. In return, the hunters make offerings to the priests, who in turn make offerings to the forest spirits.

This 'ethic of respect' towards animals is further exemplified in the Sun Dance, a ritual ceremony traditionally conducted by several First Nations peoples. In the Sun Dance, as described by Elizabeth Lawrence (1993), relationships between the tribes and the various species of animal integral to their day-to-day lives were played out and the debts accrued during the hunt repaid. For the members of these tribes, animals were regarded as totemic ancestors (see chapter 6).

The Sun Dance was a means of demonstrating respect and propitiating the spirits of those animal 'brothers' who had died so that the human population could prosper. However, because of the warrior ethos of many of the Plains peoples, the ritual involved the physical suffering of participants to demonstrate the degree of reverence accorded the animals in whose honour the ritual was conducted. Of central importance to human survival on the Plains was the buffalo (*Bison bison*), and as a result, the buffalo took centre stage in the Sun Dance:

> In the self-inflicted torture process, participants were suspended from the top of the [Sun Dance] lodge by thongs attached to skewers passing through back or chest muscles. Additionally, from incisions made in various areas of their bodies, buffalo [sic] skulls were hung from skewers. In another form of this sacrifice, instead of being suspended, a man would volunteer to 'carry four of his relatives on his back, meaning he would drag four buffalo skulls.' An Oglala who made that vow spoke of it as bearing 'my closest relatives, the ancient buffalo' (Brown, 1967: 86–95). Two

to eight skulls might be attached, and as the dancer moved, in addition to tearing his flesh by means of the skewers, the skulls and especially the horns dug into his body. (Lawrence, 1993: 9)

Practices such as the Sun Dance have led many external commentators, including anthropologists, to conclude that native peoples are inherently ecological in their ways of being in the world. Indeed, Sahlins' suggestion that 'immediate return' hunter-gatherers (Woodburn, 1982) were opportunistic foragers (a suggestion which implies exploitation), appears to be at odds with what has been observed by anthropologists in the field (for example, Brightman, 1993; Tanner, 1979). Sahlins has thus been widely criticized for attributing 'Western' motivations and norms to 'non-Western' peoples (Bird-David, 1990).

The 'respectful', reciprocal relationship that obtains between hunter and prey described above, has also led some anthropologists and environmental organizations to consider hunter-gatherers as indigenous conservationists, with an innate 'ecological wisdom' gained from their close proximity to the natural world (Ingold, 2000: 67–9; see also Nadasdy, 2005). However, as Loretta Cormier notes of Amazonian hunter-foragers, 'in Amazonian thought, personhood in no way suggests that animals are not legitimate prey. Arguably, Amazonian peoples have had little need to be conservationists except in the context of the encroachment of Western society' (2003: 155).

THE 'MYTH' OF INDIGENOUS ECOLOGICAL WISDOM?

In recent years the notion of 'primitive ecological wisdom' has been refuted as a myth by anthropologists such as Roy Ellen (1986) and Kay Milton (1996). While there are many indigenous peoples who show respect for the natural world, anthropological criticism has been directed at the consumption of 'primitive ecological wisdom' in the 'West' as another incarnation of the 'noble savage', to highlight all that is 'wrong' with modernity (Milton, 1996: 109; Thomas, 1983: 301–2). Perceiving 'primitive ecological wisdom' as dogma is also problematic because it sets up indigenous hunter-gatherers for a fall when they fail to live up to the ideal of an ecologically benign coexistence with nature.

While exchanges across cultural and geographical boundaries can be traced back to the beginnings of human history, in a post-domestic globalized world unprecedented contact with other cultures has brought with it new technologies, introduced plant and animal species, proselytizing religions and wage labour. As a result there are very few indigenous peoples whose beliefs and practices have been unaffected by contact with outsiders. Even those who have chosen to isolate themselves from the 'corrupting' influences of the outside world, such as the Colombian Kogi, have nonetheless taken on tools and domesticates (Ereira, 1990). A more productive approach for all concerned is that espoused by anthropologists such as Ingold and Milton, who recognize that individuals perceive their environments directly as they go about their day-to-day business, and respond accordingly.

To return to reindeer hunting, the Cree, Skolt Lapp or Kluane *experience* the reindeer stopping and the comparative ease with which they are able to kill them. They then *interpret* this behaviour as animals giving themselves up for human consumption. Such interpretations might be 'convenient' means by which acts of violence can be justified, but this is by no means unique to hunter-gatherers (see chapter 14). What is significant, however, is that in the process of their interactions with animals in a shared environment, these human hunters recognize that the animals in question are indeed 'people' with complex social lives, needs and desires which mirror those found in human societies. Moreover, in order to be successful in tracking the animals in the first place, the human hunter needs to be able to effectively 'think like' his or her quarry.

In many respects, the same logic applies to animals. The reindeer experience human hunters killing members of the herd, but the manner in which this is conducted means that the reindeer are not unduly spooked by the presence of humans in their midst. This recognition of continuity between humans and animals, alongside the need for successful hunters to understand the animal which they are ultimately intending to kill, is borne out of experience – the collective experience of generations of hunters. If the herd is upset they may disperse or become fearful of humans, thus making the whole enterprise impossible, with dire consequences for human survival. As a result, a respectful relationship persists, a relationship which, as Ingold has noted, changes when alternative experiences lead humans (or indeed their nonhuman quarry) to perceive the world in a different manner.

THE CASE OF THE SAAMI

Lindquist's ethnography of Swedish neo-shamans presents a useful case study with which to draw together all of the issues raised above. The Saami, an indigenous people of the Scandinavian Arctic and sub-Arctic, were traditionally hunter-gatherers (Aikio, 2006). By the 17th century, however, most Saami had given up a hunter-gatherer lifestyle in favour of reindeer pastoralism. Lindquist (2000) discusses the ongoing 'battle' between the Saami, their reindeer herds, predatory wolves (who are protected by pan-European legislation) and Swedish neo-pagans over whose rights should be prioritized. The traditional Saami way of life has become idealized – as hunter-gatherers they were perceived as living in harmony with nature. However, the commercial nature of contemporary pastoralism has led to the Saami being criticized for 'abandoning' their ecologically sound principles and their desire to hunt wolves is seen as further evidence of their disrespect for the natural world.

A closer reading of the situation reveals that, in reality, many aspects of the 'respectful' hunter-gatherer ontology have been retained by the Saami, despite the change in their dominant mode of subsistence. According to Lindquist, the introduction of Swedish laws to protect wild predators, including the wolf, in the 1960s left the Saami with no means of protecting their herds. Over the last 10 years the situation has deteriorated and Saami protests have escalated (Lindquist, 2000: 170, 182). The Saami's main argument in defence of their 'right' to hunt wolves is that, even though other predators such as bear, lynx and wolverine are responsible for more reindeer losses than are wolves, wolf predation is not only a significant challenge to their livelihood but also to their beliefs about their responsibilities to the 'natural world', including their reindeer herds (2000: 179).

First, wolves live and hunt in packs, with a hierarchical social structure not unlike that of human society (Kruuk, 2002). Consequently, wolves are accorded a greater degree of agency than other predators because of their ability to cooperate, and this is reflected in the fearful (and at times hateful) mythology surrounding wolves in Saami and other pastoralist cultures (Lindquist, 2000: 180; Vitebsky, 2005: 270–3; see also Moore, 1994).

This disproportionate fear of wolves is also based on the animals' perceived ruthlessness. Wolves are renowned for opportunistically killing more animals than they could possibly eat in one sitting (Ingold, 1980: 78). Further, they are frequently cited as cruel because they seldom kill outright, instead inflicting a slow, painful death, and frequently victims of their predations are eaten alive. There is also ample evidence of wolves historically attacking humans (Kruuk, 2002: 69–73, 76), although this is certainly not a 'normal' aspect of lupine behaviour. Their behaviour, combined with the intentionality ascribed to wolves by the Saami, makes them particularly problematic predators, whose control requires both skill and ritual preparation.

As Lindquist notes, in Saami folklore:

> The wolf-hunt was looked upon as a dangerous struggle, in which hunters risked their lives; it was often emphasised how important it was to kill the wolf with the first blow. A wounded wolf was believed to always get back at the hunter and take his life. This mysterious, frightening power of the wolf also appears in more recent folklore accounts in which ... the wolf is said to cast spells on the hunter's bullet so that it misses or on the rifle so that it fails to fire. The wolf was ascribed the ability to read a man's mind; the wolf was said to have the strength of one man and the intelligence of ten. The meat of a reindeer killed by a wolf was considered to be contaminated and inedible. (2000: 180)

Wolf predation is a major issue for the Saami reindeer herders because wolves appear to consciously undermine human activity and human spheres of influence. Like many other pastoralists, the Saami regard themselves as 'protectors' of their herds and, as Ingold notes (1980: 1) the contemporary process of reindeer herding is reminiscent of past hunting practices; the reindeer are allowed to roam beyond the control of their human owners. Further, given the Saami's continued adherence to their version of a hunter-gatherer ontology it is perhaps not so surprising that the wolf is regarded as subversive by reindeer pastoralists. The Saami's 'respectful' interactions with their herds contrast starkly with wolf predations, which, as Lindquist notes, are seen as cruel and destructive (2000: 179, 182) and therefore in breach of both the 'waste-not want-not' hunter-gatherer premise, and the perceived safety of human protective custody (Budiansky, 1999):

> 'Are the bells so you can find them?'
> 'Nye –e-et!' he answered. 'I can always find them. They're to warn wolves that the reindeer are protected – there are humans nearby.' (Vitebsky, 2005: 161)

As the indignant response given by Vitebsky's Eveny informant demonstrates, this form of domestication continues to rest on a certain degree of trust between humans and their charges and, more importantly, on the fulfilment of mutual responsibilities between some pastoralists and the animals in their *care* (cf. Ingold, 1980; see also chapters 5 and 14). Indeed, as we shall see in the next chapter, modes of subsistence do not necessarily determine the nature of human relationships with and attitudes towards animals and, while it is certainly possible to draw some general conclusions about the ways in which humans think about and interact with animals in a 'post-domestic' context or in particular 'domestic' ones, just as anthropological attitudes towards 'hunter-gatherers' have changed and are constantly being revised, the modes of subsistence and accompanying ontologies of these groups are also in a constant state of flux.

SUGGESTIONS FOR FURTHER READING

Bird-David, N. 2006. Animistic epistemology: why do some hunter-gatherers not depict animals? *Ethnos* 71(1): 33–50.

Cormier, L.E. 2001. Animism, cannibalism, and pet-keeping among the Guajá of eastern Amazonia. *Tipití: Journal of the Society for the Anthropology of Lowland South America* 1(1): 81–98.

Costa, L. and Fausto, C. 2010. The return of the animists: recent studies of Amazonian ontologies. *Religion & Society: Advances in Research* 1(1): 89–109.

De Castro, E.V. 1996. Images of nature and society in Amazonian ethnology. *Annual Review of Anthropology* 25: 179–200.

Haber, E.F. 2009. Animism, relatedness, life: post-Western perspectives. *Cambridge Archaeological Journal* 19: 418–430.

Krech, S. 1999. *The ecological Indian: myth and history*. New York: W.W. Norton.

Peterson, N. 2011. Is the Aboriginal landscape sentient? Animism, the new animism and the Warlpiri. *Oceania* 81(2): 167–179.

Sillar, B. 2009. The social agency of things? Animism and materiality in the Andes. *Cambridge Archaeological Journal* 19: 367–377.

Willerslev, R. 2004. Not animal, not *not* animal: hunting, imitation and empathetic knowledge among the Siberian Yukaghirs. *Journal of the Royal Anthropological Institute* 10(3): 629–652.

5
Domestication

'Men have forgotten this basic truth,' said the fox. 'But you must not forget it. *For what you have tamed, you become responsible forever.'* (de Saint-Exupéry, 1995 [1943]: 82, emphasis added)

A man who spends his whole life following animals just to kill them to eat, or moving from one berry patch to another, is really living just like an animal himself. (Braidwood, 1957: 122)

One of the ways in which anthropologists have traditionally classified humans is according to their mode of subsistence, placing essentialized 'types' of societies along a continuum (hunter-gatherers, pastoralists, tribal horticulturalists, peasants, feudalists, industrialists, capitalists). While in the colonial past these stages were ordered hierarchically, in the postcolonial present it is accepted that there are merits and flaws to all ways of life. It is also widely recognized that there is much variation within each of these categories and that societies do not necessarily pass through each 'stage' in linear progression.

IN THE BEGINNING ...

The earliest humans survived by hunting and gathering and, as Sahlins has noted, such a mode of subsistence has many advantages (2004 [1972]; see also chapter 4). However, between 10,000 and 12,000 years ago something happened which led some, but not all, of our prehistoric ancestors to move away from a hunter-gatherer lifestyle and bring other living things into the *domus* or household. The catalyst (or catalysts) for this change in food procurement strategy, the forms which the process took and the ways in which it impacted on human interactions with and perceptions of other animals (and themselves) all make domestication a particularly fertile area for discussion and investigation among anthropologists, archaeologists and scholars from a wide range of cognate disciplines (for example, Russell, 2007).

At the height of European colonialism, and in keeping with the influence of social evolutionism during that period, many scholars (for example, Childe, 1928; Engels, 1972 [1884]) subscribed to the view that domestication was a 'revolution' which saw Neolithic humans 'conquer' the 'wilderness' and their own savagery and move a step closer to civilization (see Anderson, 1997 for an interesting review from a geographer's perspective). The scholarship of many contemporary archaeologists however recognizes that such a position presented a more accurate reflection of the colonial mindset than of the prehistoric past. It is now widely accepted that the shift from hunting and gathering to pastoralism and settled agriculture was not a sudden event, but rather a gradual process (Wilson, 2007: 102).

The most pervasive explanation for why humans turned to domestication is the 'climate change' model. The archaeological record indicates that humans evolved into their present form in the Lower Paleolithic of the Pleistocene, a period of intense glacial and interglacial activity. This ice age caused serious climatic variation, impacting on environmental conditions and changing the fertile plains which had supported both humans and grazing megafauna such as mammoths, into forests (see Serpell, 1996 [1986] for an overview).

This prehistoric global environmental crisis led to the extinction of many large mammal species and wild cereals which were also human dietary staples (Hillman et al., 2001). As a result humans were forced to change their diets and intensify their foraging efforts, incorporating a broader spectrum of foodstuffs to compensate for the losses. Over time, an expanding population depleted resources to the extent that the cultivation of plants and domestication of animals became a necessity. This essentially functionalist approach to domestication sees prehistoric humans domesticating animals to fulfil specific human needs as a direct and conscious response to climate change. Accordingly, domesticates have been seen as 'buffers' between humans and this changing and often harsh environment (Serpell, 1996 [1986]; Shanklin, 1985: 378). However, it is now widely acknowledged that it is the gathering in a hunter-gatherer system which meets the vast majority of a society's nutritional needs, leading some anthropologists to refer to 'gatherer-hunters' in place of the conventional terminology (Bird-David, 1990).

In recent years there has been a move towards considering domestication as a trial and error, ad-hoc process which diminishes the role of human choice and agency in the whole matter. As Diamond notes:

Food production could not possibly have arisen through a conscious decision, because the world's first farmers had around them no model of farming to observe, hence they could not have known that there was a goal of domestication to strive for, and could not have guessed the consequences that domestication would bring for them. (2002: 700; see also Cohen and Armelagos, 1984)

RE-INTRODUCING HUNTER-GATHERERS

Contemporary hunter-gatherers (or gatherer-hunters) have been characterized by a nomadic existence which facilitates opportunistic hunting and foraging activities, coupled with a fluid, egalitarian but inherently unstable social structure (see also chapter 4). This lack of stability makes it difficult for any one individual to become powerful, especially among what Woodburn (1982) termed 'immediate return' hunter-gatherers. Groups such as the Hadza of Tanzania who, according to Woodburn, gathered, hunted, killed, shared and ate food as and when they needed it, were unable (due to constant movement and the conditions in which they found themselves) to store food and accrue a surplus.

Anthropologists have noted that the egalitarian nature of relationships between humans in immediate return systems is mirrored to varying degrees in relationships between humans and nonhuman others; what Bird-David (1992) terms a 'hunter-gatherer economy of knowledge' and de Castro refers to as a 'hunter-gatherer ontology' (1998; see also chapter 4). According to this ontological perspective animals and humans share a spiritual connection and other animals are accorded 'personhood' and 'agency' (see chapter 4) – loaded anthropological terms which, as has already been noted in many other contexts, do not tend to be applied to nonhumans.

Woodburn also described what he termed 'delayed return' hunter-gatherers; groups such as the Kwakiutl (Boas, 1966), who were able to stockpile materials (for example, furs, blankets and coppers). This ability to create and retain a surplus led to social, political and economic stratification, exemplified in the potlach ceremonies characteristic of the Kwakiutl and other First Nations peoples of the Pacific north-west coast of the United States (Mauss, 2001 [1954]). Archaeologists and anthropologists have suggested that delayed return hunter-gatherers would have been more likely to make the transition to pastoralism than, for example, immediate return societies because, as Juliet Clutton-Brock (1989) notes, the emergent hierarchies between humans in a delayed return system made the subjugation of animals less of an ideological leap (see also Ingold, 1994a [1988], 2000; Serpell, 1996 [1986], 2000). In addition to a recognition of continuity between species and of personhood in nonhuman others, subsistence hunters have to engage in acts of mimetic empathy, literally putting themselves in the place of their quarry (Willerslev, 2004).

When discussing the astounding 'persistence hunting' traditionally practised by the !Xo and /Gwi hunters of the central Kalahari in Botswana, where hunters track and literally run down their prey over a period of several hours, Liebenberg notes that the hunter attempts to visualize the movement of the quarry and engage in an act of empathic engagement (2006: 1024). This ontology facilitates a holistic awareness that humans are part of the 'natural' world, and are of no greater or lesser significance than any 'other'. The relationship also allows for the hunted animal to make choices and act accordingly (Kohn, 2007; Nadasdy, 2007).

Ingold (1994a [1988], 2000) has convincingly argued that this relationship is based on 'trust'; the human hunter acts in a particular manner because he or she trusts the animal to allow the hunt to be successful. The animal (as far as the humans involved are concerned) 'trusts' the hunter to behave in such a manner as to facilitate passage into the next life and so rejuvenate the herd. In the process of domestication certain restrictions are imposed, which in many cases seriously curtail an animal's ability to act as 'it' chooses. This in turn leads to a dependency on humans and represents 'an abrogation of trust, entailing as it does the denial rather than the recognition of the autonomy of the other on whom one depends' (Ingold, 1994a [1988]: 16).

THE 'CONTROL' MODEL

Animal domestication has been regarded by many scholars for many years as an example of human control over animals who constitute objects, possessions and commodities. Clutton-Brock's edited volume, *The walking larder: patterns of domestication, pastoralism and predation* (1989), considered domestication from a multi-disciplinary perspective and many contributors referred to domestication as a form of exploitation and domination.

Clutton-Brock herself defined domestication as a process 'that can only take place when tamed animals are incorporated into the social structure of the human group and become objects of ownership' (1989: 7). The definition is expanded to position domesticated animals themselves as objects which are 'bred in captivity for purposes of economic profit to a human community that maintains *complete mastery* over ... breeding, organization of territory and food supply' (1989: 7, emphasis added). Such a position builds on the writings of Marxist scholars, who saw in the process of domestication the alienation of animals and women from their own labour and autonomy; 'the domestication of animals and the breeding of herds ... developed a hitherto unsuspected source of wealth and created entirely new social relations' (Engels, 1972 [1884]: 119).

As Shanklin (1985) notes, those groups who went down the domestication route became responsible for the day-to-day care of domestic livestock. However, in addition to changes in the ways that humans interacted with what were now 'their' animals, with domestication came a new sense of power for human societies – they were no longer at the mercy of game birds and animals and instead could assume a position of dominance based on control. As 'their' animals reproduced, however, it became increasingly difficult to protect the growing herds. As a result, anthropologists have observed certain characteristics within contemporary pastoralist societies.

OF WOMEN AND ANIMALS

The gendered division of labour, high incidence of polygamy, exogamous marriage and a shift from matrilineal to patrilineal kinship systems have all been accounted for as 'functions' of the need to manage and retain large numbers of domestic livestock. For pastoralists such as the Sudanese Nuer for example, raids and the subsequent theft of animals are genuine causes for concern (Evans-Pritchard, 1940). Female relatives are therefore often 'exchanged' with neighbouring tribes and lineages in a bid to ensure harmonious social relationships with groups who might otherwise pose a threat to the integrity of the cattle herd and therefore the wealth of the patriline. Herding hundreds or even thousands of animals across open country, especially in areas which are also home to large predators, makes the ability to call on affines for extra support particularly important. For settled tribal horticulturalists such as the Kawelka of the New Guinean Highlands, keeping large numbers of domestic pigs places considerable demands on women who are responsible for the day-to-day feeding of these animals. A polygamous system therefore shares the responsibilities across a number of women who work together to care for their husbands' pigs.

While there are numerous feminist critiques of this way of representing women as universally subordinate to both male relatives and domesticated livestock (for example, Hurn, 2008a; Josephides, 1985; MacCormack and Strathern, 1980), the presence of some clear differences at a societal level between contemporary (matrilineal) hunter-gatherers and (patrilineal) 'farmers' (pastoralists, tribal horticulturalists and settled agriculturalists) suggests that the process of domesticating animals (and plants) and forming settled, sedentary communities impacted on human relationships in some rather significant ways.

For Clutton-Brock (1989), this helps account for the fact that not all hunter-gatherer societies made the transition to farming. She argues that it was the concept of 'ownership of the animals' which took early humans so long to get to grips with, resulting in the shift to domestication being a drawn out and sporadic process. There is, however, the thorny problem of using examples from the ethnographic record to try and recreate past human societies. This approach is often adopted by ethnoarchaeologists and physical anthropologists, but the use of contemporary hunter-gatherer populations as a model for past human activity raises some important issues worthy of further consideration.

ETHNOGRAPHIC ANALOGY

First, drawing on the beliefs and practices of indigenous peoples is only productive if there is an accompanying acceptance that these peoples can provide a window into our prehistoric past. However, such an approach is underpinned by the, albeit latent, tenets of social evolutionism. Even if the motivations are entirely honourable, the very act of comparing contemporary and prehistoric peoples suggests that they are sufficiently similar to make such an activity justified. Outside of academia this can have potentially damaging consequences for indigenous hunter-gatherers who can then be perceived in negative terms.

The recent eviction of the San bushmen from the Central Kalahari Game Reserve (CKGR) in Botswana is a case in point. The government of Botswana had responded to the general 'embarrassment' felt by many in Botswana towards the San's 'prehistoric' hunter-gatherer lifestyle by 'asking' the San to leave the CKGR in the 1980s and instead adopt a settled lifestyle. When the San refused they were forcibly removed; this programme of 'relocation' has been interpreted by anthropologists and human rights activists 'as a civilizing project [directed] towards the segment of Botswana's population considered to be the most "backward"' (M. Taylor, 2004: 154, quoted in J.J. Taylor, 2007).

In addition to these ethical concerns there is the question of whether it is useful to make such comparisons. While so-called indigenous 'ecological wisdom' has been called into question by many anthropologists (see chapter 4), there is general acceptance that the culturally and phenomenologically informed perception of animals as persons leads to a more respectful and sustainable coexistence. Cave paintings produced by prehistoric humans around the time some began to cultivate crops and 'tame' animals are conventionally interpreted as representing a spiritual connection between human hunters and the animals upon whom they relied and are therefore considered acts of reverence (see also chapter 1).

However, what if prehistoric humans had a very different ontology to contemporary or near contemporary hunter-gatherers? One alternative to the 'climate change' model is the 'overkill' hypothesis most commonly associated with ecologist Paul Martin (2007). Martin suggests that Paleolithic hunters were themselves responsible for the megafaunal extinctions which occurred during the Pleistocene, hunting once plentiful species such as the mammoth in a ruthless and unsustainable manner. As a result, cave paintings might represent trophies, a means by which hunters could document their hunting successes. Understandably this hypothesis has come in for some criticism, especially from Quaternary scientists and archaeologists who see interglacial climate change as the more likely explanation for mass extinctions which may have acted as a catalyst for domestication (see Haynes, 2007). However, 'overkill' raises the possibility that past hunter-gatherers experienced and thought about other animals in very different ways to their contemporary namesakes. Clutton-Brock (1989) has suggested that early hunter-gatherers resisted the transition out of respect for the animals involved. Yet it is also important to consider the possibility that the 'hunter-gatherer ontology' was lacking in early humans, and other forces were at work.

THE 'BIG MISTAKE'

In addition to the social impacts of domestication, the archaeological record reveals some rather significant morphological, pathological and nutritional changes which have come to be referred to as the 'unforeseen consequences' of domestication. This has led some academic commentators to suggest that in the process of domesticating other species, humans 'inadvertently' domesticated themselves (Clark, 2007; Leach, 2003).

In relation to why some human groups made the change and others didn't, biologist, environmental historian and geographer Jared Diamond suggests that the ad hoc nature of domestication would have provided plenty of opportunity for experimentation. Hunter-gatherer groups living alongside those who had made the transition to farming would have observed the multifarious changes which occurred and these proto-farmers would serve as cautionary tales to deter others from following suit. Diamond (1998) has been particularly vocal in asserting that domestication was 'the worst mistake in human history'. Indeed, archaeological evidence suggests that there are numerous negative consequences of domestication, including maladaptive morphological and behavioural changes in the domesticates, ideological and behavioural changes in humans themselves, and also radical changes to the standards of living for all concerned (Diamond, 2002; Leach, 2007).

The mobile lifestyle and varied diet of hunter-gatherers bestows numerous health benefits which are absent in many past and contemporary settled agricultural societies. Aside from a reduction in leisure time (as more sustained effort is required to successfully raise livestock and crops) the reduction in dietary variation (Katz, 1987) led to greater susceptibility to disease (Hulsewé et al., 1999; Ulijaszek, 2000) and a restriction in childhood development, both of which reduce life expectancy (Cohen and Armelagos, 1984). The need to store surplus food also increased human exposure to pathogens such as bacteria and moulds (Brothwell and Brothwell, 1998 [1968]).

Evidence from the archaeological record further suggests that small, nomadic hunter-gatherer groups were relatively free from contagious diseases. However, as historian Harriet Ritvo notes:

> increased population meant larger reservoirs for disease and fixed residences meant permanent proximity to waste … If people had domesticated only plants, these changes would only have exposed them more intensively to disease organisms that they already harboured. But the domestication of wild ungulates – animals which, though mobile, lived in groups large enough to incubate contagions – brought people into contact with a new set of diseases. (2004: 212)

Clark also notes what she refers to as the 'poisoned gifts' of domestication – zoonotic parasites which jumped from nonhuman to human animals (2007: 63. See also McNeill, 1998 [1976]: 69; Diamond, 1998: 207 and chapter 12). It is in light of the 'hardships' of some relationships of domestication that the 'control' model becomes increasingly salient in certain cultural and historical contexts, but less applicable in others.

DIFFERENT WAYS OF FARMING

While there are numerous examples of control-based, hierarchical relationships between humans and objectified animals in the ethnographic record – most notably contemporary industrialized farming practices in many parts of the world (for example, Thu and Durrenberger, 1998) – such a stark picture is not necessarily replicated across the board. Indeed, contemporary domestication is best thought of as a spectrum, with industrial 'factory' farming and the breeding of pedigree animals at one end a long way away from, for example, the free-range pig-keeping practised by numerous Melanesian communities (Dwyer and Minnegal, 2005), the 'respectful' herding of camelids in Latin America (Flannery et al., 2008), or the seemingly uncontrolled breeding of semi-wild horses by Kygyrz pastoralists (Cassidy, 2009a).

Decades have passed since *The walking larder*'s publication and approaches to domestication as a process contingent on a particular ideological relationship between humans and animals have been refined in light of postmodern scholarship. Clutton-Brock was arguably approaching domestication from a 'Western' perspective, as a concept with a 'problematic' history (Cassidy, 2007a: 3; Russell, 2007: 27) and she was not alone. Indeed, subsequent definitions have also emphasized the anthropogenic nature of domestication. Ellen, for example, sees domesticates as 'species which owe their current genetic composition to close encounters with human populations which harvest them for food and other products' (Ellen and Fukui, 1996: 20).

The 'control' model, as noted above, suggests that humans take control of the 'natural' behaviours of the animals in their 'care' (such as reproduction, movement, interaction with other animals, nutrition and genetic separation of domesticates from wild populations), and this model has dominated anthropological discussions of domestication. However, the process of challenging the anthropo-centric bias of 'Western' thought, which has been a consequence of the reflexive turn in anthropology or 'post-processual' movement in archaeology (Hodder, 1985), coupled with observations of the reality of human–animal interactions in contemporary domestic contexts, has led many scholars to suggest a series of alternative scenarios. Domestication is now viewed as the outcome of a series of complex relationships between humans and other animals in different places and at different times. Rather than seeing animals as victims of human actions against them, many scholars now present animals as actors themselves. As a result, the primary focus of debate has shifted to whether domestication is best thought of in terms of 'symbiosis', that is, mutually beneficial to humans and the animals involved, or as a 'change in social relationships' with humans dominating animals and the 'natural' world (Russell, 2007: 28).

ANIMAL AGENTS

The 'symbiosis', 'self-domesticating' or 'co-evolution' models (Budiansky, 1999; Leach, 2007; O'Connor, 1997; Simoons, 1994) posit that it was actually beneficial for certain animal species to coexist with humans and, because of this, the animals themselves took an active role in instigating or influencing the relationship. For example, biologists Raymond and Lorna Coppinger (2001) have argued that dogs are the descendants of self-domesticating wolves who sought to exploit the middens which accompanied Mesolithic human settlements. This suggestion stands in opposition to that espoused in the past by writers such as Serpell (1989) and Grandin and Dessing (1998), who have both suggested that domesticated dogs were descendants of wolf cubs captured by opportunistic humans.

The Coppingers see the human–dog relationship as one of symbiosis as opposed to domination (see also Serpell, 1995), but what of the domestication of animals whose sole purpose was and is to feed and clothe their human owners? It is difficult to conceive of the domestic relationship between humans and pigs, sheep, cattle, reindeer or any other primarily 'edible' animal as symbiotic. Journalist Stephen Budiansky (1999) does just that, however, arguing that if there were only minimal benefits in the shift for humans (and a great deal of hardship), there must have been something in it for the animals involved. Budiansky presents as an example circumboreal peoples such as the Saami, who were traditionally hunter-gatherers but now herd reindeer as pastoralists. Budiansky argues that the relationship between humans and these ungulates is mutually advantageous. Both species are nomadic, so humans (and their 'tame wolves') provide protection from predators but also provide valuable and otherwise inaccessible dietary supplements such as salt in the form of human urine (Budiasky, 1999: 51).

Such 'advantages' may go some way towards offsetting the 'costs' of entering into what has come to be referred to as the 'domesticated animal contract' (Anderson, 1995, 1997, 1998; Larrère and Larrère, 2000; Palmer, 1997) or the 'ancient contract' (Dawkins and Bonney, 2008). In many respects the 'domesticated animal contract' (the belief that humans have a moral responsibility to treat domesticated livestock fairly and with respect) can be viewed as an extension of 'hunter-gatherer ontology' and the widespread hunter-gatherer view that hunted animals offer themselves up as 'gifts' to human hunters (Nadasdy, 2007; see also chapter 4). Humans took or take animals into their social lives and, in return for human protection, animals 'allow' humans to utilize their bodies.

However, as Budiansky has noted, although there are potential benefits to cohabiting with humans for some animals, referring to the relationship as a form of 'social contract' implies that the animals themselves (or the prehistoric ancestors of current domesticates) have, or had, the capacity to think through the implications of domestication and make an informed choice. Given the fact that humans were unable to foresee the consequences of domestication, it is unlikely that their animal 'partners' would have been able to either.

One important area where there has been comparatively little academic attention to date is the liminal space between control (domination) and mutual benefit (symbiosis), and between the 'wild' and the 'tame' (Suzuki, 2007). For example, the ethnographic record contains material relating to numerous pastoralist peoples who exhibit many aspects of a 'hunter-gatherer ontology' (see chapter 4; de Castro, 1998), but who do not engage in the sort of 'business' relationship implied by the 'domesticated animal contract'. The latter is arguably the product of Judaeo-Christian ideology, capitalist modes of production and the European legal tradition and so, while this concept has been utilized and engaged with convincingly by geographers considering contemporary 'Western' domestic relationships (Anderson, 1995, 1997, 1998; Palmer, 1997), its relevance for most non-Western contexts is limited. Llama herders on the Punas of Ayacucho in the Peruvian Andes, for example, believe that *wanami* (mountain spirits), are responsible for the life and death of the llamas and they seek to appease them in order to preserve their flocks (Flannery et al.,

2008). These herders also go to great lengths to ensure that all of the animals they sacrifice during ritual ceremonies are utilized in a manner reminiscent of the 'respectful' and propitiatory practices of many hunter-gatherer peoples.

SYMBIOSIS

In his ethnographic study of the Sudanese Nuer, Edward E. Evans-Pritchard noted that while the Nuer obviously relied on their cattle for sustenance, cattle also had immense symbolic value and were implicated in maintaining social cohesion. For example, cattle served as bridewealth payments and were given to children during important rites of passage. Moreover, in cases of homicide, cattle would be paid as compensation ('bloodwealth') to the bereaved family. This synonymy between humans and cattle, whereby cattle could be accepted in lieu of a human life, not only demonstrates how important cattle were to the Nuer but also highlights the often volatile social context within which Nuer and their cattle existed:

> Nuer say that it is cattle that destroy people, for 'more people have died for the sake of a cow than for any other cause'. They have a story which tells how, when the beasts broke up their community and each went its own way and lived its own life, Man slew the mother of Cow and Buffalo. Buffalo said she would avenge her mother by attacking men in the bush, but cow said that she would remain in the habitations of men and avenge her mother by causing endless disputes about debts, bride-wealth, and adultery, which would lead to fighting and deaths among the people. So this feud between Cow and Man has gone on from time immemorial, and day by day Cow avenges the death of her mother by occasioning the death of men. Hence Nuer say of their cattle, 'They will be finished together with mankind', for men will all die on account of cattle and they and cattle will cease together. (1940: 49)

In relation to my own fieldwork in a rural farming community in west Wales, I have discussed the breeding and exhibition of indigenous equines (Welsh ponies and cobs), as a form of domination or control and simultaneously a symbiosis, as owners are completely preoccupied with breeding and exhibiting their animals (Hurn, 2008a, 2008b). In the case of my Welsh farming informants, or Melanesian 'Big Men' (and their wives), or Nuer cattle pastoralists, the humans concerned effectively 'live off' their animals both physically and emotionally, by consuming their flesh or by exchanging them for financial or social reward. However, the animals too 'consume' human resources (time, feed, money, physical labour) and have some ability to effect change (see chapter 10). Thus while the relationship might appear to be disadvantageous and even damaging to both parties, it is simultaneously advantageous in other respects (Clark, 2007). These are very different relationships to those which play out between a factory farmer and his or her shed of caged chickens or pigs. Factory farming is of no discernible benefit to the animals involved and is more accurately thought of as parasitic rather than symbiotic; the relationship is one-sided and abusive, with the parasite (humans) benefiting at the expense of the host (livestock).

POST-DOMESTICITY

As noted in previous chapters, in much of the contemporary world humans have entered a phase which Bulliet (2005) refers to as 'post-domesticity'. Post-domestic societies are characterized by the removal of most consumers from the reality of intensive livestock production, a close but inherently anthropomorphic relationship with pets and a suppressed sense of guilt about industrialized farming practices and the widespread exploitation of animals. It is difficult to reconcile such a position with the shopping habits of the general public. However, the growing demand for organic produce, free-range meat and eggs, and the steady increase in vegetarianism and veganism in the 'West' suggests that some post-domestic consumers may indeed feel uncomfortable or 'guilty' about the nature of mainstream contemporary agricultural practices.

Even farmers themselves are not immune. Farmers who practise industrialized or intensive, exploitative production methods often blame their actions on market forces and the greed of members of the general public who demand cheap meat and 'force' farmers to cut corners (Serpell, 1999b). In a bid to assuage guilt it is post-domestic consumers who become scapegoats, while the specialization of aspects of production which remove farmers from the final stage means that others in the chain can take the blame for the ultimate fate of livestock.

This collective 'guilt' was expressed, rather surprisingly, in public responses to the 2001 outbreak of foot and mouth disease in the UK. Indeed, as Sarah Franklin (2001) has demonstrated, while modern domestication is greatly removed from subsistence agriculture, it seems that some 'post-domestic' humans are still grappling with similar ethical dilemmas to those faced by both the hunter-gatherers and the pastoralists for whom the 'domination' of other animals was or is problematic.

Media coverage of public responses to global and national zoonotic epidemics such as SARS, foot and mouth, BSE and salmonella suggest that they are widely perceived as nature's way of punishing humans for our disrespect and exploitation. Franklin notes that, as a rule, these nagging doubts are suppressed (a point also made by Bulliet, 2005), but the intense media coverage following the foot and mouth outbreak in the UK in 2001 made it impossible to deny the fact that millions of animals would be slaughtered as a result of human negligence; the cause of the outbreak was linked to poor standards of hygiene. That all of these animals had been bred specifically to be slaughtered was not the point. What affected popular consciousness was the fact that their deaths were in vain, resulting in waste – something which hunter-gatherers avoid at all cost, or else risk the devastating consequences of spiritual retribution.

Another interesting point raised in Franklin's article is that of all the 'victims' of foot and mouth it was most notably sheep who came to symbolize the tragic nature of the epidemic and not the human farmers, several of whom committed suicide as a result of the government's culling policy. These human 'stewards' were readily demonized while animals who were formerly regarded as objectified livestock became worthy of human empathy and respect: 'Once as unremarkable as hedgerows, sheep have assumed a prominently visible role as doppelgangers for a confused citizenry' (Franklin, 2001: 4). Although now, many years on from the crisis, sheep appear to have been reassigned to their insignificant, objectified status, it is interesting that (even if just for a short time) the ethic of respect could re-emerge in a post-domestic context and in relation to the 'lowliest' of domestic animals.

SUGGESTIONS FOR FURTHER READING

Alvard, M.S. and Kuznar, L. 2001. Deferred harvests: the transition from hunting to animal husbandry. *American Anthropologist* 103(2): 295–311.

Campbell, B. 2005. On 'loving your water buffalo more than your own mother': relationships of animal and human care in Nepal. In: J. Knight (ed.) *Animals in person: cultural perspectives on human–animal intimacies*. London: Routledge.

Cassidy, R. and Mullin, M. (eds) 2007. *Where the wild things are now*. Oxford: Berg.

Jones, O. 2003. 'The restraint of beasts': rurality, animality, actor network theory and dwelling. In: P. Cloke (ed.) *Country visions*. Harlow: Pearson Education.

Milliet, J. 2002. A comparative study of women's activities in the domestication of animals. In: Henninger-Voss, M.J. (ed.) *Animals in human histories: the mirror of nature and culture*. Rochester: University of Rochester Press.

Russell, N. 2002. The wild side of animal domestication. *Society & Animals* 10: 285–302.

Shanklin, E. 1985. Sustenance and symbol: anthropological studies of domesticated animals. *Annual Review of Anthropology* 14: 375–403.

Shipman, P. 2010. The animal connection and human evolution. *Current Anthropology* 51(4): 519–538.

Tsovel, A. (2005) What can a farm animal biography accomplish? The case of 'Portrait of the burger as a young calf'. *Society & Animals* 13(3): 245–262.

6
Good to Think

There is nothing in the external world which demands that certain things go together and others do not. (Tyler, 1969: 7)

Classification has long been regarded a 'prime and fundamental concern of social anthropology' (Needham, 1963: viii) because, as Emile Durkheim and Marcel Mauss demonstrated in their seminal book *Primitive classification* (1963), not only are classificatory systems key to understanding human social organization, they also function to help people (anthropologists included) make sense of the world around them. Systems of classification also serve to differentiate between the humans in question and the 'others' with whom they interact. According to 'scientific' 'Linnaean' taxonomy, the system which is commonly followed in a 'Western' context, humans are animals (members of the kingdom *Animalia*). They are also vertebrates, mammals, primates, hominids and *Homo sapiens*. Yet there are numerous alternative classificatory systems which anthropologists often refer to as 'folk' models. Some of these 'folk classifications' invoke aspects of a Linnaean system, and others do not. According to the Christian Church, for example, humans are not animals, while for some vegetarians the fact that humans are mammals renders other members of that class inedible (see chapter 7). The folk classifications that anthropologists have observed in many cultural contexts are of interest in their own right, as windows into the societies in question but also, with the benefit of hindsight, because of the attitudes which anthropologists themselves have expressed in relation to their inherently 'unscientific' nature.

TOTEMISM AND THE BORORO CASE

Probably one of the most famous examples of folk classification is the Brazilian Bororo's identification with Red Macaws (*Ara chlopteras* or *Ara macau*). This identification has figured in the anthropological consciousness so prominently as a result of the Bororo statement 'We are red macaws' recorded in 1894 by Karl

70

von den Steinen. The various ways in which the statement has been interpreted by anthropologists over the years provides a useful starting point for considering a wide range of important theoretical issues of relevance to human–animal interactions.

Von den Steinen himself interpreted the statement as proof of what was referred to at the time as 'primitive mentality' (Lévy-Bruhl, 1923) and later 'undomesticated thought' (Lévi-Strauss, 1966 [1962]); that the Bororo, as a 'primitive' people, could not make even the most rudimentary distinction between humans and birds. For Lévy-Bruhl and his contemporaries, influenced by the tenets of social evolutionism, 'non-Western' thought was inherently inferior to 'Western' thought. 'Western' science represented the epitome of rationality, while the animistic or totemic beliefs of the 'primitives' were superstitious and irrational. Such views were only slightly revised with the advent of empirical field research, and for Malinowski totemism was still irrational by 'Western' standards. It could, nonetheless, be explained in functionalist terms, with relationships determined according to how 'useful' particular plants or animals were to the people who associated with them. But this was still evidence of an inferior, 'savage' mode of thought, as evidenced in Malinowski's functionalist explanation of Trobriand totemism:

> The road from the wilderness to the savage's belly and consequently to his mind is very short. For him the world is an indiscriminate background against which there stands out the useful, primarily the edible, species of animals and plants. (Malinowski, 1974: 44)

Durkheim, on the other hand, saw totemic thought as a symbolic mirror reflecting human social organization and reinforcing the status quo. Of course the 'natives' themselves didn't recognize this 'fact' because they lacked the necessary cognitive abilities. It was the job of the anthropologist to interpret and demonstrate the ways in which indigenous ideas about 'nature' were merely outward projections of human society (see also Willerslev, 2007: 18).

Radcliffe-Brown (1951, 1952), drawing and expanding on Durkheim's structural-functionalism, also took steps away from Malinowski's explanation and suggested that while totems could indeed be useful, there were also numerous prohibitions associated with them which required further explanation. He concluded that totems played an integral role in maintaining social order *because* of the specific *symbolic* (*metaphorical*) relationships which they were thought to exhibit. Radcliffe-Brown attempted to account for totems, then, on the basis that they expressed social divisions, with higher-ranking groups or individuals being associated with particularly charismatic totems such as predators or key game species, while those of lower rank were associated with less significant totems.

In a similar vein the French structuralist Claude Lévi-Strauss thought the question could be answered by considering the social system as a whole, rather than by simply focusing on the specific characteristics of totemic animals (and the people they were supposed to represent). Therefore totem animals could not be accounted for in utilitarian or economic terms (i.e. whether they were edible, or provided valuable materials). Instead, Lévi-Strauss argued that certain animals achieved totemic status because they were 'good to think' in the sense that they offered 'conceptual support for social differentiation' (1963: 101), meeting 'intellectual requirements rather than ... satisfying needs' (1966 [1962]: 9). This may appear to be very close to Radcliffe-Brown's explanations, and in some ways it is. According to Lévi-Strauss animals were chosen as totems because of the ways that their differences (as perceived by the society in question) corresponded to differences between groups within that society. It is at this point in 'history' that we can bring the discussion back to the Bororo, as most anthropological commentators thereafter saw the by-now infamous statement as a manifestation of metaphorical associations, in the style of Lévi-Strauss.

So, totemism is often described as the symbolic expression of social relationships between human groups and particular totemic 'others' (see for example, Descola, 1992; Saunders, 1994). The chosen totems (macaws in the Bororo case) have ritual or symbolic importance and, in some contexts, are thought to share distant ancestry with the human group in question. However, as James Fernández (1991) has convincingly argued, totemic relationships can be either metaphorical or metonymic (or, on occasion, both).

A metaphoric relationship exists when anthropologists recognize clear semantic distinctions between categories (in the Bororo case, between humans and parrots) but the parties are united by some shared symbolic attribute. A metonymic relationship is suggestive of continuity or even shared ancestry between the different parties in the relationship. Fernández uses the example of a caterpillar and a butterfly to denote a metonymic relationship (they represent different stages in the life cycle of the same animal), whereas a lion and a king would constitute a metaphorical relationship (they share certain symbolic associations: power, strength, courage and so on). If the Bororo really did believe they were red macaws and, as von den Steinen and Lévy-Bruhl claimed, were unable (or rather didn't see the need) to differentiate between species – or even self and other – the relationship would actually be metonymical.

As far as the Bororo themselves are concerned, on death human souls can enter the bodies of the living and parrots are the preferred hosts for these wandering spirits (Fernández, 1991: 132). This 'fact' has led some anthropologists to conclude that the Bororo believe they will be reincarnated as parrots when they die, hence the statement 'We are red macaws' is actually 'We will become red macaws' (Smith, 1972: 393) and is thus indicative of a metaphorical relationship; macaws are distinct entities who act as vessels for human souls. However, depending on just how the Bororo perceive this process, it could be metonymical if the souls *become* (rather than just enter) parrots.

In 1985, Crocker suggested a series of alternative interpretations of the Bororo–macaw conundrum. He also concluded that the relationship was metaphorical, but for different reasons. Crocker observed that the statement was only made by or applied to men, who would adorn themselves with the feathers of the birds during important rituals. He also noted that parrots were frequently kept as pets by women, and that the Bororo's was a matrilineal society. Thus he saw the statement as an ironic comment on the status of Bororo men who were, in effect, the property of their female relatives. These interpretations have come in for criticism from Fernández (1991: 134–5), who suggests that the relationship is, in fact, metonymical *and* metaphoric depending on the aspect under consideration. This may appear to be a rather trivial semantic distinction, but when it comes to understanding how humans *actually* think about other animals, it becomes very important indeed.

Fernández asserts that:

> just as metaphor creates the meaningful relation between its members [the elements in a common whole, for example Bororo, parrots, feathers/plumes, spirits], so metonymy may create the semantic and intentional whole to which its members are defined, for purposes of the trope, as belonging [society]. Outside or prior to the metonymy itself, they may well be seen as belonging to separate wholes [spirit world or mortal world, human species or parrot species] ... [However] metaphors in effect also constitute themselves as metonymies because the emergent common meaning

they create constitutes a new 'whole' [the ritual context] of which the two otherwise disparate members of the metaphor equally become parts. [However] Metonymy does not imply metaphorical identification, and two dissimilar entities [men and parrots] may be constituted as parts of a tropic whole without any implication that they share any specific common property.

In other words, there may be no metaphorical relationship between men and parrots as has traditionally been assumed. However, Fernández (1991: 135) argues that *aspects of* the Bororo relationship with parrots are at times metaphorical and at times metonymical, and the relationship is overall synecdochic, meaning a figure of speech with numerous potential applications such as: (1) a part used to refer to the whole (as *feather* for *parrot*), (2) the whole used to refer to a part (as *parrot* for *feather*), (3) the specific to refer to the general (as *ancestor* for *spirit*), (4) the general to refer to the specific (as *parrot* for *red macaw*) and (5) the material from which a thing is made as opposed to the thing itself (as *men* for *Bororo*).

For Fernández, the statement has been misinterpreted and should actually read 'We make ourselves araras [parrots]' or 'We become araras' (as per Smith, 1972) rather than 'We are araras.' This is because there is only one traditional context when the men alone don the feathers of their 'totems' to engage in ritual activity and this is key to understanding the complexity of the relationship as far as Fernández is concerned:

> Ceremonial performance is a most important part of Bororo life and appears to be the most highly valued form of social activity. Since only men perform the ceremonies, this figures as the most culturally distinctive feature, the most valued attribute, of maleness for the Bororo. (1991: 137).

Fernández uses this as an explanation for why 'outsiders' may have come away with the impression that it was the men only who 'are' red macaws:

> Bororo men might well be proud to describe themselves for this reason to an outsider as those who 'become araras' by donning their feathers in communal ritual, even though they would have few spontaneous occasions to use the expression to one another. (1991: 137)

Because the red plumes are the most significant material objects utilized in these ritual contexts (rituals can be postponed if insufficient plumes are available), and performance in the ceremony is integral to their collective identity as 'Bororo', the conclusion could be drawn (as it is by Fernández) that the men who participate have to 'become' macaws (by donning feathers) in order to 'become' Bororo (through ritual performance). Another point of relevant ethnographic detail noted by Fernández is that the Bororo term for 'plumes' also means 'spirit' and 'ancestor' (1991: 138). The Bororo, as with many other animistic peoples, see the 'spirit' as the animating force of 'things', including humans (see chapter 4), and so:

> By detaching plumes from their original source ... and applying the plumes to themselves, Bororo men *metonymically* create a new external form for themselves as spirit beings, 'ancestors representing spirits,' who are themselves called *aroe* (plumes-spirit). By creating for themselves the external form of spirits and thus playing the role of form-creating spirit toward themselves, Bororo men empower themselves, as spirit-actors, to play the same role toward society at large through their ritual performance. The metonymic assumption by the ritual actors of feathered form as plumed 'spirits' becomes the *metaphoric* basis of their power to reproduce the forms of society through collective ceremony. (1991: 139, emphasis added; see Strathern and Strathern, 1971: 176–7 for a similar example from Mount Hagen, Papua New Guinea)

The macaw plumes as both feathers and spirits, ancestors and spirit beings, mediate between the metonymic and metaphoric components of the ritual, enabling Bororo men to 'become macaws' in order to 'become spirits' in order to reproduce society in order to 'become themselves' (Fernández, 1991: 139).

THINKING ABOUT TOTEMS

The various interpretations of the Bororo case as outlined above demonstrate more general theoretical trends in anthropological thought about humans and other animals. The 19th- and early 20th-century 'armchair anthropologists' such as Lévy-Bruhl thought in ethnocentric terms, seeing the Bororo as irrational 'primitives', little more than animals themselves. For Malinowski, human relationships with animals were grounded almost exclusively in the latter's functionality, a view which failed to take into account the perspectives of the people who actually made totemic associations with other animals, and for whom nonhumans were also spiritual beings who connected with humans in multifarious and complex ways which were not always apparent to the outside observer.

The later symbolic 'totem as metaphor' explanation also failed to take into account the complexity of human interactions with, and perceptions of, nonhuman 'persons', and, more importantly, undermined the views of the people themselves. What if, rather than all this symbolism, metaphor and metonymy the simple fact of the matter is that the Bororo, as they themselves have stated, really are macaws?

Indeed, the use of metaphor can, in many respects, be regarded as a form of anthropomorphic ethnocentricity, entailing the 'attribution' by outsiders of symbolic relationships to the humans and the animals involved, relationships which (according to anthropological interpretation) could only be comprehended or perceived by human actors: anthropologists to be precise (see also chapter 4; Ingold, 2000; Willerslev, 2007). Fernández's recognition of the *complexity* of the Bororo/araras relationship in ritual context, and the interplay between metaphor and metonymy, is certainly an improvement on previous interpretations, but is flawed nonetheless. Fernández still approaches the relationship from an anthropocentric perspective, while his Bororo informants do (or did) not.

SEEING PERSONHOOD

As de Castro (1998) among others has argued (for example, Fausto, 2008; Kohn, 2007; see also chapters 4, 10 and 16), many South American peoples (including the Bororo) see animals (and other nonhuman entities) as persons who perceive reality, and themselves as persons, in ways which differ profoundly from human perceptions. From this perspective, all persons have a shared essence which unites them, a point which Fernández himself also notes, but it is their external, physical form which differs and effects their being in (and therefore perception of) the world. For anthropologists to project their own etic interpretations onto the situation, seeing metaphor where the indigenous subjects actually see continuity is, as Willerslev (2007: 19) and Ingold (2000: 76) both note in relation to Bird-David's (1992) analysis of Nayaka animism, problematic to say the least:

When hunters use terms drawn from the domain of human interaction to describe their relations with animals, they are said to be indulging in metaphor (Bird-David, 1992). But to claim that what is literally true of relations among humans (for example, that they share), is only figuratively true of relations with animals, is to reproduce the very dichotomy between animals and society that the indigenous view purports to reject. We tell ourselves reassuringly that this view the hunters have, of sharing with animals as they would with people [or, in the Bororo case, that they are parrots], however appealing it might be, does not correspond with what actually happens. For nature, we say, does not *really* share with man [and humans cannot *really* be parrots]. When hunters [or Bororo] assert the contrary it is because the image of sharing is so deeply ingrained in their thought [or because parrot feathers are so visible during ritual activity] that they can no longer tell the metaphor from the reality. But *we* can, and we insist – on these grounds – that the hunters [or the Bororo] have got it wrong. (Ingold, 2000: 76)

Added in to the equation, but overlooked in discussions of the Bororo statement, are the possible effects of psychoactive drugs, which are commonly used in Amerindian ritual contexts. As Rosengren notes, the use of hallucinogens further complicates (and blurs) the relationships between humans, animals and spirits (2006). In the Bororo case then, men might indeed see themselves and red macaws (and other animals in the forest) as one and the same thing as a result of spirit possession or shamanic journeying following the ingestion of psychoactive drugs, or simply because they recognize parrots (or jaguar – Kohn, 2007; Saunders, 1994; or monkeys – Cormier, 2003) as fellow living beings, so a distinction between these two Linnaean categories is unnecessary.

As Eduardo Kohn notes in relation to his fieldwork with the Runa:

Dogs really become human (biologically and in historically very specific ways) and the Runa really become puma; the need to survive encounters with feline semiotic selves requires it. Such becomings change what it means to be alive; they change what it means to be human just as much as they change what it means to be a dog or even a predator. (2007: 18)

Kohn's Runa informants talk about 'becoming jaguars' (*runa puma* where 'runa' is both an ethnonym and the term for 'person') as a result of successful (i.e. non-fatal) interactions between individual humans and feline predators encountered in the forest (see chapter 10).

Another oft-cited ethnographic example where folk classification comes into conflict within many an etic world view is the insistence of the Karam, a people from the Papua New Guinean highlands, that Cassowaries (*Casuarius bennetti*) are not birds. The Karam classify animals according to their experiences of them. Therefore for the Karam birds such as the cassowary are not birds at all (because they are bipedal and flightless), whereas winged mammals such as bats are (Bulmer, 1967). This may seem like a common-sense approach to classification. However even within the same cultural context, the experiences of individuals do not always tally, leading to contradictory attitudes towards the classificatory status of particular animals; for other New Guineans, who arguably coexist with animals in similar ways to the Karam, the Cassowary is a bird just as it is in Linnaean taxonomy (Bulmer, 1967: 22 n. 5).

As Ingold notes, 'to individuals who belong to different intentional worlds [even if they belong to the same or a similar "ecological" or "cultural" world], the same objects in the same physical surroundings may mean quite different things' (2000: 40; see also Milton, 2002, 2005). These discrepancies have caused anthropologists some conceptual difficulties when attempting to understand how others construct or perceive the world. Because there are always exceptions or disagreements within as well as across cultural 'boundaries', then the traditional 'constructivist' assumption – that culturally specific classificatory systems enable people to organize their sensory data – is not particularly satisfactory (Ingold, 2000: 153). While 'culturally grounded' received wisdom certainly has a part to play, the role of individual experiential engagement with other beings (human and nonhuman) is now widely recognized by anthropologists as an important consideration (Ingold, 2000; Milton, 2002, 2005).

TRANSGRESSIVE BOUNDARY CROSSING

One way in which animals become problematic is when humans are unable to exert direct control over them. This is increasingly the case as humans encroach into the natural habitats of their nonhuman neighbours, resulting in intensified competition for food and resources (see for example, Knight, 2000a). In the majority of cases, however, it is the animals who are regarded as problematic and subsequently classified as anomalous or transgressive because they do not fit into appropriate cultural categories. Their transgressive status might be due to their physiology, their behaviour, or the environment in which they find themselves; they are perceived as 'matter out of place' and need to be dealt with accordingly. Pigs, for example, are anomalous (and therefore their flesh is taboo in certain religious contexts) because they are perceived as 'dirty' (Mandel, 1989, 1990, 1994; see also chapters 1 and 7) or 'incomplete' (Douglas, 1966). Behaviourally, certain animals act in ways which are deemed inappropriate and therefore 'unacceptable', for example by killing livestock (Marvin, 2000), raiding crops (Hill, 2000) or attacking humans (Peace, 2002). These 'transgressive' animals become sources of conflict between human groups and individuals because of the ideological associations that each makes with the animal in question, which, in some cases, are grounded in the traditional wisdom of cultural constuctivism and in others are grounded in embodied experiences, both good and bad.

Transgressive animals and the debates which grow up around them are fertile ground for anthropological investigation (see Knight, 2000a). An interesting example from the ethnographic record concerns the shifting classification of dingoes (*Canis lupus dingo*) in Australia before and after the tragic death of a young boy on Australia's Fraser Island (Peace, 2002). Prior to the attack, dingoes on Fraser Island had been used to promote it as a 'natural wilderness' tourist destination. The presence of the dingoes, who were classified and promoted as a rare and endangered species, was a considerable lure for tourists and dingoes were therefore regarded as integral to the island's economic and ecological prosperity. However, the history of Fraser Island's development in the run-up to the dingo attack reveals some contradictory and troubling representations of the animal. Between the 1970s and 1990s the island was a source of conflict between commercial organizations that were keen to exploit its natural resources and conservationist groups who opposed such activity.

In the early 1990s the conservationists emerged victorious and the island was declared a World Heritage Site. The population of pure-bred dingoes was a significant contributing factor in this accreditation. As a result, Fraser Island has become an extremely popular tourist destination, commoditized via the promotion of its natural resources (which included the dingoes), rather than through their exploitation, or so it seemed (see also chapter 13).

As Peace notes (2002: 15), the island is marketed as an unpredictable, natural wilderness, devoid of human intervention. Although the dingoes are 'wild animals', the way that they were represented (or, as Peace suggests, misrepresented) in the island's promotional literature undeniably contributed to the attack. Despite their wild status, dingoes strongly resemble domestic dogs – a fact emphasized in the advertising aimed at tourists. These adverts misled holiday-makers into associating with an anthropo-morphic, caricatured image of the dingo. Indeed, even where the dingoes' 'wildness' was emphasized, it was in a non-threatening manner, via images of the animals lounging on picturesque beaches. On the island tourists were confronted with warnings from the Department of the Environment, but even these were played down and the positive elements of a dingo encounter emphasized (through assertions that dingoes are 'beautiful', 'natural treasures' and could provide visitors with 'treasured memories').

In 2009 a 9-year-old boy was killed by two young dingoes while he played near to a camp site with a 7-year-old friend. The same dingoes also attacked the boy's father and brother who rushed to his aid (Peace, 2002). In the wake of the attack the way dingoes were classified and represented changed, but, as Peace notes, this was a process which had already been evolving on the island. With the booming tourist industry came increased development, with camp sites, car parks and picnic areas spreading into areas of dingo habitat:

> This made them [dingoes] accessible as photographic subjects, and therefore most welcome to many tourists; but their popularity was more than offset over time by their taking food from restaurant tables, forcing entry into expensive tents, chewing up costly hiking boots, defecating around swimming pools, and running off with bathers' clothing. (Peace, 2002: 16)

These forays into human settlements provided dingoes with easy access to food, which they came to rely on – losing their natural hunting abilities and 'wildness' in the process, and becoming a threat to their human providers (for a similar example involving baboons in South Africa, see Hurn, 2011b).

In this example of human–animal conflict, the transgressive animals were arguably victims of human exploitation, retribution and manipulated representation: the 'wildness' and natural beauty of the dingo was used to initially protect and then to promote Fraser Island. The burgeoning tourist industry, based on the ideal of an unspoilt natural wilderness, of which the dingo was an integral part, paradoxically 'spoilt' the island's wilderness through the development of areas to accommodate tourists. Because human settlement then encroached into the dingoes' habitat they, in accordance with their 'wild' and 'natural' status as hunters and scavengers, crossed the human constructed socio-spatial boundaries between nature and civilization, but the dingoes' 'wildness' was only acceptable in the wild.

CRYPTOZOOLOGY AS A WAY FORWARD?

As we have seen, 'scientific' systems of classification focus on taxonomic data, in other words what is perceived to be the innate nature of things which may or may not be visible to the naked eye. For example, cetaceans are mammals because, while they are aquatic creatures, they are warm-blooded and give birth to live young who feed on milk. 'Folk' models on the other hand, focus on the 'class', the observable 'common attributes'. In many important respects 'scientific' classification is problematic because of its rigidity. It does not accommodate or allow for anomaly or different ways of being, different ways of knowing. Quotidian ontology on the other hand allows for that plasticity of identity and understanding. An orca (*Orcinus orca*) may be a mammal, but why does that mean it can't also be a fish (Dupre, 2006)? Or, for that matter, a reincarnated tribal elder (Norman, 2009)?

John Dupre (2006) notes that whales are physiologically and evolutionarily closer to land-mammals than other aquatic creatures, but wonders why this should mean they are denied entry into the category 'fish'. He believes this is because:

> people believe that both mammals and fish are natural kinds, and as such form part of a divergent hierarchy of kinds such that no kinds overlap: any two kinds are either disjoint or one includes the other. This is indeed a principle of most biological taxonomies. But by no stretch of the imagination is 'fish' a term of such taxonomy. An enormously diverse group of organisms are included under the category of fish and I can imagine no convincing reason for excluding the cetaceans (whales and

porpoises) from this broad church. In fact, a salmon, say, is less distantly related to a porpoise than it is to an ancient and 'primitive' fish such as a lamprey. (2006: 3)

The belief in 'natural kinds', identified by 'science' according to 'innate' and defining characteristics doesn't stand up in practice, and also hinders the ability of many to see other animals as people; the 'nature' of animals is not deemed to include continuities with people, and therefore this aspect is overlooked or ignored. Ethnographic engagement, and daily personal experience informs us that living beings do not fit neatly into boxes. Our experiences of other animals frequently cause us to reconsider how we classify them. Pets, for example, are often reclassified as individual persons as opposed to incarnations of an ideal type (see also chapter 8).

One last point relates to an important, albeit under-theorized area of anthropological concern; so-called 'cryptids' or crypto-zoological entities. The very existence (or perceived existence) of these 'mythical' creatures, which often defy scientific classification or explanation, challenges the normative discourse which such taxonomy seeks to maintain. According to Dan Sperber (1996), folk taxonomies can deal with anomalies because they are not bound by the rigid confines of scientific modes of classification, which locate animals in a particular class or genus. Cryptids do not belong to the categories of science; were-wolves for example are neither human nor lupine but something between these species and, as a result of their liminality, they are accorded supernatural powers. Kohn's discussion of were-jaguars in Amazonia provides a contemporary return to the 'problems' presented by the Bororo case, and demonstrates again the need to resist the projection of etic values and classifications onto unfamiliar ways of being (as per Descola, 1994):

Many Runa, especially those that have developed shamanistic powers, acquire a kind of jaguar habitus. This gives them predatory power when they are alive and allows their souls to inhabit the bodies of jaguars at death ... when a person 'with jaguar' (Quichua, *pumayu*) dies, his or her soul goes to the forest to 'become a dog.' Were-jaguars become the dogs of the spirit animal masters. That is, they become subservient to them in the same way that the Runa, in everyday life, enter into subservient relations when they go to work as field hands for the estate owners and priests who serve as this-world models for the spirit beings. The were-jaguar, then, is simultaneously Runa, a potent feline predator, and the obedient dog of a white animal master. (2007: 11)

Kohn's description demonstrates that categories are not mutually exclusive. So, humans can be human, persons, spirits, jaguars and dogs – these categories are contingent on context and 'come into being' as a result of interactions with others.

SUGGESTIONS FOR FURTHER READING

Atran, S. 1990. *Cognitive foundations of natural history*. New York: Cambridge University Press.

Forth, G.L. 2003. *Nage birds: classification and symbolism among an eastern Indonesian people*. London: Routledge.

Forth, G.L. 2009. *Images of the wildman in Southeast Asia: an anthropological perspective*. London: Taylor & Francis.

Köhler, A. 2000. Half-man, half-elephant: shapeshifting among the Baka of Congo. In: J. Knight (ed.) *Natural enemies: people–wildlife conflict in anthropological perspective*. London: Routledge.

Marks, J. 2007. Anthropological taxonomy as both subject and object: the consequences of descent from Darwin and Durkheim. *Anthropology Today* 23(4): 7–12.

Marvin, G. 2001. Cultured killers – creating and representing foxhounds. *Society & Animals* 9(3): 273–289.

Milton, K. 2000. Ducks out of water: nature conservation as boundary maintenance. In: J. Knight (ed.) *Natural enemies: people–wildlife conflict in anthropological perspective*. London: Routledge.

Ritvo, H. 1997. *The platypus and the mermaid, and other figments of the classifying imagination*. Cambridge, MA: Harvard University Press.

Rye, S. 2000. Wild pigs, 'pig-men' and transmigrants in the rainforest of Sumatra. In: J. Knight (ed.) *Natural enemies: people–wildlife conflict in anthropological perspective*. London: Routledge.

Willerslev, R. 2004. Spirits as 'ready to hand': a phenomenological analysis of Yukaghir spiritual knowledge and dreaming. *Anthropological Theory*. 4(4): 395–418.

Willis, R. (ed.) 1994. *Signifying animals: human meaning in the natural world*. London: Unwin Hyman.

7
Food

Nothing more strongly arouses our disgust than cannibalism, yet we make the same impression on Buddhists and vegetarians, for we feed on babies, though not our own. (Robert Louis Stevenson)

Processes of food production and consumption involve a multitude of human interactions with other animals. These interactions culminate in perhaps the most significant of all (from the animal's perspective at least) – death and the subsequent consumption of flesh and associated by-products. Which animals get eaten, how they get eaten and why are questions of huge import and interest for anthropologists and consequently the reasons underlying dietary preferences and prohibitions have been the focus of anthropological attention and debate for many years.

The discussion of classification in the preceding chapter established that animals are 'good to think'. However, animals can also be good to eat – or not, as the case may be. The classificatory systems that different societies and indeed individuals use to differentiate between animal species can also help to determine an animal's edibility; one person's meat is another's poison. Indeed, food taboos and dietary preferences are what Marvin Harris called 'riddles of culture'. He illustrated the point as follows:

> Everyone knows examples of apparently irrational food habits. Chinese like dog meat but despise cow milk; we like cow milk but we won't eat dogs; some tribes in Brazil relish ants but despise venison. And so it goes around the world. (1974: 28)

While such cultural stereotypes are problematic, anthropologists generally agree on the basic sentiment being expressed here – that there are certain food stuffs associated with particular national cuisines and identities. The real debate occurs when we try to understand why such 'apparently irrational' food habits exist and persist. There are several different schools of thought which have dominated the discussion. Traditionally the structuralist or symbolic perspective, following Lévi-Strauss, locked horns with the cultural materialists, following Harris, but in recent years the debate has become much wider, inclusive and on occasion rather heated.

THE STRUCTURALIST OR SYMBOLIC PERSPECTIVE

Proponents of the structuralist or symbolic perspective advocate that animals are good to think and good to prohibit. They tend to see culture as an ideological system whereby meaning is ascribed to 'things' according to seemingly arbitrary symbolic values. For Sahlins, for example, animals (and their resultant edibility or inedibility) are categorized according to classic structuralist oppositions. He argued that, as a rule, humans (and his paper focused on humans living in the USA in the 1970s) eat animals who are far removed from their culturally constructed notion of humanity. Such an approach built on the work of Douglas (1966), Leach (1964) and Tambiah (1969), who also noted that social and ideological distance positively corresponds with an animal's edibility. Sahlins suggested that North Americans refrain from eating animals who are physically close to them, dogs and cats for example, because to do so would be tantamount to cannibalism. These animals are quasi-humans, sharing American homes in the capacity of friends or family members. It is, on the other hand, perfectly acceptable to eat cows, sheep, pigs and chickens because, while they are also domesticated animals, they live outside of the human household, and are not, as a rule, personified (given names) or thought of in anthropomorphic terms.

Sahlins' 'model of edibility' might be conceived of as a series of concentric circles with humans and the animals they hold dear to them (and whose flesh is therefore taboo) in the centre. Horses, like pets, are also taboo in the American food system and inhabit the second concentric ring of familiarity; they are named and treated as quasi humans, but according to Sahlins are of a lower status than pets because they are servile animals, traditionally employed in agriculture and now predominantly used for recreational activities. The edible animals (such as cows, pigs, sheep and chickens) are those contained within the third concentric ring – they are domesticates living under human 'control' (see chapter 5) and are objectified as 'livestock', 'things' which (it is implied) lack the intelligence, personality or feelings shared by those fortunate enough to dwell inside the first two circles. Edible game animals are located in the next circle. The animals beyond the outer circle are those such as foxes, rats and mice regarded as 'transgressive' (see chapter 6) and therefore for the most part deemed taboo. Their anomalous status (often as pests or vermin) can be accounted for, in many cases, on the grounds of their behaviour; they act in ways which make them difficult to classify or control. Rats and mice for example enter human homes uninvited and, it is often thought, spread disease (Edelman, 2002). Foxes enter chicken coops and fields of newborn lambs and wreak havoc (Marvin, 2000). Badgers interact with cattle and may or may not spread tuberculosis (Caplan, 2010). Yet these actions alone do not account for why badger or fox or rat are not national dishes, or even occasional meals in areas where their populations flourish – they are theoretically 'edible' but culturally (and psychologically) 'uneatable' in most, if not all post-domestic societies.

When discussing hunting in Europe anthropologist Bertrand Hell states that animals such as these (which he refers to as 'stinking animals') are not eaten because:

> their meat is regarded as too black; they are carnivorous animals and their small digestive systems do not allow them fully to digest the fresh blood they consume. This is why the consumption of their meat is forbidden while that of the other game animals, herbivores all of them, is permitted. But stinking animals are also associated with uncleanliness since, as carrion-eating animals, they transgress an important biblical taboo – 'Thou shalt not eat of a dead or wounded animal' (Leviticus, XVII). They are therefore considered impure. (1996: 211–12)

So, along structuralist lines these animals are 'inedible' because they are deemed 'like us' in the sense that they too consume the flesh of other animals. Moreover they do so in a manner which, as Hell notes, renders them unclean.

While there is some merit to the structuralist or symbolic interpretations discussed above, it is important to recognize that each case needs to be considered on an individual basis and in relation to the context within which particular food preferences occur. For example, while Sahlins' model has some currency in some Euro-American cultural contexts, it falls short in many other ethnographic situations where quasi-humans, 'impure' or anomalous animals are eaten. In Malawi for instance, as Brian Morris (2000: 191–9) has noted, the meat of most animals, including rats, is consumed with relish and while large carnivores such as lion (*Panthera leo*) and hyena

(*Crocuta crocuta*) are referred to as *chirombo* (dangerous) and therefore deemed inedible, the meat of smaller carnivores such as servals (*Leptailurus serval*) is edible and considered a delicacy.

Mary Douglas (1966) famously approached religious dietary taboos from a similarly structuralist perspective. Douglas also argued that food prohibitions were based on maintaining purity and social order, exemplified in the classificatory systems used to distinguish between certain opposites, such as clean/dirty, pure/impure, edible/inedible. Douglas suggested that pork is a taboo meat for Jews because pigs are anomalous; in Genesis there are very clear categories into which animals must fit in order to be considered 'clean' or 'pure'. Fish for example must have scales and swim in the sea (hence the taboo on shellfish) and birds must have feathers and fly in the sky (so flightless birds are also deemed 'abominable'). For Douglas (1966), some animals constituted 'matter out of place' because they failed to fit into this culturally prescribed system. Pigs were inedible on account of their impurity; they were neither one thing nor the other because they 'part the hoof but do not chew the cud'. In other words, while pigs have cloven hooves they are not ruminants like cows, sheep and goats and are therefore 'unclean' and taboo because they contravene the laws of creation.

In a religion whose followers are exhorted to strive towards purity and the attainment of unity with God, the act of eating an anomalous 'impure' animal would be polluting indeed. According to Douglas, the root meaning of 'Holy' is 'wholeness' and 'completeness'.

The instruction to be holy precedes each item in the list of prohibited animals in the Old Testament, so the prohibitions must therefore be explained in terms of holiness: individuals will prosper if they conform to holiness and perish if they deviate from it.

CULTURAL MATERIALISM

Another theoretical school whose proponents have made numerous contributions to the debates concerning food taboos is cultural materialism. Cultural materialists such as Marvin Harris (for example, 1979) have looked at the 'material infrastructure' of a given society, or the conditions from which particular cultural practices (such as institutionalized dietary restrictions) emerge. For Harris and his followers this etic infrastructure plays a deterministic role in shaping the 'structure' of social or cultural institutions (economy, political organization and so on), which in turn determine the emic 'superstructures', the internal behaviours and ways of thinking about the socio-cultural reality of the world 'out there'. In relation to religious prohibitions on the consumption of pork, Harris suggested that pigs were simply not suited to the climate and ecology of the ancient Middle East, where the Abrahamic faiths developed.

Archaeological evidence points to widespread deforestation in the Middle East approximately 9000 and 4000 BCE. Without forested areas to keep them cool (as pigs cannot regulate their own body temperatures, hence their need to wallow in mud), swine production would have become a labour-intensive activity – 'ecologically maladaptive', to use Harris's terminology. Because Harris saw the domestication of animals in functionalist terms, providing material benefits in times of hardship, this change in the agricultural environment may well have led to pork becoming a luxury food and, as such, it would have been counter-productive for early pastoralists to expend much effort and resources on keeping pigs. Also worthy of consideration are the difficulties associated with storing pork in a hot climate and the high numbers of pathogens and parasites which can be transferred to humans from pigs via the consumption of undercooked pork. But does such an approach convincingly explain why the ancient Hebrews subsequently deemed it necessary to place a taboo on pigs in general? Harris believes it does, stating 'the greater the temptation, the greater the need for divine interdiction' (1974: 44). In other words the material infrastructure determined the superstructure.

Harris, then, took a very different view to Douglas. Whereas Douglas argued that it was the religious importance ascribed to 'purity' which rendered certain animals taboo, for Harris animal domestication originated in an attempt to ensure a steady food supply for the growing population (a view shared by many others – see chapter 5). Harris therefore saw humans as maximizing individuals, *Homo economicus* in the formalist tradition, or as Hobbesian 'possessive individuals', making religious proscriptions on material grounds and banning labour-intensive animals. Yet the formalist approach to human subsistence strategies was challenged and usurped by a substantivist critique in the 1960s (led, coincidentally enough, by Sahlins – see also chapter 4). The substantivists argued that seeing human activity in what were essentially capitalist terms was ethnocentric. Moreover, the deterministic nature of the cultural materialist model is something which contemporary anthropologists tend to shy away from because it denies human choice and agency in shaping cultural practices. That is not to say, however, that Harris's argument is without merit or that the two positions (symbolic/

structuralist and cultural materialist) are mutually exclusive. On the contrary, Harris may well have a point that the conditions of the ancient Middle East were such that pig keeping became difficult, but it might also be the case that pigs were regarded as 'impure' because they had cloven hooves but were not ruminants.

'HOLY COW'

Another example discussed by Harris is the veneration of cattle in Hinduism. Pigs are taboo in the Abrahamic tradition because their presence can threaten the status (and eternal life) of the devout human, but cattle are 'sacred' (though not worshipped as such) because they create and support life. Bhishma, one of the main heroic characters in the Hindu epic *Mahabharata*, provided the following explanation: 'Cows are guileless in their behaviour and from them flow sacrifices ... and milk and curds and butter. Hence cows are sacred....' From a cultural materialist perspective, the milk-producing capacity of cows means they are worth more alive than dead, while from a structuralist perspective, cows represent life and are a symbolic surrogate mother of sorts. Indeed, Gandhi commented that 'the cow' was revered because, in addition to producing milk, 'she made agriculture possible'. Cattle are important traction animals and Harris noted that it made no economic sense to kill animals required in other aspects of food production (such as the growing of crops). Yet cows also compete with humans for scarce resources, so while 'productive' animals are venerated the older generations are not so fortunate. As Maya Warrier notes; 'cows in modern India are usually abandoned after their reproductive years and can be seen wandering the streets of India's towns and villages in conditions of malnourishment and neglect' (2009: 276 n. 14). Harris (1979) also noted the inherent contradictions between attitudes and actions during his own fieldwork. In Kerala, southern India, Harris's farming informants would indirectly allow male calves to starve by restricting their access to food, despite the prohibition on killing cattle:

> When I asked farmers to explain why male calves got sick more often, several suggested that the males ate less than the females. One or two suggested that the male calves ate less because they were not permitted to stay at the mother's teats for more than a few seconds. But no one would say that since there is little

demand for traction animals in Kerala, males are culled and females reared. (1979: 33)

Psychologist Drew Western (1984) notes that the prohibition on killing cattle is a 'cultural' ideal, which permeates all aspects of Hindu life and yet not all Hindus observe this ideal in practice. As a result, cultural materialism and symbolic or structuralist explanations both offer some insight, but neither model offers a completely satisfactory explanation. Indeed, the cultural materialist explanations cannot account for the contradictions experienced within communities (for example, Hindu farmers 'allowing' male calves to die) and between communities that live in very close proximity. Take for example Hindus and Muslims living on the borders between India and Pakistan. Even Harris diverted from his materialist course to suggest that eschewing cow slaughter as a form of *ahimsa* (non-violence) was a means by which Hindus could differentiate themselves from neighbouring Muslims.

This emphasis on the symbolic importance of animals (which could, in Harris's materialist model, constitute the 'emic' or 'mental superstructure') comes to the fore in contemporary debates over the status of cattle. In India cows have become iconic 'markers' of Hinduism, and cow protection is closely associated with Indian nationalism (Warrier, 2009). That is not to say that all people living in India are Hindus, or that if they are, they venerate the cow. Nonetheless, the symbolic association with cattle is sufficiently widespread and entrenched that when historian Dwijendra Narayah Jha published his book *The myth of the holy cow* (2002), which convincingly argued that the sacrality of the cow in Hinduism was a myth (or rather an 'invented tradition'), the Indian government banned the book, Jha's life was threatened by right-wing extremists and there were numerous well-attended public book-burnings. This furore demonstrates that it is the 'idea' or symbolism of the sacred nature of the cow, rather than the reality, that is important to many contemporary Hindus.

The symbolic approach helps to account for the large numbers of Hindus who do consume beef but still identify themselves as 'Hindu' (Warrier, 2009: 276 n. 14) – indeed, beef is the most widely consumed meat in India (Chigateri, 2011) – or for the covert killing of male calves by farmers observed by Harris. In *The myth of the holy cow*, Jha demonstrates that cattle were not regarded as 'sacred' until quite recently in Indian history (a point also made by Harris, 1966 and Serpell, 1996 [1986]). Through an exploration of Vedic and Hindu texts, Jha shows that cows were integral to religious ritual and that cow slaughter was widespread in ancient and classical India. The Hindu notion of *ahimsa* (non-violence) was and is an ideal which has come to be engaged with in an increasingly literal manner in contemporary and near-contemporary forms of Hinduism. Moreover, Hinduism is not a unified, organized religion with a central text dictating belief and practice. Rather, 'Hinduism' encompasses a plurality of ideas and teachings and is (like any spiritual practice and religious *belief*) open to interpretation and re-interpretation. The debate over the sacrality of cattle for Hindus reveals that there are numerous factors at play and, while a particular cultural practice may have begun in response to ecological conditions, the underlying reasons for the persistence of that practice may change over time and will vary according to the particular circumstances of individuals and wider social groups.

JUXTAPOSING SYMBOLISM AND MATERIALISM

In contemporary anthropological scholarship, the flaws of a materialist perspective are frequently offset by combining a materialist's focus on the resources available with a reflexive awareness of the constructivist nature of symbolic explanations, a recognition of individual agency and the emotional engagement of individuals with their environments. In many post-domestic contexts, for example, consumers have ready access to a wide range of foodstuffs reasonably cheaply. From a cultural materialist perspective this means individuals can be choosy about what they do and do not eat. The determining factor has become money – whether people can afford to buy particular items, such as free-range eggs or organically grown produce. Yet, even so, the 'culture' within which people live constrains choice to some extent; supermarkets in the UK do not stock dog meat for example, and there remain certain foods which carry particular symbolic meanings which are widely understood, even outside of academic scrutiny. Take, for example, the following account from Danny Miller's ethnography of shopping in north London, which demonstrates the continued prominence of symbolic thought: 'this family's shopping basket has mainly items such as mint sauce, chops, shortbread, corned beef, sage and onion stuffing, vinegar, pork belly and chipping potatoes, which together form a portrait of "Britishness" in the rather "bulldoggy" sense' (1998: 26).

The association of particular 'nationalities' with specific (often meat-based) cuisine can cause some problems for those who, for whatever reason (religious, ethical, health) choose to eschew the 'norm'. In Germany, for example, large numbers of Turkish immigrants for whom the consumption of pork is *haram* (forbidden) find themselves confronted with a situation where pork in the form of the ubiquitous *würst* (sausage) is a key aspect of 'national' cuisine. Anthropologist Ruth Mandel found that for these German-Turks the issue was essentially symbolic in nature. She states:

> I became aware of [the strength of feeling about pork] after having been asked by Turks on numerous occasions if I ate pork. The intensity of their concern led me to pursue the issue, and in many cases the act of eating pork or abstinence there-from served as the demarcation line between acceptance as one of 'us' and rejection of 'them'. (1990: 170)

Mandel goes on to consider the metaphorical relationship between pigs and those who consume them:

> The way it is often phrased, *'domuz kiskanmaz'* ('pigs are not jealous') euphemistically signifies that pigs are promiscuous animals, not monogamous, and that therefore those who partake of pork also become promiscuous, shameful, lacking in honour and virtue. It is the moral extension of 'you are what you eat'. (1990: 170)

This symbolic association has been discussed by numerous anthropologists and other commentators on the socio-cultural significance of food. Nick Fiddes (1991), for example, refers to the process as 'incorporation', whereby the perceived 'qualities' or characteristics of the 'meat' when it was alive can be appropriated by others in the act of consumption. These qualities are often of a sexual nature, such as the consumption of pork leading to promiscuity or red meat leading to increased libido and sexual virility (see for example, Adams, 1990; Fiddes, 1991), but often relate to morality more generally (such as pigs being impure or unclean). Anthropologist David Sutton (1997, 2001), who conducted fieldwork on the Greek island of Kalymnos looking at food as a mnemonic device, found that his vegetarianism rendered him effeminate in the eyes of his informants for whom meat was a way of life.

In the case of Mandel's informants, the notion of incorporation, of taking on the characteristics of the animals concerned, was abhorrent in a manner which completely inverts the ideal of incorporation. The same applies in other ethnographic contexts too. According to Manuel Lizarralde for example, the Venezuelan Bari regard red howler monkeys (*Alouatta seniculus*) and sloths (*Bradypus variegatus*) as slow and stupid – distinctly undesirable qualities. As a result, the Bari do not eat howlers 'because they would not want to acquire these characteristics through the ingestion of their flesh' (2002: 93).

EATING PEOPLE

The conflict between dominant post-domestic ideas about edibility and many indigenous or minority beliefs and practices is perhaps best illustrated in relation to cannibalism. As Eriksen has noted, the ways in which anthropologists have thought about cannibalism is as a form of classification. He makes the observation that discussions and differences of opinion about cannibalism (in both academic and popular consciousness) are not really about food at all but are rather based on conflicting approaches to the classification of *people* (2001: 234). As has already been noted on numerous occasions, the standard post-Enlightenment view holds that only humans can be 'persons', and so for classificatory systems rooted in Judaeo-Christian doctrine cannibalism is taboo. For many other peoples, whose classificatory systems are grounded, albeit often in the distant past, in animistic belief systems, the consumption of 'persons' both human and nonhuman is not so problematic. In her account of pre-colonial cannibalism in Africa, for example, Kajsa Ekholm-Friedman notes that, for many of the peoples who themselves claimed to be cannibals, part of the allure was the ability to take on the life force of a fellow human, especially a vanquished enemy (1991: 222; see also chapter 3).

Loretta Cormier's fieldwork among the Amazonian Guajá presents an interesting contemporary comparative. Like many Amazonian peoples, the Guajá eat particular species of monkeys while keeping others as pets (see chapter 8). As Cormier notes 'given that Guajá animistic beliefs involve social relations with nonhuman life forms, consuming them can be considered a form of symbolic cannibalism' (2002: 135). Cormier suggests that Guajá symbolic cannibalism can be understood when considered in relation to their wider cosmological beliefs which rest on two principles:

(1) a recognition of kinship between all living things and (2) the belief that like eats like. So, for the Guajá, it is the underlying and observable similarities between humans and monkeys which render monkeys edible.

As psychologists Knight and colleagues (2004) have noted, the experiences of individuals can inform their perceptions of animals and lead them to acquire what they term 'Belief in Animal Mind' (BAM). BAM is one factor which can increase the likelihood of individuals becoming vegetarian in a post-domestic context; they recognize the 'personhood' of other animals, and so do not want animals to suffer. BAM can be compared with the perspectivism of de Castro, and with Milton's 'ecology of emotions'; as a result of experiencing the sociality of animals (de Castro, 1998) through interactions which trigger emotional responses (Milton, 2002), individuals perceive in other animals qualities which they themselves can empathize with (Milton, 2005). This is significant in relation to food choice, and especially what might be termed 'inverse incorporation', that is, the decision not to eat certain foods because of the qualities perceived in their living forms. For many elective vegetarians for example, meat is taboo because the personhood of other animals is recognized. It therefore becomes a moral issue – why should other sentient, feeling, intelligent beings be killed to ensure the survival of humans who can meet their nutritional requirements by a whole host of other non-fatal means? Yet once again the emotional engagements of individuals with other animals are shaped to some extent by their 'culture' and the material resources at their disposal. The Inuit for example revere polar bears as quasi-humans and recognize their physical likeness to the human form when flayed. They also recognize that polar bears are carnivores, but traditionally hunted bears and ate their flesh (d'Anglure, 1994). To take a materialist approach, in Arctic conditions, available sustenance cannot be dismissed lightly.

There are certain mechanisms that individuals have at their disposal so that even when the personhood of other animals is recognized this recognition can be dismissed or over-ruled. As previously noted, the dominant post-domestic cultural construct is that humans and other animals exist within a hierarchy. As Milton has recently argued (2009), for many people 'science' is accepted as an arbiter of 'truth'. With the foundations of science firmly rooted in Cartesian dualisms, individuals can overlook the personhood of other animals by deferring to this 'higher' wisdom, especially when it serves political or economic ends. So farmers who have to make their living by 'exploiting' other animals cannot afford to recognize the personhood of their 'livestock'.

Nonetheless in some contexts farmers share close bonds with 'their' livestock, but argue that individual animals have to be sacrificed for the collective good (where collective applies to the herd, and also the human community). Dimitrious Theodossopoulos' (2005b) study of Greek subsistence farmers' attitudes towards their animals is a prime example of such an approach. However, one particularly enduring rationale is the deterministic belief that eating meat is 'natural' for humans, and this has been the focus of a recent debate in the anthropological press.

MEAT TO LIVE?

A cogent critique of a deterministic approach to human 'behaviour' in relation to food choices was levelled at the genetic determinism of some evolutionary biologists, anthropologists and Meat and Livestock Australia (MLA – the corporation responsible for promoting and supporting the meat industry in Australia) by social anthropologist Adrian Peace (2008). Peace's article opened with a presentation of the key points from a paper published in the medical journal *The Lancet* (McMichael et al., 2007) which had in turn responded to the Stern *Review of climate change* (2006). Both of these earlier publications had assessed the role of meat production and consumption in the global environmental crises and found serious cause for concern. The primary focus of Peace's article however, was an advertising campaign run by MLA which drew on the published work of a whole host of 'specialists', including anthropologists, to suggest that eating meat is a genetic imperative. The MLA linked the evolution of modern humans (*Homo sapiens sapiens*) with the consumption of meat and suggested that this continues to be an essential nutritional requirement and genetically rooted driver of contemporary 'natural' human behaviour.

Peace's aim was to question the role of anthropology in promoting a particular practice (the increased consumption of red meat) which could in actual fact have dire consequences for the future well-being of the species. This is not to say that meat eating *per se* is bad for human health, but rather the fact that, in the wake of the advertising campaign, endorsed by prominent anthropologists, public expenditure on meat in Australia rose by a staggering $1 billion (Peace, 2008: 9). The industrialized farming practices which must be employed to sustain such a demand have considerable negative implications for the health of the global environment.

After the publication of the Stern review of climate change, one of the main issues latched onto by the media was Stern's assertion that: 'Meat is a wasteful use of water and creates a lot of greenhouse gases. It puts enormous pressure on the world's resources. A vegetarian diet is better.' This example clearly shows that cultural materialism cannot adequately explain contemporary food choices. If it could, everyone in post-domestic societies would be vegetarian. Many are, but the adherents to the various permutations of vegetarianism constitute a minority on a global scale. Moreover, not every post-domestic consumer knows and fully comprehends the negative environmental consequences of large-scale farming, or cares about it enough to change their shopping and eating habits.

A return to the archaeological record and recent (albeit controversial) revisions to what is referred to as the 'hunting hypothesis' (see chapter 14) might present an interesting way forward. While meat eating has long been presented as the 'natural' state of humans, marking a turning point in our evolutionary history (see for example, Cartmill, 1993 and Dart, 1940), it is more likely that our prehistoric ancestors were opportunistic omnivores who foraged and consumed a wide variety of foodstuffs (Binford, 1981 and see chapter 14). There are grounds to suggest that while it did contain some animal protein, what is referred to as the 'Pleistocene diet' of early humans (Milton, 1993) was predominantly based on vegetation (see also Popovich et al., 1997). It is arguable, therefore, that the move to a heavily meat-based diet, which is widely regarded as 'natural' today, was driven by symbolism and economics as opposed to necessity in the historical period.

The historical context within which early human remains were found made the hunting hypothesis particularly attractive (see chapter 14), and the profitability of the livestock industry (to humans at least – see chapter 5) has transformed agricultural 'institutions like MLA … [into] powerful players in the global market place; they are the agricultural equivalent of oil companies and chemical firms' (Peace, 2008: 6). The 'cultural' importance of meat, or indeed any other foodstuff, therefore becomes bound up in the complex history of international trade relations, making it virtually impossible to extricate the material and symbolic factors which have traditionally been the focus of anthropological attention from the political and economic drivers of contemporary post-domestic relationships of consumption.

SUGGESTIONS FOR FURTHER READING

Bourque, N. 2001. Eating your words: communicating with food in the Ecuadorian Andes. In: J. Hendry and C.W. Watson (eds) *An anthropology of indirect communication*. London: Routledge.

Caplan, P. (ed.) 1997. *Food, health and identity*. London: Routledge.

Caplan, P. 2000. 'Eating British beef with confidence': a consideration of consumers' responses to BSE in Britain. In: Caplan, P. (ed.) *Risk revisited*. London: Pluto Press.

Counihan, C.M. 1999. *The anthropology of food and body: gender, meaning, and power*. London: Routledge.

Hutchinson, S. 1992. 'Dangerous to eat': rethinking pollution states among the Nuer of the Southern Sudan. *Africa* 62: 4.

McDonald, B. (2000). Once you know something, you can't not know it: an empirical look at becoming vegan. *Society & Animals* 8(1): 1–23.

Morales, E. 1995. *The guinea pig: healing, food, and ritual in the Andes*. Tucson: University of Arizona Press.

Murcott, A. (ed.) 1984. *The sociology of food and eating*. Aldershot: Gower.

Potts, A. and While, M. 2008. New Zealand vegetarians: at odds with their nation. *Society & Animals* 16(4): 336–353.

Rigby, K. 2011. Getting a taste for the Bogong moth. *Australian Humanities Review* 50: 77–94.

Ross, E.B. 1980. *Beyond the myths of culture: essays in cultural materialism*. New York: Academic Press.

Stanford, C.B. 2001. *The hunting apes: meat eating and the origins of human behaviour*. Princeton, NJ: Princeton University Press.

Tobias, M. 1996. The anthropology of conscience. *Society & Animals* 4(1): 65–73.

Vialles, N. 1994. *Animal to edible*. Cambridge: Cambridge University Press.

Willerslev, R. 2007. Feasting on people: eating animals and humans in Amazonia. *Current Anthropology* 48(4): 497–530.

Williams, J. (2003) Vegetarian biographies in time and space: vegetarians and alternatives in Newport, west Wales. In: C.A. Davies and S. Jones (eds) *Welsh communities: new ethnographic perspectives*. Cardiff: University of Wales Press.

8
Pets

Pets are commodities that many people use, like other consumer goods, as a means of constructing identities. (Mullin, 1999: 215–16)

Pets differ from other domesticated animals in several respects. The *Oxford English Dictionary* has numerous entries for 'pet' but the key aspects of these definitions are: a tame or hand-reared animal, an animal kept for pleasure or companionship, an individual singled out for preferential treatment in a manner which induces the disapproval of others, a person who is good natured and obedient, or a favourite. The dictionary definition does not mention, however, the fact that in many post-domestic contexts pets are seen as the property of their human owners. They are bought and sold (often in response to consumer trends, see Bettany and Daly, 2008; Hurn, 2011a) and therefore constitute commodities of sorts (Mullin, 1999). This objectifying attitude towards the ownership of animals is transcended to a degree in cases where pets are considered members of the family, another commonplace occurrence also omitted from the dictionary definition. Yet even where this is the case, the socio-cultural (and legally sanctioned) expectation is that pets belong to individual humans who have certain responsibilities towards these animals, but also the power over the animal's life and death.

THE FUNCTIONAL ROLES OF PETS

Many commentators have concluded that the human–pet relationship is essentially functional in nature, based on domination and control. However, as with anthropological approaches to domestication (see chapters 5 and 7) the reality is much more complicated. While pets can indeed fulfil utilitarian roles, the functional approach does not help to account for inconsistencies in attitudes towards pets, nor does it explain why people keep pets when they appear to fulfil no obvious utilitarian role.

There have been numerous commentaries on pet keeping from a social science perspective (for example, Bulliet, 2005; Franklin, 1999; Herzog, 2010; Serpell, 1996 [1986]; Tuan, 1984) and some of the key points will be summarized here. The main concern, however, will be with reconsidering some of the established explanations for pet keeping in light of an ever-growing body of ethnographic material and postmodern theoretical perspectives to demonstrate the wider anthropological relevance of what are often dismissed as insignificant (or even objectionable) relationships between humans and their pets.

An example of the functionality of pets comes from Brian Morris's extensive fieldwork in rural Malawi. Morris summarizes Malawians' multiple relationships with and attitudes towards dogs as follows:

> When asked, hunters suggest several reasons for keeping (ku-sunga) a dog: as a guard dog for protection against thieves and wild animals, for beautifying the household as a flower (amakongolesa pakhomo ngati maluwa), and, most importantly, to help a man in his hunting pursuits. (2000: 86)

Morris's informants present many functional interpretations themselves, which suggests that in some cases the utilitarian value of animals is indeed a contributing factor. What is important to note, however – and Morris's account nicely illustrates this – is that most of these functional reasons are not mutually exclusive, nor do they exclude other non-functional motivations for the human–pet relationship. Like all aspects of social life, human interactions with pets are fluid and highly complex. Anderson (1986) discusses a similar example: the relationship between Saami reindeer herders and their dogs. These dogs are essentially working animals, but the relationship becomes complicated in the sense that they will be returned to their breeder at the end of their working lives for 'retirement' as quasi-pets.

PETS AS EDUCATORS

In many traditional hunter-gatherer societies children are given small mammals, birds, insects or lizards. These animals may be found while adults are out foraging, or, as in the case of the Amazonian Guajá, baby monkeys will be collected and brought home when their mothers are killed during hunting expeditions (Cormier, 2003). Cormier discusses the functional, educational aspects of keeping monkeys as pets for Guajá children with clear gender divisions. For girls, they provide practical experience of caring for an infant. Unlike other pet animals (agouti [*Dasyprocta leporine*], for example), monkeys cling on to their human carers and this simulates the level of responsibility that a mother has to take for her newborn baby. For boys, pet monkeys are important for learning vocalizations and behaviours which will enable them to become more proficient hunters (see also Laughlin, 1968; Morris, 1998, 2000).

It is often argued that children are given pets to teach them compassion and responsibility through caring for another living thing (Fifield and Forsyth, 1999), yet the converse can also be true; among the Guajá, again, children will often take pot-shots at pets in the household. Pet ownership also introduces children to the facts of life, or, more specifically, the facts of death. However, the assumption that accustoming children to the death of pets softens the blow when a human family member dies is misguided, and undermines the genuine feelings of love which children often have for pets. It also rests on the assumption that all children will develop positive associations with animals, but the statistics on animal abuse enacted by young people indicates that some have very different relationships with their pets (Ascione, 1993; Ascione and Arkow, 1999; Paul and Serpell, 1993). As Milton (2002) has noted in relation to why some individuals 'care' about environmental conservation and others do not, emotional experiential engagement is crucial and, as experiences of pet animals vary between individuals, so too will children's perceptions of and attitudes towards them.

PETS OFFER SOCIAL SUPPORT

Another explanation for the prevalence of pets in pre-domestic, domestic and post-domestic societies is that they can become substitutes for humans, acting as surrogate children, friends or protectors (Serpell, 1991: 13). Such relationships are often frowned upon by those who observe a clear demarcation between humans and animals (Franklin, 1999; Sartre, 1966; Thomas, 1983). This negativity surrounding close, affectionate interactions between humans and pets has deep historical roots (Menache, 1997, 1998; Serpell, 1987).

In medieval Europe, for example, pet keeping was actively discouraged by religious authorities, at least among the lower classes, for several reasons. First, pets were regarded as wasteful because they diverted their owners' time and attention away from God (see Menache, 1998) and, second, because so many people were struggling to exist, pets were thought to divert resources away from humans whose need, by virtue of their species, was greater. As Serpell and Paul (1994) note, familiarity with animals was regarded by the devout as proof of a dirty, beastly and unholy life. The fact that many poor or elderly people took comfort in the companionship of animals was seen as dehumanizing because it elevated the animals to human status. According to Serpell (1996 [1986]), this blurring of the distinction between humans and animals challenged accepted socio-cultural norms and was therefore viewed with suspicion. Indeed, pet ownership was often the only 'evidence' in the trials of alleged witches for example, so some pet owners literally risked their lives by engaging in non-utilitarian cross-species relationships (see Serpell, 2002a). Throughout the same period, however, pet keeping was also an accepted preserve of social elites, and therefore demarcated status, wealth and privilege.

While there is no doubt some validity in these explanations, structural-functionalist approaches to historical or indeed contemporary human–animal interactions are problematic on two grounds. First, structural-functionalism fails to acknowledge that some social elites may have chosen to keep pets for a whole host of reasons other than simply because they could, or because to do so differentiated them from the hoi poloi. Second, structural-functionalism does not account for the numerous individuals from the lower echelons of society who chose to keep pets despite the many difficulties such an activity presented for them. Indeed, even in the contemporary world humans often opt to keep pets when the relationship may appear to make their lives more complicated. For example, large numbers of homeless individuals prefer to stay on the streets than relinquish their canine companions (see for example, Burley, 2008: 16; Singer et al., 1995). Elderly people are also less likely to seek medical care when they need it for fear that they will be hospitalized and forced to give up their pets (McNicholas et al., 2005). Such dogged determination to maintain a relationship with a pet animal, even when it places the human owner at risk, has traditionally been dismissed as irrational or even self-harming behaviour. However the therapeutic properties of pets, and the psychological support which socially isolated people can obtain from the non-judgemental and constant companionship of an animal, are increasingly being recognized.

PET KEEPING BRINGS HEALTH AND THERAPEUTIC BENEFITS

Many recent psychological studies into the human–pet bond have suggested that pets can have a range of positive effects on human health and well-being, from lowering blood pressure to improving post-operative recovery rates (see also chapter 12). Cohabiting with certain animals, dogs for example, also encourages owners to exercise more than they otherwise might (Cutt et al., 2007, 2008; Serpell, 1991). However, many existing studies which extol the virtues of pet ownership have themselves been subjected to critical analysis (McNicholas, 2005), with questions being raised as to the validity of results, the difficulty of accounting for all variables which may impact on the health of individuals and the fact that the health risks posed by close interactions with animals in the home (such as exposure to zoonotic parasites and pathogens or attacks from aggressive animals) are often overlooked. Nonetheless, these criticisms are aimed more at the methodological approaches and orientations of researchers and the extent to which claims may have been exaggerated; the general consensus is still in favour of there being many positive outcomes for specific individuals interacting with specific animals in specific contexts.

Perhaps more anthropologically relevant is research which has demonstrated that pets are valuable social catalysts. Dog owners in particular recognize that their pets can be effective 'ice-breakers' when it comes to forming new social relationships. While the mediatory capacity of pets can enhance the self-esteem and social integration of their owners, this is often contingent on the culturally perceived 'value' of the pet in question. A friendly dog can help alleviate social awkwardness, a snarling, slavering Rottweiler – a breed perceived by many to be potentially 'dangerous' – will have the opposite effect. This anti-social identity may make certain animals desirable 'pets' for certain individuals (for example, Caglar, 1997; Forsyth and Evans, 1998).

PETS AS STATUS SYMBOLS OR MARKERS OF IDENTITY

A point consistently made in relation to pets is that in many cultural contexts they can become markers of status. Such metaphorical relationships (Belk, 1996) see humans attributing to animals certain symbolic characteristics which are perceived by the pet owner (or the social group to which they belong) in a particular light. Consequently the relationship itself might be construed as less important than the overall image which the human–animal combination portrays to onlookers. For Guajá women for example, Cormier has observed that the '[pet] monkey functions as a type of body art such as Burmese neck rings or Euro-American high-heeled shoes, creating a culturally desirable image of female attractiveness, even at the cost of physical impediment' (2002: 71; see also 2003: 115). But not just any monkey will do; as for many post-domestic pet owners who choose to buy particular breeds of animals, the animal fits with the image of themselves they want to portray, and that representational quality is sufficient grounds for sustaining the relationship regardless of the actual 'personality' of the individual animal.

This sort of symbolic reductionism has been widely criticized by anthropologists such as John Knight (2005) for whom it represents the portrayal of animals as mere objects, denying them agency as persons in their own right. This is certainly a very valid point, and academics who are cognizant of the complexity of human–animal interactions should recognize and be wary of applying this particular trope. Yet it is also true that many humans who are not theoretically engaged with the issue will continue to see animals, including their own animals, as symbols (see Hurn, 2008a, 2008b, 2011a; and chapter 6). Anthropologists are well positioned to document and theorize these relationships in cultural context, and highlight how they appear to the different onlookers, both lay and academic, individual and collective.

In post-domestic societies, many individuals are seen to be divorced from 'nature' and bound up in the pursuit of fetishized commodities and ephemeral social relationships. Regardless of academic recognition of the subjectivity of nonhuman individuals, for many post-domestic pet owners, these animals are objects imbued with symbolism and therefore redolent of their own sense of self. In relation to clothing, which anthropologists widely recognize as deeply symbolic (see for example, Hansen, 2004; Küchler and Miller, 2005), philosopher Lipovetsky comments that: 'the materialism of contemporary societies is widely deplored. But why do the critics not stress that consummate fashion also helps detach human beings from objects? Under the régime of use value, we no longer become attached to things' (1994: 147). In other words, contemporary consumers have no qualms about replacing clothes and objects as and when they wear out or are superseded by the latest gadget or trend. Referred to as 'planned obsolescence', consumer goods (such as mobile phones and other digital media devices) are designed to have a limited life-span to encourage further consumption. Lipovetsky asks 'how can we continue to talk about alienation at a time when, far from being dispossessed by objects, individuals are dispossessing themselves of objects?' (1994: 148).

There are parallels here with contemporary pet ownership in post-domestic societies. This throw-away mentality can also be observed in relation to animals, evidenced by the large numbers of unwanted pets living (and dying) in animal shelters. In the minds of many contemporary consumers, then, pets are seen as potentially disposable material accessories in much the same way as cars, jewellery or clothing. Caglar writes about the use of pet dogs as lifestyle accessories by Turkish immigrants in post-unification Germany. One specific type of dog – *kampfhunde* ('fighting dogs') were particularly popular among young single men for defensive and offensive purposes in the 1990s. These dogs became:

> one of the constituents of a life-style by means of which groups of German Turks are defined ... Dogs are integrated into their self-image. In that respect they constitute sites around which they articulate desire and pleasure. These pets become part of the 'life spaces' ... they try to create. (Caglar, 1997: 82)

Kampfhunde were given names such as 'Gangster' and 'Rambo' to further emphasize their characteristics, both real and symbolic. But what is particularly relevant here is the comment made by one of Caglar's informants that: '"nowadays everyone wants to wear one [a dog] on his hand". He uses the verb "to wear one" [*eline takmak*] as if dogs were jewellery or part of the owner's body' (1997: 82). The way in which Germans perceive German Turks' interactions with their pets serves to strengthen the divisions between these wider cultural groups (cf. Mandel, 1989). *Kampfhunde* are, in the eyes of most of Caglar's informants, objects of commodified material culture or fetishized commodities rather than loved members of the family (see also Nast, 2006).

COMMODITY FETISHISM

Commodity fetishism is a state of socio-economic relations characteristic of the capitalist systems which predominate in post-domestic societies. In the capitalist market the value of social relations is influenced by the perceived value of commodities, but this value often rests on the symbolic qualities that 'things' are thought to possess. Commodity fetishism is typically engaged with by scholars looking at the impact of capitalism outside of the developed world. For example, Michael Taussig's (1980) study of peasant workers on Colombian sugar cane plantations and in Bolivian tin mines considered their responses to the displacement of traditional community-based subsistence activities by the introduction of wage labour. Taussig discussed the development of a belief that workers who bought into the capitalist system had entered pacts with the devil in a bid to increase production and therefore income. However, Taussig observed that it was only when workers were proletarianized (i.e. alienated from the actual products of their labour) that the devil assumed importance. When working their own land or working for their own subsistence they did not invoke the devil. Taussig noted the widespread belief that, while it brought material wealth, the devil contract had undesirable consequences and contracted workers would die a premature and painful death.

Animals imbued with symbolic value become commodities in contexts where individuals are alienated from processes of production, because they can be used for financial gain (to breed more animals to be sold, for example). But what of the large numbers of pets who are viewed as commodities and status symbols by their owners, but who do not actually yield any monetary profit? Pets might also be regarded as commodities when they generate *social* profit for their owners (see for example, Horst and Miller, 2006; Miller, 2001, 2008 for discussions of material culture in relation to status, identity and changing socio-economic relations).

Seeger (1981) made a similar point in relation to the 'Amerindian' concept of ownership or mastery, governed by asymmetrical social relations (which reveals the misconception that Amazonian peoples are egalitarian and governed by symmetrical reciprocity, see also Fausto [1999, 2008]). Humans living and working within the confines of other economic systems pursue fetishes (such as fertility or cattle), but outside a capitalist context these are not necessarily related to financial gain. The nature of the relationship then bears some correlation to the dominant mode of subsistence, a variation on the theme of Marshall Sahlins' aphorism that 'money [and commodities] is to the West what kinship is to the rest' (1976: 216). Among hunter-gatherers or foragers such as the Guajá (Cormier, 2002, 2003), for example, kinship, expressed in the fertility of women, in turn expressed in the appropriation and display of pet monkeys, is prioritized – or rather fetishized – to the extent that women carry monkeys around when it is highly inconvenient and even detrimental to the conduct of their daily subsistence activities.

The ephemeral nature of many contemporary relationships with commoditized pets is also assumed to be a post-domestic phenomenon; within a capitalist system humans frequently 'discard' pets (see also Arluke, 1994; Frommer and Arluke, 1999; Swabe, 2005; Taylor, 2010; Tuan, 1984). Philosopher Raymond Gaita (2004) has discussed the morality of contemporary pet ownership and concluded that many owners see euthanasia as the easy way out when pets become burdensome. However the situation is not necessarily so cut and dried. As Joanna Swabe (2005) observed in her ethnographic study of veterinary professionals in the Netherlands, there are numerous reasons why an owner may opt for euthanasia, some of which have the animals' best interests at heart (such as to alleviate terminal pain and suffering) while others do not (for example, because it is a cheaper option than paying for kennels during the holiday period). What is particularly relevant from an anthropological perspective however, is that there is evidence to suggest that this 'throw-away' attitude is also held elsewhere, including in pre-capitalist settings purportedly governed by a 'hunter-gatherer' ontology.

In relation to the Guajá, Cormier (2002; 2003) herself acknowledges that pet monkeys have a limited life-expectancy, both in terms of their survival rates and also in relation to how long they are accorded privileged status. While very young monkeys are prized and treated as quasi-human children, hormonal changes and the negative consequences of provisioning and social isolation result in monkeys becoming aggressive and destructive as they grow older. To limit the incidence of anti-social behaviours they are frequently tied up and contact with human carers is reduced, exacerbating the problem and leading to self-harming behaviours. Such examples serve as a corrective to the view that the objectification of pets is exclusively found in 'Western' contexts, but does little to counter the next 'explanation' which has been commonly asserted: that pets enable humans to exert control over a subordinate and dependent other.

CONTROLLING PETS

The transient nature of some human–pet relationships has been theorized by many scholars on the grounds of control and dominance. Pets are dependent on their owners or carers for food, water, exercise, companionship and so on. Philosopher Yi-Fu Tuan (1984) has forcefully argued that pets fulfil the innate human desire to be needed and this, coupled with the element of control that responsibility for a dependent brings, accounts for the ubiquity of pet keeping in the modern world and the high incidence of pets being abandoned or killed when that desire either wanes or becomes difficult to enact in practice.

Yet not all pet owners desire 'control' (although Tuan asserts this desire may be unconscious) and control is not necessarily something which is coveted in all cultural or individual contexts. Post-humanist critics have responded to Tuan's binary juxtaposition of freedom and dominance by discussing examples where the converse is true and interactions are mutually beneficial, with decisions made by all parties, human and nonhuman alike. Julie Ann Smith (2003) for example counters Tuan's claims on the basis of her experiences as a foster carer for the House Rabbit Society (HRS). For Smith the relationships she shares with the rabbits in her life emerge from a willingness to see the rabbits as her equals. Admittedly they are in captivity, but Smith's whole life and domestic space, as with other HRS members, is geared to fulfilling the needs of the rabbits, often in ways instigated by the animals themselves and which seriously compromise the activities of the humans involved.

Engaging with Tuan's assertion that neutering of pets is a supreme act of control, Smith suggests that, provided it is carried out humanely (under anaesthetic and coupled with the administration of post-operative analgesics), neutering can be regarded as an attempt to control humans who would otherwise breed rabbits out of ignorance or a desire to make money. There are also health benefits for female rabbits as spaying prolongs their lives by several years, reducing their susceptibility to potentially fatal uterine conditions. As a result, Smith suggests that 'paternalism that instantiates control' needs to be distinguished 'from a paternalism that attempts to make the best of already compromised situations for the animals' (2003: 192). Thus Smith is not discounting the possibility that some human–pet relationships are based on control, rather, while she recognizes that equality between humans and animals is oxymoronic in many post-domestic settings, not all ways of being with pet animals are defined in this manner. Moreover, there are often conflicting ways of interpreting the same events or interactions. Consider the following example presented by Tuan:

Perhaps the hardest test required that the dog should be brought into the ring hungry and, when given a plate of his favourite food, sit by it until he was told to eat; the time was four minutes and the owner had to go out of sight, leaving the dog alone with his tempting plate. Hundreds of people were watching when, on one occasion, Beeswing [a tiny Pekinese] came into the ring. He was ravenous and the four minutes must have seemed interminable; he endured for two and then, without moving from his post, slowly got up and … 'sat on his bottom and begged'. The crowd roared but he did not move a muscle. He had not broken the rules but instead of sitting on four legs sat on two; after another two minutes the judge called her; Beeswing saw his mistress come into the ring but he knew he still must not move as she walked up and stood beside him. She had to wait for the word from the judge. It came, she released Beeswing who literally jumped on the food and gobbled it. (1984: 107–8)

Tuan uses 'poor Beeswing' to illustrate the extremes that some humans go to – this is presented as extreme control over an animal and therefore morally questionable. However it could also be interpreted as a positive relationship between dog and human, and the ability of the former to understand the expectations of the latter on the basis of mutual respect and intersubjectivity (see also Goode, 2006; Haraway, 2008; chapter 10).

PETS ARE GOOD PEOPLE TO BE AROUND

According to Ingold:

Many people who are convinced that, as a general rule, animals cannot be persons, are quick to make an exception of their pets. But if you ask them why pets are persons, or at least rather like persons, whereas other animals are not, they will probably say that on account of having been raised in human households, virtually as members of the family, these particular animals have become almost human themselves. They are credited with human feelings and responses, spoken to and expected to understand, given names, put through life-cycle rituals, and sometimes even dressed in clothing. Thus, far from softening or obscuring the boundary between humanity and animality, the special treatment of pets constitutes the exception that proves the rule: namely that, in the West, to be a person is to be human. (2000: 90–1)

Ingold is referring here to the anthropomorphism which informs some human attitudes towards, and interactions with, their pets. However, such a picture does not necessarily represent the attitudes of all 'Westerners'. Indeed, while some human–pet relationships are transient, based on control, dictated by 'fashion' or the symbolic qualities of the animal, others are defined by mutuality and the recognition of animals as active subjects (see chapter 10 and Milton, 2005; Nast, 2006). Like Smith, with her account of her shared life with house rabbits, post-humanist philosopher Donna Haraway (2003, 2008) along with Mark Rowlands (2008) and Raymond Gaita (2004), to name but a few, have passionately demonstrated just how all-encompassing living with other animals can be. In these accounts the pets are not 'owned' but rather share and enrich the lives of their human companions. To ask why some humans keep pets, then, is tantamount to asking why they have friends. While there are functional roles which friends fulfil, most of us would baulk at the suggestion that we are friends with other human individuals because they are useful to us. They may well be on occasion, but many would argue there must be more to it for the relationship to count as genuine friendship. Indeed in his *Nicomachean ethics* (Books 8 and 9) Aristotle differentiated 'good' men from 'bad' on the grounds that the latter were friends out of utility.

Pets can thus be considered 'friends' in many cultural contexts, and for many individuals who recognize their personhood this is perhaps a better way of conceiving of some instances of the relationship than the 'kinship' metaphor that is traditionally invoked. Indeed, as a general rule humans cannot choose who is in their family and because families are effectively imposed, there is no guarantee that individuals will like each other. There is more scope for choice when it comes to friends, so when humans choose to take responsibility for the welfare of another animal one of the reasons for doing so is because of some spark of mutual attraction, or a recognition of personhood across the species barrier.

IMPLICATIONS OF PET KEEPING

There are many reasons why humans keep pets, but what do the animals involved stand to gain? Some pets certainly benefit from human hospitality and care. Others are not so lucky and appear to have been forced into 'pacts with the devil'. As Taussig (1980) noted, while the devil contract provided Colombian plantation workers with short-term gains, they were ultimately alienated from the products of their labour, denied the opportunity to engage in the sociality upon which their community structure and cohesion depended and they were fated to die premature and painful deaths. Like domesticates more generally (see chapter 5) most pet animals are kept in isolation, or in confined spaces, are reliant on their owners for the satisfaction of all of their needs and often have to substitute the companionship of their own species for interactions with humans. For some species such as dogs, who readily accept humans as 'pack' members, this is less problematic than it is for other highly social, active or nervous animals who can be placed under considerable stress if their human carers are unable to adequately meet their requirements. Rabbits, for example, have traditionally been housed in small cages and, while commonly kept as pets, do not always respond well to confinement and handling. However the phenomenon of 'house rabbits' noted above, where animals are given much greater freedom and the ability to socialize (albeit not necessarily with their own kind) leads to a much healthier and happier pet (Smith, 2003). These alternative approaches to keeping companion animals, which are grounded in a recognition of them as individual members of a nonhuman species as opposed to an anthropomorphic projection onto a commoditized object, are gradually becoming more mainstream.

I close this chapter by coming full circle and revisiting the nomenclature and definitions of pets presented at the outset. The tendency of social scientists to reduce the human–pet relationship to a series of functions or oppositions needs to be countered by a recognition of the diversity that exists in reality. Pets can be companion animals, working animals and friends, mascots, accessories, mediators and victims of human control; greater care needs to be taken to differentiate between these different sub-categories. This is easier said than done, however, as the membership criteria for the category 'pet' are extremely fluid and, on occasion, temporary, leading to what may appear from the outside as contradictory and random attitudes towards, and treatment of, animals classed as 'pets'. Indeed, the status of the individual animals to whom the term is applied is dependent on a whole host of factors, and should any one of these change, privileges can be either revoked or extended. This makes it difficult for anthropologists to generalize about why people keep pets but rather, in line with the postmodern rejection of grand theories within the discipline more generally, highlights the need to consider occurrences on a case-by-case basis and in relation to the life histories and experiences of both the humans and animals involved.

SUGGESTIONS FOR FURTHER READING

Beck, A.M. 1983. *Between pets and people: the importance of animal companionship.* New York: Putnam.

Erikson, P. 1997. On Native American conservation and the status of Amazonian pets. *Current Anthropology* 38(3): 445–446.

Fox, R. 2006. Animal behaviours, post-human lives: everyday negotiations of the animal–human divide in pet-keeping. *Social & Cultural Geography* 7(4): 525–537.

Irvine, L. 2004. Pampered or enslaved? The moral dilemma of pets. *International Journal of Sociology and Social Policy* 24(9): 5–17.

Mullin, M.H. 2007. Feeding the animals. In: R. Cassidy and M. Mullin (eds) *Where the wild things are now: domestication reconsidered*, pp. 277–304. Oxford: Berg.

Nast, H. 2006. Critical pet studies? *Antipode* 38(5): 894–906.

Podberscek, A., Paul, E.S. and Serpell, J.A. 2005. *Companion animals and us: exploring the relationships between people and pets.* Cambridge: Cambridge University Press.

Power, E. 2008. Furry families: making a human–dog family through home. *Social & Cultural Geography* 9(5): 535–555.

Wrye, J. 2009. Beyond pets: exploring relational perspectives of petness. *Canadian Journal of Sociology/Cahiers canadiens de sociologie* 34(4): 1033–1063.

9
Communication

All behaviour is communication. (Grandin, 2008: 101)

Recent research in the field of microbiology (Keller and Surette, 2006) has found that bacteria can communicate through the diffusion of 'signal molecules' between cells. Moreover, it is now recognized that not only do bacteria communicate with members of their own species, they can also sense and respond to signal molecules which they themselves do not synthesize, suggesting an ability to 'eavesdrop' on the discussions of other organisms in their environments (Ryan and Dow, 2008). If communication can transcend the species barrier at the molecular level, then it stands to reason that 'higher-order' animals might also be able to 'understand' what other animals are 'saying'. Yet communication, and language in particular, is another of the traditional defining characteristics of 'humanness' and as a result there has been some reluctance to consider the communicative competences of species other than humans.

Anthropologists have prioritized language as the dominant form of communication because of the widespread belief that 'language expresses cultural reality ... language embodies cultural reality ... [and] language symbolizes cultural reality' (Kramsch, 2008: 3). In other words, humans use language, the meaning of which is shared by other humans, to convey information. They use language to create and convey their experiences and emotions to other humans and they imbue things with value, creating a symbolic language of signs. So, 'culture', that marker of humanness and of intra-human difference, is rooted in language. Language has also often been considered a prerequisite for thought. Such assumptions are now regularly challenged as our understandings of the workings of other species increases (see for example, Bermúdez, 2003; Griffin, 2001: 258; Vigo and Allen, 2005), but agreement about the communicative and requisite cognitive abilities of animals remains unresolved.

SYMBOLIC LANGUAGE

While many animals can produce acoustic vocalization, human physiology allows us to form and utter the vast array of sounds which constitute human speech, and our neurological make-up provides us with the capacity for syntactical (grammatical) language. Some mimetic birds such as African grey parrots (*Psittacus erithacus*) are also able to articulate (and comprehend) some aspects of human speech (Pepperberg, 2002) and while we share some neural mechanisms with a selection of other animals – the great apes for example – human language is undeniably complex in comparison with the communicative abilities of other species. As a result, anthropologists and scholars from cognate disciplines often conclude that these innate attributes differentiate humans from other animals (for example, Cheney and Seyfarth, 2007; Kramsch, 2008; Lieberman, 1994).

Yet we still have so much to learn about the communicative, linguistic and semantic abilities of other animals, especially those species whose forms of communication are so 'alien' in relation to our own abilities that we haven't always had the methodological tools to be able to translate them. Advances are being made all the time though. For example, it is now widely accepted that dolphins communicate by a combination of whistles and body movements. The significance and complexity of whistles however, and signature whistles in particular (which, so it is hypothesized, effectively serve as 'names' to represent individuals), divides researchers. Some see signature whistles as proof of symbolic thought and linguistic ability, while others are more dismissive, fearing over-analysis and anthropomorphism (see Barton, 2006 for an overview erring on the side of scepticism, and Janik et al., 2006 and Marino et al., 2007 for more favourable reviews and analyses).

Biological archaeologist Robin Dunbar has argued that human language and the capacity for symbolic thought had particular evolutionary advantages, enabling our primate ancestors 'to form long-lasting, tightly bonded coalitions' (1996: 68) through 'a kind of vocal grooming [gossip] to ... bond larger groups than was possible using the conventional primate mechanism of physical grooming' (1996: 78). That may have been the case, but grooming is just one of the many ways in which primates communicate with each other. When discussing the suitability of baboons as models for human evolution Cheney and Seyfarth (2007: 251) state that while baboons communicate with each other and other species, they are incapable of language *per se*. This is a controversial point because baboons have perceptive and cognitive abilities which show *continuity with* human language. Moreover, baboons are capable of forming complex mental representations (see for example, Noser and Byrne, 2007). As a result, when many other species of animal are denied language, what they actually seem to lack is spoken language and the ability to use abstract or symbolic signs (words) in almost infinite combinations to convey meaning about things, events and experiences which are not confined to the here and now.

Ethologists led by Karim Ouattara (Ouattara et al., 2009) have recently found that Campbell's monkeys (*Cercopithecus campbelli*) in East Africa engage in 'affixation', a process of meaningful acoustic modification to alter and broaden the meaning of standard alarm calls. Whereas in the past researchers thought these monkeys had a very limited repertoire of calls, the recognition that a variable stem is sometimes followed by an invariable suffix to broaden the meaning of a call has effectively doubled their vocabulary. Psychologist Klaus Zuberbühler has also found that Diana (*Cercopithecus diana*) and Campbell's monkeys consistently respond to the distinct predator alarm calls of the other species in the same way that they do to the vocalizations of the predators themselves. This suggests that 'nonhuman primates are able to use acoustic signals of diverse origin as labels for underlying mental representations' (Zuberbühler, 2000: 713). In comparison to the linguistic and representational abilities of humans this is still very limited, but these are just a few examples demonstrating that animals other than humans can communicate in ways which we are only just beginning to appreciate, and with members of species other than their own. As a result, the whole debate raises interesting issues for anthropologists and scholars from the biological sciences.

INTER-SPECIES COMMUNICATION

Regardless of the scientific support for different forms of interspecies communication, humans in ethnographic regions around the world engage in communications with animals on a day-to-day basis; in many cases, their very survival is contingent on the success of this communication. That large and potentially dangerous animals such as elephants (*Elaphas maximus*) can be trained to work with humans in the logging industry, or as transport for tourists in many parts of south Asia is possible because of the elephants' abilities to understand what they are being asked to do by their Mahouts, and the Mahouts' abilities to read and respond to the messages being communicated by their elephant charges (see for example Hart, 2005). Elephants are social animals, and sociality is often cited as a key factor in the development of communicative abilities (see chapter 3) and cooperative strategies, but there are also examples of humans communicating and working with typically solitary creatures.

Many indigenous groups in areas of sympatry (habitat sharing) across Africa, such as the Borana in Kenya (Isack and Reyer, 1989), or the Tsonga, Ndebele and Zulu of South Africa (Dean et al., 1990) have a mutualistic relationship with the Greater Honeyguide (*Indicator indicator*) based on the ability of human and bird to communicate with one another and recognize in the other a means to an end (in this case honey) which would be more difficult to attain without the input of a collaborator or 'symbiont'. On locating a hive the birds solicit the assistance of a symbiont, which tends to be either a human or a Honey badger (*Mellivora capensis* [Isack and Reyer, 1989]). The Honeyguides draw attention to themselves by flying close and calling, 'inviting' the symbiont to follow them by flying on a short distance, then returning, calling, circling and so on until the human or badger responds:

> The modern relationship between the Honeyguide and man [sic] is now developed to the extent that the birds will follow humans in motor vehicles and boats, and can be attracted by the sound of chopping wood, a specific human activity. (Dean et al., 1990: 100)

TRAINING

One area of particular anthropological significance is in relation to training. Humans train other animals of various species to perform a wide range of behaviours. 'Training' implies the imparting of practical, often vocational (i.e. functional) skills, knowledge or practices. These skills are not necessarily useful to the animals themselves, but are a consequence of their domestication and subsequent enrolment within an anthropocentric world. For example, the training of elephants by Mahouts to facilitate their roles as traction and transport in the logging and tourist industries in Asia utilizes, or rather harnesses, variations of naturally expressed behaviours (Hart, 2005). The association of the term with discipline and control (as in the physical preparation required by athletes) and relationships of dominance (as in the military) makes its application to some human–animal relationships especially pertinent.

The 'traditional' approach to training horses in the UK for example, which can be traced back to the manual *On horsemanship* authored by military historian Xenophon in c. 350 BCE, demands that horses be 'broken' so as to accept the will of their human handler or rider. In a bid to facilitate this process, various tools are utilized by traditionalists ('tack' such as saddles, bridles and bits, and 'artificial aids' such as whips and spurs), which can be seen to deny horses any genuine freedom, choice or agency. More importantly, however, these tools are often used to punish unwanted behaviours (Birke, 2008; Hurn, 2011a). As cultural geographer Owain Jones observes:

> Cows, pigs, horses, poultry and sheep often have to be coerced by violent means into rural production networks. As Ingold shows, dealing with animals has produced a whole range of 'tools of coercion', such as the whip or the spur, designed to inflict physical force and very often acute pain (2000: 307). (2003: 296)

While it has existed in other informal incarnations for centuries, 'Natural Horsemanship' (NH), whereby humans seek to develop a partnership with their horses based on mutual trust and respect as opposed to domination, is a comparatively recent trend in many post-domestic societies. NH draws on the work and teachings of 'horse whisperers' such as Monty Roberts and Pat Parelli, who came to prominence as a result of their respective success in 'training' notoriously difficult and uncooperative horses. Both Roberts and Parelli have developed their own forms of inter-species communication based on horse body language and behaviour. Roberts (2008: 30) refers to his version as a 'silent' language called 'Equus' which he learnt from observing herds of wild Mustangs in the USA. When applied to human–horse communication, 'Equus' is successful because, rather than expecting horses to understand human language, NH proponents communicate with horses on their terms.

Using a 'traditional' approach, horses would be trained to respond to vocal commands such as 'stand' or 'trot' or 'whoa', or to force such as a kick or a pull on the reins. Horses learn to follow these commands (often as a result of negative reinforcement) and so the spoken words or physical gestures acquire meaning as a result of experience. However, because verbal language is not shared by horses, the process is biased in favour of the human trainer, resulting in a long and often confrontational and stressful learning process. When humans attempt to communicate with other animals on their own terms (using body language for example, and taking into account the behaviour and physiology of the species and individual in question), the playing field is levelled and, in theory at least, the process should be a great deal more humane.

Horse owners who identify themselves as proponents of NH may follow a particular branch (for example, Roberts or Parelli), but many others take a more syncretic approach, adopting the general philosophy of NH (cooperation rather than domination, trying to think like a horse rather than expecting the horse to think like a human) but adapting methods to suit their own particular needs. As a school of thought NH advocates only limited use of paraphernalia such as halters, training ropes and sticks. The latter are never to be used to hit the horses, but rather serve as extensions of the trainer's body, facilitating physical touch at a safe distance. Certain branches encourage horse owners to eschew conventional tack (saddles and bridles) altogether, encouraging riders to do a great deal of ground work and when they do ride to go 'bareback' (without saddle), 'bitless' (without a metal bit in the horse's mouth) and 'barefoot' (without nailing metal shoes to horses' feet).

Lynda Birke (2007, 2008), Keri Brandt (2004, 2005) and Joanna Latimer (Latimer and Birke, 2009) have all conducted ethnographic fieldwork with proponents of NH, or in Brandt's case, as practitioners themselves. Birke in particular argues that while proponents of NH are seeking a more humane approach to training their horses, with the desire to create a partnership as opposed to a dominance-based hierarchy, in reality a complex and at times contradictory tension between control and freedom is experienced. Not all owners have the requisite knowledge and skill to enable them to communicate effectively with their horses, nor do they have the requisite understanding of equine behaviour. As a result, in NH communication between humans and horses can become confused.

Despite certain limitations, the increasing popularity of NH is symptomatic of a paradigm shift in attitudes towards animals, and domesticated animals in particular, within a post-domestic setting. While it is often dismissed as anthropomorphism, the genuine desire to read, understand and respond appropriately to the needs of the animals in their care is a driving motivator for many humans. The emergent phenomenon of 'house rabbits' – which sees these animals taken out of their cages and integrated within the human household, with often significant implications for human daily praxis – is driven by an increasing recognition of the 'personhood' of these highly social animals (see also Davis and DeMello, 2003 and chapters 8 and 10). For example, when discussing her commensal relationship with house rabbits Smith provides a vignette detailing how the mimetic behaviour of one rabbit, Hattie, caused her to re-think human–rabbit communication. Smith describes what happened after she herself had accidentally dropped and broken the rabbit's water bowl as follows:

> I cleaned the mess and fetched another crock, which I filled and set on the top shelf. I walked away for a moment, then turned to retrieve the crock and watched ... as Hattie ran up the ramp and pushed it off the shelf – causing another huge crash and mess. To my mind, this was an example of Hattie's seeing my behavior as a performance, as an act directed toward her, and enacting a response ... rabbits often replicate each other's acts. They also appear to love to make noise by throwing objects around. Still, I was astounded that Hattie treated me like a rabbit. Her act brought me to see us in a relationship as she might see it. Even though each of us experienced the interaction differently, it gestured toward a cross-species form of communication that I deeply valued. My rabbits execute actions all the time that convey their understanding that they are in a relationship of some kind with me. They constantly shove their noses under my hands to demand petting. (2003: 195)

In a recent study of mushers (racing-sled drivers) and sled dogs in the USA, Gail Kuhl (2011) found that the majority of her informants believed that the process of sledding, and especially success in races, was contingent on the efficacy of a two-way communication between humans and dogs. The mushers were able to read the body language of the dogs, but also readily acknowledged that the dogs were highly attuned to the verbal and non-verbal messages being conveyed by humans and each other. This canine ability to empathize was presented by some of Kuhl's informants as quasi-psychic; the dogs appeared to be able to read minds.

EMPATHY

The examples of inter-species companionship précised in the preceding section are all suggestive of some level of empathy. But this too has long been regarded as an exclusively human preserve. Biologist and primatologist Frans de Waal (2009), however, has recently discussed empathy and provided a large body of evidence in support of its presence in animals. De Waal argues that many species are able to empathize not only with members of their own species but also with members of other species too. As a result, the paucity of documented instances of inter-species social relationships in wild animals may be due to the fact that they have simply not been systematically observed rather than because they do not occur (see chapters 3 and 11 for similar points in relation to culture in animals).

Empathy, the ability to read emotions or body language and recognize how another is feeling, leads to much more effective and meaningful communication and is evolutionarily advantageous (de Waal, 2009; see also Langford et al., 2006). For example, success in the hunt (for both parties) is contingent on the ability not just to read the behaviour of the other involved, but then to correctly anticipate the next move, to put oneself in someone else's shoes (or paws or hooves – see chapters 4 and 14).

Dogs are particularly good at reading humans and vice versa. For example, studies carried out by psychologist Peter Pongrácz and colleagues (2005, 2006) consistently found that humans were able to read the emotional states of dogs from listening to recordings of dog vocalizations and that this ability was shared by participants regardless of their experiential familiarity with dogs. Sociologist Clinton Sanders (2003) and ethologists Allen and Bekoff (2005) discuss play as a form of communication between humans and dogs, which involves the ability to empathize with the other's position, as well as an ability to utilize and interpret facial expressions, vocalizations and eye contact.

The importance of eyes when it comes to assessing how an individual is 'really feeling' emerges regularly in the literature relating to human communication and human–animal interactions in general (see Servais, 2005: 222 for example in relation to the importance of eye-contact in human–dolphin interactions) and dogs have also learnt the importance of following the gaze of humans as a result of the lengthy relationship between these two species (Viranyi et al., 2008). Dogs and humans have a long history of co-evolution and symbiotic commensalism (see chapter 5) and as a result the level of effective inter-species communication between humans and dogs has been a regular focus of academic inquiry and interest. Dogs are routinely 'employed' in a working relationship with humans, as hunting hounds (Hufford, 1992; Marvin, 2000, 2002), guide or hearing dogs (Naderi et al., 2001) or shepherds (McConnell and Bayliss, 1985) for example, and while some of the behaviours exhibited during these interactions are 'innate', they are refined and developed to quite a precise degree as a result of training and shared embodied experience.

The previous chapter was concerned with pet keeping and all of the 'explanations' given focused almost exclusively on the human perspectives. It is obviously much easier to ascertain what humans get from these interactions and relationships because researchers can ask them, or draw on their own experiences. However, the move towards 'bringing in the animal', which is gaining momentum across the social sciences, necessitates the recognition of animals as active subjects in (but also frequently victims of) relationships with humans, and the attempt to give these muted individuals a voice (see also chapters 5, 10 and 16). While humans may instigate or maintain a relationship with a pet or indeed any other animal on the grounds of recognition of personhood, the same applies to some nonhumans too. The Algers (2003), for example, in their ethnographic study of a cat shelter, found that some cats enjoy human companionship and actively solicit affection (in addition to food) from specific human carers or potential adopters. This often worked in their favour, and the Algers note that 'adopters tended to respond very favourably to the cats who showed an interest in them' (2003: 161).

INTER-SPECIES SOCIALITY AND 'ADOPTION'

While many pet animals may benefit from being pets, pet keeping is frequently given as another exclusively human activity (for example, Herzog, 2010). However, positive inter-species interactions, as the previous two cases suggest, are not necessarily always instigated by humans. They may exclude humans altogether. Perhaps the most significant, but also most contested, instance of inter-species communication relates to the ability of animals to successfully raise the young of another species. The case of a lioness (*Panthera leo*) at the Lewa wildlife reserve in Kenya who repeatedly 'adopted' Oryx calves *(Oryx gazella)* over a period of several years (Schmidt, 2007) suggests the desire for 'pets' (or rather that the caring, empathic drivers which motivate some human pet owners) may extend beyond the human species.

Another arresting example has been documented by wildlife film-makers Dereck and Beverly Joubert (2009). The Jouberts followed a leopardess and her cub, who they named Legadema, and on occasion observed Legadema being brought a live calf so she could learn how to hunt (in a manner reminiscent of the educational aspects of pet keeping in some human cultural contexts, albeit it within a much shorter time frame). What was particularly noteworthy, however, was the outcome of Legadema's first baboon kill. Attached to the dead body of its mother was a small baby baboon and, rather than killing it or ignoring it to eat her meal, Legadema picked up the infant when it reached out to her and carried it up a tree where she groomed it, carrying it higher each time it cried. The pair eventually curled up together and slept, but the baby died in the night and it was only then that Legadema returned to the mother baboon's body to eat.

Such examples might be dismissed as the exceptions that prove the rule, or as confused young females indulging their maternal instincts towards a vulnerable infant. Because of the species involved the relationships do not last very long, so there is no opportunity to study their maturation. However, there is one well documented case of what has been regarded as a form of inter-species adoption by primatologists Izar et al. (2006). This particular case involved a baby marmoset (*Callithrix jacchus*) being adopted and cared for into adulthood by a group of wild (but provisioned) capuchins (*Cebus libidinosus*).

Such events are only possible if the animals in question can recognize the needs of the other, and the ability or even inclination to (attempt to) raise the young of another species is perhaps an indicator of inter-species communication and continuity. Indeed, even if Legadema was merely responding to an innate maternal instinct, the fact that she engaged with the baboon as a 'baby' as opposed to a potential food source was as a result of some form of communication which took place between them; the baby reached out to her, and she responded to its request for comfort (see Serpell, 2002b for a related discussion on neoteny as an evolutionary advantage).

FERAL CHILDREN

The abilities of animals to raise human children has ancient antecedents in the legends surrounding the foundation of Rome. Throughout history accounts of so-called 'feral children' have captivated public and academic attention alike (see Benzaquén, 2006; Newton, 2002). The 'wolf children of Mindapore' and 'Luke the Baboon boy' (Foley, 1940; cf. Zingg, 1940) are particularly well-known historical cases. However, the persistence of isolated but documented instances of humans raised by or alongside animals in the contemporary world make interesting food for thought.

In 1988 John Ssebunya, a 3-year-old child in Uganda, ran away from home after witnessing his father murder his mother, was 'adopted' by a troop of vervet monkeys (*Cercopithicus Aethiops*) and taught by them how to forage. What makes John's story different from many other accounts is the fact that he had some human socialization prior to his incorporation into a nonhuman social group, and was thus able to communicate his experiences on his reincorporation into 'humanity' (Du Bois, 2007).

ANTHROPOZOOMETRICITY

Cases of feral children are widely disputed by anthropologists because the ability of animals other than humans to raise human children (albeit according to their own 'cultural' and behavioural norms) again calls many long-standing assumptions about human uniqueness into question. Moreover, despite the wealth of material in support of proto-symbolic and more complex forms of representational thought in animals, especially in language-trained primates, for whom human symbolic systems provide tools to communicate about referents in more detail than their own (unaided) systems allow (see Call, 2011 for a recent overview including studies dating back to the 1970s), these findings do not appear to have caught the attention of social anthropologists. Kramsch for example, in her recently published textbook *Language and culture* confidently asserts that 'the crucial feature that distinguishes humans from animals is humans' capacity to create signs that mediate between them and their environment' (2008: 15).

There is a long-standing tendency to use a human yardstick when measuring the abilities of nonhuman animals (what might be referred to as anthropozoometricity), but focusing on human capacities as the marker of cognitive ability is inherently anthropocentric (see also chapters 3, 10, 11, 16). There are many abilities unique to other animals which humans lack, or which humans and animals share but in which humans lag behind in terms of proficiency. Among many animals, Ring-tailed lemurs (*Lemur catta*) for example (Bolt, 2010), olfactory communication is an important sensory modality for the transmission of meaningful information between individuals in a social setting. While humans can glean some information from the odour of another human, this sense plays a comparatively insignificant role in our communicative systems in general. Rather than saying that humans have an inferior communicative repertoire in relation to other animals with a more developed sense of smell however, we just say that we are 'different' and attribute less value to areas where we lack proficiency.

ALTERNATIVE COMMUNICATION

In many parts of the world, humans communicate with the spirit realm via trance, meditation or the ingestion of hallucinogenic drugs. Such activities serve to enhance the sensory and perceptive abilities of individuals, and facilitate communication with beings who would otherwise be unreachable. Among the Runa of Ecuador, for example, humans ingest hallucinogens in order to converse with the spirit master (Kohn, 2007). Runa hierarchical ontology sees the spirit master in a superior position to humans, and this relationship is mirrored in Runa relationships with their dogs. Humans can understand dog vocalizations, along with the non-verbal communications of other animals (such as the stare of a jaguar, who is the 'dog' of the spirit master; see also Fausto, 2008). However, for dogs to fully understand human speech they have to enter into an altered state of consciousness. By administering hallucinogens to dogs, Runa are able to communicate with them to a more sophisticated degree than they otherwise could in the mortal realm (Kohn, 2007: 13).

The apparent 'need' to organize animals hierarchically on the basis of how much like humans they or their communicative (or cultural) abilities are seems unnecessarily crude, and yet it is a pervasive discourse, as seen in the Runa case. The issue is probably one of degree, as with many of the characteristics perceived to be exclusively human. While many humans find ways around this, such as through the administration of hallucinogens, or by attempting to 'speak horse' (Birke, 2007), others remain resolute in their belief that human spoken language is paramount. Because human language and cognition is far more complex than that documented in other animals, anthropologists have felt able to dismiss it out of hand. Such an approach is no longer excusable, however, because some animals do create and use representational signs within their own 'cultural' systems. Yet the perception that they do not will only be challenged when (or rather if) anthropologists engage with research being conducted by ethologists in this field. This is another reason why anthrozoology or the anthropological study of human–animal interactions is so important, because it can facilitate inter-disciplinary as well as inter-species communication.

SUGGESTIONS FOR FURTHER READING

Crist, E. 2004. Can an insect speak? The case of the honeybee dance language. *Social Studies of Science* 34(1): 7–43.

Gärdenfors, P. 2008. The role of intersubjectivity in animal and human cooperation. *Biological Theory: Integrating Development, Evolution and Cognition* 3(1): 51–61.

Grandin, T. and Johnson, C. 2006. *Animals in translation: using the mysteries of autism to decode animal behavior.* New York: Harcourt.

Greenbaum, J.B. 2010. Training dogs and training humans: symbolic interaction and dog training. *Anthrozoös* 23(2): 129–141.

Haraway, D. 2008. *When species meet.* Minneapolis: University of Minnesota Press.

Hearne, V. 2007. *Adam's task: calling animals by name.* New York: Skyhorse Publishing Inc.

Jerolmack, C. 2009. Humans, animals, and play: theorizing interaction when intersubjectivity is problematic. *Sociological Theory* 27(4): 371–389.

Laule, G., Bloomsmith, M.A. and Schapiro, S.J. 2003. The use of positive reinforcement training techniques to enhance the care, management, and welfare of primates in the laboratory. *Journal of Applied Animal Welfare Science* 6(3): 163–173.

Sanders, C.R. 1999. *Understanding dogs: living and working with canine companions.* Philadelphia, PA: Temple University Press.

Schapiro, S.J. 2003. Positive reinforcement training as a technique to alter nonhuman primate behavior: quantitative assessments of effectiveness. *Journal of Applied Animal Welfare Science* 6(3): 175–187.

Shapiro, K. 1990. Understanding dogs through kinesthetic empathy, social construction, and history. *Anthrozoös* 111(3): 184–195.

Serpell, J.A. and Hsu, Y. 2005. Effects of breed, sex, and neuter status on trainability in dogs. *Anthrozoös* 18(3): 196–207.

Wait, C. and Buchanan-Smith, H. 2002. The effects of caretaker–primate relationships on primates in the laboratory. *Journal of Applied Animal Welfare Science* 5(4): 309–319.

10
Intersubjectivity

No one who looks into a gorilla's eyes – intelligent, gentle, vulnerable – can remain unchanged, for the gap between ape and human vanishes: we know that the gorilla still lives within us. Do gorillas also recognise this ancient connection? (Schaller, 2007: 84)

As Lévi-Strauss noted, animals are convenient symbols for humans because they are 'good to think' (1963). In other words, humans are able to communicate important messages about themselves through animals, provided that the recipients of those messages share the same semiotic understanding or system of classification (see chapter 6). In the process of 'standing in' for humans, animal 'objects' can also become active subjects with the capacity to impact on the relationships between the humans involved, leading some researchers to refer to these multi-species interactions as 'intersubjective' (for example, Alger and Alger, 2003; Cassidy, 2002; Hurn, 2008a, 2008b). While such assertions are typically grounded in ethnographic data, researchers seldom discuss the long-standing philosophical debates on intersubjectivity, nor the implications of intersubjectivity for anthropological studies of humans and animals. Such issues need to be raised because not only do they have serious ramifications for the ways in which anthropologists think about animals (and how they think their informants think about both themselves and animals) but also they impact more generally on anthropological methodology and disciplinary identity.

ANIMALS AS SYMBOLS

An interesting example of the symbolic use of animals as markers of identity comes from fieldwork by anthropologist Ayse Caglar (1997). Caglar's Turkish informants, who found themselves marginalized by mainstream German society, viewed the *kampfhunde* (fighting dogs) they owned and interacted with simultaneously as extensions of their 'selves' and as objectified 'accessories' which communicated an aggressive and macho image to the outside world. Elsewhere, foxes have been seen as representative of English 'incomers' for some Welsh farmers (Hurn, 2009) because, as far as these individuals are concerned, foxes, like the large numbers of incomers who relocate to the Welsh countryside, encroach uninvited upon their territory and undermine their traditional way of life. While these metaphorical associations with animals reveal information about the perceived characteristics of both the humans and animals concerned, characteristics which can often be appreciated and understood by external observers (such as members of mainstream German society), or exclusively by members of specific 'subcultural' groups (such as Welsh farmers), they do not necessarily constitute intersubjective relationships.

THE PHENOMENOLOGICAL TRADITION

Intersubjectivity is an integral aspect of the philosophical movement known as phenomenology, which has a long history within philosophy and the social sciences more generally. The 20th-century philosopher Edmund Husserl is widely recognized as the principal founder of the phenomenological movement, but it is the work of later phenomenologists such as Heidegger (1962) and Merleau-Ponty (1962) which has had the most overt influence on anthropology as the practice of theory. Anthropologists such as Chris Tilley (1994), Tim Ingold (2000) and Michael Jackson (1998), and sociologists such as Alfred Schutz (1967) have adopted and adapted their conceptions of phenomenology for practical application. For these academics it is the subjective, self-conscious notion of 'being-in-the-world' which provides the key to understanding human lived reality. The creation of meaning is an active, intentional process and each individual interprets the world and relays that interpretation to others through his or her own language and actions. Thus, intersubjectivity occurs when individual actors consciously recognize and attribute intentionality to each other. As a result, there is a requirement for actors to be self-aware, conscious beings if they are to participate in intersubjective exchanges.

However, as Cohen and Rapport note, 'Western social thought is built upon the Cartesian notion of self-consciousness (as expressed in the *cogito*) *as the distinguishing characteristic of humanity*' (1995: 1, emphasis added). Such a view is received anthropological wisdom and yet many researchers who work closely with other animals find that experience tells them otherwise. For example, when discussing the nature of relationships between laboratory chimpanzees and their carers, referred to as chimpers, Taylor notes that:

> both the chimper and the chimp interact with each other with a view of themselves which is gained from the others' perception of them ... In other words the world shared by chimper and chimpanzee is essentially an intersubjective one *based on mutual perceptions of mindedness*. (N. Taylor, 2007: 60–61, emphasis added)

In their ethnographic experiences many anthropologists find that certain animals are perceived in a similar manner by their informants.

OBJECTS VERSUS SUBJECTS

Anthropologist Rebecca Cassidy, for example, in her ethnographic study of the horse racing industry in Newmarket, UK, suggests that 'an intersubjectivity between the thoroughbred and its human attendants' often exists (2002: 9). This is because Cassidy's informants accorded their horses both object and subject status, depending upon the context within which interactions occurred. When horses were perceived as objects (for example by the vet when taking routine blood tests), intersubjectivity was impossible. Yet when horses were recognized as active subjects, situated along a continuum which also included humans, then some form of inter-subjective relationship could result (such as when horses reacted directly to the actions of human riders or grooms).

Cassidy goes on to suggest that, in this particular ethnographic situation, the relationship between humans and racehorses in Newmarket can take 'the form of an intersubjectivity whereby gains or losses in status of the racehorse accrue to those with whom it is associated' (2002: 124). In this example, however, it is more difficult to qualify the relationship as intersubjective because the possibility of the individual racehorse being *aware* of the potential impacts that winning or losing a race might have on his or her human associates is unlikely to say the least. While horses may well come to associate winning or losing races with certain treatment after the event (such as rough handling when they finish behind other horses, or praise and positive treatment if they finish ahead), it is unlikely that they could recognize that their performance may affect the status of humans in relation to other humans. That's not to say that humans and horses can't engage in intersubjective relationships, but rather that it is unlikely in this particular example.

EMPATHY AGAIN

In order to be able to engage in intersubjective relationships, individuals must also be able to empathize, to make the conceptual leap to appreciate how the situation may be for whoever they are interacting with. That is not to say that they must be able to 'correctly' perceive and appreciate this 'other' way of being, but rather they must have some sense that it may be different in relation to their own experience. With other humans, we have various ways of ascertaining whether or not we have managed to achieve an empathic appreciation of another's world view. We can ask questions, observe facial expressions or other outward displays of emotion (Milton, 2002). When it comes to animals however, the situation is more complex, or so we are led to believe, because we do not have commonality of species on which to base our observations.

The philosopher Ludwig Wittgenstein famously observed that 'If a Lion could speak, we could not understand him' (1958: 223) because, for Wittgenstein, language, and therefore meaning, was relative. As a result, our empathic interpretations can never be adequately put to the test. We can never really *know* what it is like to be a lion, or another human being for that matter. This is a perennial problem for anthropologists whose job it is to try and do just that, and yet we all, anthropologists included, make assumptions about what we imagine it must be like to be a lion or another human being every day; anthropologists just undertake this mundane practice in a more sustained and theoretically rigorous manner.

Anthropologists attempt to learn the cultural language of their subjects and thus enter into their 'language-games', to use Wittgenstein's terminology (1958: 7), so as to better (but not *completely*) understand them through the shared embodied experiences characteristic of participant observation. Wittgenstein's statement is also interesting for philosopher and animal trainer Vicki Hearne because: 'Wittgenstein does not leap to say that his lion is languageless, only that he is not talking ... a profundity rarely achieved, because of all it leaves room for' (2007: 169). In other words, rather than denying lions (or other animals for that matter) language, consciousness and other important faculties, Wittgenstein leaves the possibility of possibilities. Hearne refers to the statement as an 'interesting mistake' because for some humans, lions do talk in ways which they can understand, for example the founders of the Born Free Foundation, Joy and George Adamson (see also Wolfe, 2003).

INTERSUBJECTIVITY IN ANTHROPOLOGY

In anthropology, the postmodern trend of insider ethnography leads researchers to claim greater authenticity of experience and thus authority when it comes to understanding and translating what it means to be, say, a Goth (Hodkinson, 2002) or, to use an anthrozoological example, a participant in dog agility classes (Haraway, 2008), on the grounds of their membership of the group in question. This illustrates to some extent the fact that *shared* experience and world view make it easier for individuals to empathize and engage in intersubjective exchanges. However, insider ethnography is not without its challenges and criticisms (Hastrup, 1987; Hodkinson, 2002), and even individuals who share the same socio-cultural upbringing may have very different and, at times, diametrically opposed perceptions of the world (see Milton, 2002). This recognition of the diversity of experience within, let alone across, cultural groups has led anthropologists in two seemingly opposing directions.

On the one hand, the recognition that 'any mind beyond the ethnographer's own is other and requires to have interpretive work done on it' (Cohen, 1986) means that anthropologists can no longer make sweeping generalizations about what it means to be a member of a particular culture or society because all humans are unique. On the other, the diversity of *individual* human perception of the world means that anthropologists need now, more than ever, to reflexively draw on their own subjective experiences and ability to empathize, to try and put themselves in the shoes of their informants. This emphasis on empathy, on accepting that we can never really know what is going on inside the mind of another, but recognizing that sometimes we can make a pretty good guess, should enable anthropologists to think seriously about the possibility of human–animal intersubjectivity, an activity which, in the past (as discussed in chapter 3), would have been dismissed as mere anthropomorphic projection. However, intersubjectivity still requires the acceptance of 'mindedness' in the nonhuman other.

ETHOLOGY

Numerous ethologists who work with animals, observing and analysing their behaviours, have also found that engaging in ethnographic participant observation of sorts with animals in the wild, or as close to a natural situation as possible, yields positive results (for example, Goodall, 1986, 1990; Sapolsky, 2006; see also chapters 11 and 16), an approach which in the not too distant past would have been dismissed as 'unscientific', allowing as it does for subjective interpretation verging on anthropomorphism (de Waal, 2001). Yet even when working with species far removed from the higher primates, researchers find it possible to draw conclusions based on an ability to empathize with their subjects (Hayward, 2010; see also chapter 16). When such an approach is combined with what is conventionally regarded as more scientific practices such as monitoring brain activity or measuring hormone levels, and the results corroborate the researcher's subjective observations, then the conclusion that empathy is possible across the species barrier can be convincingly made (de Waal, 2009).

In the social sciences, intersubjectivity is often conflated with the symbolic interactionism of pragmatist philosopher George Herbert Mead (1934). Symbolic interactionism is based on the belief that an individual's sense of 'self' develops as a result of their linguistic interactions with other humans within a social context. This self-awareness or self-consciousness is required if individuals are to engage in intersubjective interactions with other self-aware individuals. Because most animals are widely thought to lack a sense of self, then they are, by Mead's standards, unable to participate in intersubjective exchanges. Yet there is a wealth of evidence from ethologists which demonstrates convincingly that many animals are conscious with often exceedingly complex cognitive abilities (for example, Griffin, 2001; see also chapter 3).

SELF-CONSCIOUSNESS

Perhaps the most conclusive evidence for other animals having 'self-consciousness' and the ability to empathize comes from research into 'pointing'. An animal's ability to recognize the significance of a pointing gesture of another provides a pretty clear indication that not only are they self-aware, but that they can recognize that the 'other' who is doing the pointing is also self-aware (White, 2007: 68–9). For example, if individuals look at what it is the other is pointing *at* rather than the tip of the pointing finger, then they are showing what cognitive psychologists call 'theory of mind'. Some animals, such as certain primates, dogs and corvids (for example, crows and ravens), take this to another level and follow the eye-gaze of others (Bugnyar et al., 2004; Hare and Tomasello, 2005; Miklósi et al., 2000; Virányi et al., 2008). In relation to social transmission of behaviours in nonhuman primates Perry has noted that:

> Being sensitive to the emotional states and gaze directions of others enables joint attention of the model and the observer on the same aspects of an activity pattern, thereby enhancing the probability that some aspect of the model's knowledge and/or behavior will be acquired by the observer. (2006: 184)

SYMBOLIC LANGUAGE

In addition to self-consciousness, complex syntactic language is often thought to separate humans from other animals (see chapter 9). Language is also an essential aspect of Mead's symbolic interactionism because it allows for perceptions and experiences to be shared with others who, by dint of their own socially developed 'selves' and linguistic competence, will be able to appreciate and understand what is being communicated to them. So animals are excluded on this count too, despite the fact that 'language' has been documented in a wide range of animals from chimpanzees and dolphins through to chickens (for example, Blumstein and Armitage, 1997; Evans, 1997; Greene and Meagher, 1998; Manser, 2001; Marler and Evans, 1996; Ouattara et al., 2009; Rogers and Kaplan, 2004: 189). However, there is more to communication than language. As non-verbal 'embodied communication' between anthropologists and their human subjects is widely accepted as a legitimate tool in the pursuit of anthropological understanding, then it might also present a partial solution to the 'problem' presented by claims of human–animal intersubjectivity. Consider the following passage from Haraway's *When species meet* with reference to the work of anthropologist and psychologist Barbara Smuts:

> Smuts defines a greeting ritual [between beings who know each other well] as a kind of embodied communication, which takes place in entwined, semiotic, overlapping, somatic patterning over time, not as discrete, denotative signals emitted by individuals. An embodied communication is more like a dance than a word. The flow of entangled, meaningful bodies in time – whether jerky and nervous or flaming and flowing, whether both parties move in harmony or painfully out of sync or something else altogether – is

communication about relationship, the relationship itself, and the means of reshaping relationship and so its enacters. (2008: 26)

In addition to utilizing non-verbal communication and empathy when it comes to considering human–animal intersubjectivities, however, anthropologists might be wise to follow the lead of colleagues elsewhere in the social sciences and consider what Actor Network Theory (ANT) can contribute. Indeed, in a survey of recent anthropological perspectives on agency (with particular reference to human–animal interactions) anthropologist Casey High (2010) has also noted the potential of ANT when it comes to anthropological understandings of nonhuman agency in, for example, shamanic practices.

ACTOR NETWORK THEORY

Most typically associated with French philosopher, sociologist and anthropologist Bruno Latour, ANT was developed by Latour along with sociologists John Law and Michael Callon. For Latour, culture is a network of associations between individual 'objects' he termed 'actants', and these actants can be both human and nonhuman (Latour, 1996: 373; see also Barron, 2003).

As its alternative title (Material Semiotics) suggests, ANT considers relationships between material objects (actants) and symbolic concepts within a particular cultural context or social network. So, for example, a sheepdog trial might be considered a network which includes a human shepherd, a flock of sheep, a sheepdog, a pen and the shepherd's crook, and all of these 'actants' would be accorded 'agency', that is, an ability to impact on the other actors within the network.

ANT has not really been fully utilized by anthropologists precisely because of the equal standing and ability to effect change which Latour gave to all actors within any given network – for some, while there might be some scope for considering animals such as dogs actants, the need to position the 'inanimate' shepherd's crook and the 'mindless' sheep on a level playing field with the human shepherd is problematic. Indeed, Latour's assertion that other nonhuman beings or 'material objects' are actants in their own right has formed the basis of many critiques of ANT (for example, Fuller in Barron, 2003), and was one of the contributing factors which eventually led Latour to question the validity of ANT himself (Latour, 1999). Nonetheless, ANT has been utilized as a conceptual tool to allow researchers to bring animals into human social networks most successfully and with most frequency by geographers (for example, Fitzsimmons and Goodman, 1998; Jones, 2003; Philo and Wilbert, 1999, 2000; Whatmore and Thorne, 1998, 2000; Woods, 1998). ANT presents a particularly useful model for anthropologists of an anthrozoological orientation because it recognizes the transient and flexible nature of relationships between all actants in a network and accords nonhuman as well as human actants agency, a widely discussed concept in anthropology.

AGENCY IN A NETWORK

As Laidlaw notes (2002: 315), anthropologists tend to think about agency in terms of the capacity of actors (or agents or actants) to impact upon others and, as a result, agency has been used by anthropologists as a tool to think about power relations. Because animals, at least in most post-domestic systems of production and consumption, are enrolled in ways which more often than not deny them any opportunity to change the circumstances within which they find themselves (such as battery cages), they are also denied agency. Yet this predominantly socio-cultural view of agency is not necessarily accepted across the entire breadth of the anthropological spectrum and, from within the field of material culture studies for example, more open and inclusive definitions can be found. Ahearn's definition of agency as 'the socio-culturally mediated capacity to act' (2001: 110) for example allows anthropologists to consider the fact that even (what may appear to outside observers to be) passive 'inanimate' objects can be agents in the world, with social lives of their own (Appadurai, 1986). But more to the point, these objects influence both action and thought (Thrift, 2003: 312).

While conventional wisdom within many post-domestic contexts holds that particular human interactions with other animals (or nonhuman 'things') can be expected to have particular outcomes (i.e. the sheepdog obeys the shepherd, the sheep respond to the movements of the dog, the shepherd uses the crook to catch hold of any stragglers, and all the sheep end up in the pen), in reality the situation may play out differently. The sheepdog may misinterpret or ignore the instructions given by the shepherd or, to bring another actant into the network, the wind may prevent the shepherd's instructions from reaching the dog's ears (see Ingold, 2011a, for a discussion on the importance of weather in our interactions and ways of being). The sheep may respond in an 'unpredictable' manner to the situation, they may evade the reach of the crook, outrun the dog, or 'spook' at the pen and refuse to go in. The crook may fall out of the shepherd's hand, and the pen may collapse when the sheep eventually do go into it and jostle against its sides. The actual outcome of the interactions between all of these actants, human and nonhuman, 'animate' and 'inanimate' is by no means predetermined precisely *because* of the individual 'agency' of all actants within the network and their respective abilities to impact on the actions of the others involved. Therefore, at least in terms of considering human–animal relationships, ANT is particularly useful because it forces us to reconsider the perceived primacy of the human animal, who is not necessarily always in control, and recognize that other actants influence human action and the outcomes of social interactions.

Such a position is also much more in sync with the ways in which many peoples actually view human–animal interactions on the ground. Indeed, while in Cartesian thought animals are 'mindless', this position is, as Ingold also notes, almost diametrically opposed in a 'hunter-gatherer economy of knowledge' for example, whereby 'it is as entire persons, not as disembodied minds, that human beings engage with one another and, moreover, with nonhuman beings as well' (2000: 47 and chapter 4).

This comparison between opposing conceptions of animals is indirectly touched on by Michael Jackson (1998: 7), who identifies three useful aspects of intersubjectivity which destabilize the conventional prioritizing of the (literate, intentional) human in much contemporary philosophical and anthropological thought by recognizing that, for many indigenous peoples, 'Western' categories (such as subject and object, human and animal) do not apply.

Jackson emphasizes the relative nature of 'subjectivity', which allows for alternative ways of viewing intersubjectivity and, as a result, the inclusion of animals in the realm of the self-aware (although it should be noted that Jackson himself doesn't refer to animals explicitly). Jackson highlights the fact that if 'subject' and 'object' are human (cultural) constructs, then they can be reformulated, noting that the conception of self as exclusively human and constructed in opposition to all that humans are not is 'anthropologically atypical'. This state of affairs is, as far as he is concerned, disadvantageous because:

> in withholding or retracting intersubjectivity from human relations with material *and natural* things in the name of scientific rationality, one risks discarding those *anthropomorphic* corre-

spondences that enable people, in moments of crisis, to cross between human and extrahuman worlds, and thereby feel that they can imaginatively if not actually control the universe as a particular extension of their subjectivity, much as tools allow one to manipulate matter as an extension of one's own body. (Jackson, 1998: 6 emphasis added)

Here Jackson highlights the need for anthropologists to adopt and apply indigenous systems of classification when it comes to their own perceptions of intersubjective relationships. Like many of the traditional subjects of anthropological attention in the colonial past, animals are 'others' whose worlds some anthropologists (and many of their human subjects) attempt to rationalize and understand, yet in relation to both human and nonhuman subjects alike such an approach requires subjective interpretation. Even if anthropologists are able to think using unfamiliar terms of reference, to imagine what it must be like to be an Ilongot headhunter (Rosaldo, 2004) for example, there remains a need to abandon, or at least see for what they are, the categories which govern much anthropological thought. Such an approach is part and parcel of reflexive awareness, but while anthropologists have become accustomed to thinking in a reflexive manner about their interactions with other humans, applying the same principles to their interactions with other animals may not come so naturally. Yet to many anthropological informants, it is second nature.

REFLEXIVE THINKING

As a result of fieldwork with the Kluane First Nations in the sub-Arctic Yukon, anthropologist Paul Nadasdy (2007) demonstrates that this particular case of 'indigenous' hunting constitutes a form of reciprocal exchange between humans and 'other-than-human' persons. What makes Nadasdy's work particularly relevant here is his observation that the relationship between his First Nations informants and the nation state, played out through land claims and the enrolment of the Kluane in the state-controlled management of wildlife, necessitates their 'learning to speak new languages'; the languages of biologists, wildlife managers, politicians and lawyers, which do not make sense in the Kluane world view (Nadasdy, 2003). Moreover, Kluane ways of thinking about and interacting with animals are frequently at odds with those of the (dominant) Euro-Canadian state.

For many people, the 'personhood' of animals makes viewing them as 'numbers' (in terms of wildlife conservation) or as 'resources', removed from a holistic, reciprocal (and respectful) system of inter-species exchanges, anathema (see chapter 4). As a result, it might be possible to suggest that, in some ethnographic contexts, there is more evidence of intersubjective relationships occurring between humans and animals (for example, between the Kluane and the animals they hunt) than between humans (for example, between the Kluane and the state). Such situations present opportunities for anthropologists to act as mediators or cultural translators, which many do, often to good effect (for example, Nadasdy, 2003). However, what becomes blatantly apparent is the fact that there is scope for alternative conceptions of intersubjectivity to inform the ways in which outsiders (be they state officials or anthropologists) think about human–animal interactions and the possibility of inter-species intersubjectivity.

A recent re-examination of Husserl's ideas about intersubjectivity in relation to anthropology provides an interesting position from which to consider intersubjectivity between humans and animals. When coupled with an awareness of advances in the scientific understanding of other species and the animistic world view of many indigenous peoples, which share some points of reference with ANT, intersubjectivity becomes a particularly useful theoretical model. Indeed, Duranti argues that, from a Husserlian perspective, 'intersubjectivity is more than shared or mutual understanding and *is closer to the notion of the possibility of being in the place where the Other is*' (2010: 1, emphasis added).

There is an increasing body of ethological material which convincingly argues for the ability of numerous animals to empathize not just with members of their own species, but with members of other species (de Waal, 2009; see also chapter 9). While there is also plenty of evidence to suggest that many animals do not demonstrate empathy, the same could be said of humans. That they don't always empathize or demonstrate empathic engagement is a very different issue to whether they are *able* to empathize. Not all human relationships with others, human or nonhuman, are inter-subjective, because even with members of our own species we do not always make the necessary connection, that is, we do not or cannot empathize with that other enough for intersubjectivity to follow. Either that, or we refuse to empathize and employ various distancing devices which allow us to 'objectify' the other in order to carry out actions which would otherwise cause us psychological trauma, such as viewing other humans as animals to justify genocide, or viewing other animals as objects to justify their slaughter.

PERSPECTIVISM

What de Castro has termed 'perspectivism' demonstrates that other animals see and experience the world differently to humans (see also Bermúdez [2003] for a discussion on how animal thought differs from human thought) but these other ways of being (or thinking) are no less valid than our own. More to the point, humans are capable of empathizing with these other ways of being because of a shared past which facilitates inter-species exchanges, both in the material and the spiritual realms. This 'relational epistemology' or engagement between humans and other animate beings is comparable to inter-subjectivity (Bird-David, 2006: 44; Hornborg, 2006: 29; Kohn, 2007: 4). According to Kohn, when interacting with each other humans and animals 'partake in a shared constellation of attributes and dispositions – a sort of shared transspecies habitus' (2007: 7).

For many Amazonian peoples, for example, it is an individual's external form which determines how they come to perceive the world. Yet this external form is changeable, as humans are thought capable of shapeshifting into nonhuman entities and vice versa. Such views can be traced to origin myths where humans and animals coexisted, undifferentiated, often as siblings with shared character-istics. Species then separated out over time, with animals 'losing' some of the traits which were retained by humans. This is what de Castro refers to as 'nature distancing itself from culture', and as such it represents the inverse of 'Western' origin myths which see culture distancing itself from nature.

What is particularly interesting about this take on animism is that it provides alternative ways of thinking about some of the issues raised by intersubjectivity between humans and animals. If continuity between humans and animals is accepted (as it is by many) then it is no more difficult to empathize with, say, a jaguar or a dog (if you are a Runa for example [Kohn, 2007]) than it is with another human. De Castro's observation that the external form which determines the way in which an individual human or animal perceives the world can be changed *across the species barrier* means that, in many 'hunter-gatherer' societies, intersubjectivity between humans and animals is not only possible, it is a key aspect of a holistic cosmology which has been lost in many domestic and post-domestic contexts.

SUGGESTIONS FOR FURTHER READING

Alger, J.M. and Alger, S.F. 1997. Beyond Mead: symbolic interaction between humans and felines. *Society & Animals* 5(1): 65–81.

Berry, B. 2008. Interactionism and animal aesthetics: a theory of reflected social power. *Society & Animals* 16(1): 75–89.

Goode, D. 2006. *Playing with my dog Katie: an ethnomethodological study of dog-human interaction.* West Lafayette, IN: Purdue University Press.

Haraway, D.J. 2003. *The companion species manifesto: dogs, people, and significant otherness.* Chicago: Prickly Paradigm.

Haraway, D. 2006. Encounters with companion species: entangling dogs, baboons, philosophers, and biologists. *Configurations* 14(1–2): 97–114.

Jerolmack, C. 2009. Humans, animals, and play: theorizing interaction when inter-subjectivity is problematic. *Sociological Theory* 27(4): 371–389.

Konecki, K.T. (ed.) 2007. *Special Issue: Animals and people. Qualitative Sociology Review* 3(1).

Latour, B. 2009. Perspectivism: 'type' or 'bomb'? *Anthropology Today* 25(2): 1–2.

Myers, O.E. Jr. 2003. No longer the lonely species: a post-Mead perspective on animals and sociology. *International Journal of Sociology and Social Policy* 23(3): 46–68.

Sanders, C. 2003. Actions speak louder than words: close relationships between humans and nonhuman animals. *Symbolic Interaction* 26(3): 405–426.

11
Humans and Other Primates

The scientific practices and discourses of modern primatology participate in the pre-eminent act in western history: the construction of Man. (Haraway, 1984: 489)

Primatology is an extraordinary complex field in which there are many ways of being a baboon, of being a chimpanzee, of being a gorilla. (Latour in Barron, 2003: 86)

The study of nonhuman primates (henceforth primates) is primarily the preserve of primatologists, although in some academic institutions primatology falls under the remit of anthropology departments as a sub-discipline of physical or biological anthropology (Pavelka, 2003). Primatology itself can be broken down into sub-disciplines, such as ethnoprimatology and cultural primatology. Despite the similar nomenclature, ethnoprimatology and cultural primatology are two distinctly different areas of academic interest and enquiry. Ethnoprimatology looks at the human–nonhuman interface and involves researchers observing and documenting human interactions with primates on the ground. Cultural primatology on the other hand involves the investigation of 'culture' in primates (see chapter 3). It has been suggested that cultural primatology is akin to cultural anthropology (McGrew, 2007), to the extent that Whiten et al. (2003) coined the term 'cultural panthropology', while ethnoprimatology is more comparable to social anthropology. Ethnoprimatology, cultural primatology, cultural anthropology, social anthropology and anthrozoology all share methodological and theoretical common ground, and this facilitates some interesting dialogue, debate and comparison across disciplinary boundaries (see also chapter 16).

CULTURAL PRIMATOLOGY

Cultural primatology was developed in the 1950s by Japanese primatologist Kinji Imanishi who encouraged researchers to look for regional variation in primate behaviours which might shed light on the evolution of human culture (Imanishi, 1952). During the course of its comparatively short academic life to date, cultural primatology has gone through three distinct phases; natural history, ethnography and ethnology (McGrew, 2007: 168). The first phase saw researchers produce descriptive accounts of a wide range of primate behaviours in the field (see Itani and Nishimura, 1973). Studies tended to focus on monkeys (primarily *Macaca fuscata* – Japanese Macaque – endemic to Japan and therefore a ready subject). During this first phase researchers tended towards deterministic explanations for primate behaviour, assuming that either 'instinct' (biological) or environmental factors were responsible (see McGrew, 2007).

The second phase started in the 1960s with key figures such as Jane Goodall setting up research sites in Africa (for example, Boesch, 1996; McGrew, 1992; Whiten et al., 1999). Chimpanzee researchers in Africa adopted the ethnographic techniques of anthropological fieldworkers and made a series of important, even ground-breaking 'discoveries' about chimpanzee behaviour and behavioural variation, such as the performance of 'rain dances' (van Lawick-Goodall, 1975) and the use of stone tools. That is not to say that prior to the 1960s chimps did not engage in these behaviours; on the contrary, archaeological evidence suggests that they have been using tools for over 4,300 years (Mercader et al., 2002). Rather, prior to Imanishi's call and the systematic documentation which came out of Africa in the 1960s most scientists had been either unwilling or unable to consider the existence of 'culture' outside of the human species. Although researchers such as psychologist Wolfgang Köhler (1925, 1929) had suggested that the higher primates *might* be able to develop cultural practices analogous to those of humans on the basis of experiments into the problem-solving abilities of captive chimpanzees, the question of whether such abilities would come to fruition without human intervention and in a 'natural' setting aroused considerable scepticism within the scientific community (see also chapter 3).

Like their forebears, these 'second phase' researchers adopted a rather deterministic approach to explaining behaviours. 'Culture' itself also came to be seen as a determinant as specific processes were thought to be learnt within particular social contexts. However, as a result of their sustained ethnographic immersion in the field researchers in this second phase differed from their predecessors in a key respect. They began to consider not only the impact of subtle ecological variations on 'culture', such as the need for different tools to collect different species of ants (Humle and Matsuzawa, 2002), but the potential for the *experiences* of *individuals* to result in asocial learning, albeit framed within or constrained by particular ecological and social conditions (Perry, 2006: 178–9). Indeed, Itani and Nishimura (1973) emphasized the need to consider the life histories of individual animals as this would impact on their subsequent behaviours (for example, animals who had been provisioned in the past and moved to another troop would be more open to experimenting with new food sources than their new conspecifics).

Contemporary cultural primatologists tend to refer to the 'personalities' of individual primates (for example, whether they are gregarious or inhibited), comparing this information with the social dynamics of the group within which individuals reside. Such recognition of individual agency is in line with the postmodern emphasis on phenomenology in anthropology. Phenomenology focuses on the experiential nature of learning (for example, Ingold, 2000; Jackson, 1998; see also chapter 10), and the individual nature of *emotional* responses to external stimuli (Milton, 2002, 2005). This allows for individuals who experience the same 'environment' to perceive it, and therefore respond to it, in different ways.

INDIGENOUS PRIMATOLOGISTS

In this important respect the parallel theoretical evolution between cultural primatology and socio-cultural anthropology is striking. What is particularly noteworthy, however, is the fact that some scientists took so long to recognize the cultural behaviours of other primates, while the peoples who coexisted with these animals were cognizant of nut cracking, drumming, rain dances and a whole host of other behaviours which have now come to be recognized as 'cultural'. As Nyanganji et al. (2011) note, the Hausa name for chimpanzee is '*biri mai ganga*' or 'the monkey with the drum' because of a local awareness of the ritualized buttress-drumming performances that chimpanzees engage in, while anthropologist Paul Richards found that chimpanzee nut cracking and other 'cultural' behaviours were common knowledge among his Mende informants:

During fieldwork in the Gola Forest 1988–1990 I collected several hunters' accounts of chimpanzee behaviour. On various occasions I was told how the animal hunts, uses leaves to treat skin complaints, and teaches its young to crack nuts with stones and anvil. Informants often commented on the animal's high social intelligence. 'Drumming' in the forest was one such manifestation. A hunter opined that the chimpanzees made drumming noises 'for display' (i.e. to claim rank). Another informant told me he had witnessed a female chimpanzee cracking and piling nuts and then provisioning her young charges 'just like a [human] mother dishing food'. At the time I was inclined to treat this material as fanciful, but later discovered it was consistent with accounts in the primatological literature. (2000: 80)

Anthropologist Loretta Cormier suggests that, on the basis of their intimate knowledge of the range of primate species with whom they coexist, her informants, the Guajá gatherer-hunters of the Amazon, should be regarded as 'indigenous primatologists because their view is similar to the traditional goal of scientific primatologists in anthropology: to look to nonhuman primates in order to understand ourselves' (2003: xxiv).

During the second phase of cultural primatology the nonhuman 'ethnographic record' was populated with material attesting to the presence of 'social traditions' which could be construed as 'cultural'. Perhaps most notable is the work of Jane Goodall (1986) at Gombe, Tanzania, but numerous other studies soon made it possible for comparative analysis across and between sites and troops to be undertaken. This led in the early 1970s into the third phase, ethnology (the comparative analysis of ethnographic data), when the growing body of data allowed for a theory-driven 'compare and contrast' approach to be adopted.

Contemporary cultural primatologists study primates in both laboratory and field settings. However, while captive animals in zoos and other research facilities can help shed light on many important questions about the capabilities of primates, there remains a strong bias towards studying primate communities in their 'natural' setting. Such research is becoming increasingly difficult because of anthropogenic activity. Wild populations of primates are in rapid decline through human population expansion, habitat loss, poaching and zoonotic disease. It is here, then, that the sub-field of ethnoprimatology takes the reins.

ETHNOPRIMATOLOGY

Ethnoprimatologists are concerned with precisely the sorts of issues that arise as a result of human contact with other primates. The term was first coined by anthropologist Leslie Sponsel (1997) to refer to the multi-faceted interactions which occur between human and nonhuman primates in places where there is sympatry (habitat sharing) between species. Ten years after this initial definition, the research of primatologists (for example, Wolfe and Fuentes, 2007) has demonstrated that ethnoprimatology is a holistic field of enquiry that can also cover regions of allopatry (where there are no endemic nonhuman primates), although here interactions tend to be more limited as humans come into contact with primates in controlled situations (for example, as pets).

In zones of sympatry interactions can include human consumption of primates (including the use of body parts for ethnomedicinal practices; Alves et al., 2010), keeping primates as pets (Cormier, 2003), zoonotic disease transmission (for example, Wallis and Lee, 1999), adaptive and maladaptive behaviours in response to habitat loss and alteration (such as crop raiding; Hill, 2000, Strum, 1994; see also Hurn, 2011b), folk knowledge about primate behaviour (Cormier, 2003) and the inclusion of primates in human culture (in terms of symbolic associations, mythology and so on, for example, Cormier, 2006; Riley and Priston, 2010).

The contemporary focus of ethnoprimatological attention makes its relevance to social anthropology immediately apparent. However, anthropological primatologist Erin Riley (2006) has posited that ethnoprimatology also represents a way to 'bridge' the 'gulf' between socio-cultural and biological anthropology. Riley's suggestion warrants closer scrutiny because it may also help to reconcile the seemingly disparate aspects of anthropologically grounded anthrozoology.

BETWEEN BIOLOGICAL AND SOCIAL ANTHROPOLOGY

According to Riley:

> Many see the source of the dislike and tension between cultural and biological anthropology as a function of the two competing traditions that have existed in anthropology since its inception: the objective approach, which stems from the biological sciences, and seeks to discover causes or laws to explain phenomena, and the humanistic approach, which seeks to explore more subjective knowledge through interpretation and the search for meaning. (2006: 75)

'Dislike' is probably a bit strong, but there is often (although not always) an academic rift between anthropologists who hail from these competing sub-disciplines. As Riley notes, the theoretical and methodological orientation of biological anthropology is a product of the Cartesian scientific tradition and, while this is also true of social anthropology, the reflexive turn in the social sciences has led to a much greater emphasis on the need for reflexive awareness when engaging in research of any kind (see also chapters 1 and 3). The inherently experiential and therefore subjective nature of qualitative ethnographic fieldwork is at odds with the detached, objective, quantitative focus which predominates in the natural sciences (see also chapter 12). This is not to say that all biological anthropologists are unreflexive, but rather that the academic culture within which they work, and which undoubtedly informs their theoretical and methodological approach, is such that there is little room for deviation from the norm.

The fear of being accused of anthropomorphic projection has not helped scientists consider alternative positions. As Riley notes, this is where social anthropologists can help to develop biological approaches to primates, while the work of cultural primatologists and ethnoprimatologists can facilitate an awareness of the cultural capabilities and sociality of our closest nonhuman relatives, thereby enabling us to reconsider our ideas about humans. This has certainly been the case in relation to the use of primates as models for reconstructing early human societies. The 'baboon model' is a case in point, as Riley explains:

> within primatology, reflection on our biases resulted in the questioning of the baboon model that overemphasized the importance of male dominance in social organization and ignored female roles other than mother–infant relationships ... Such reflection has also contributed to the development of alternative perceptions of primate aggression, including expansion from a more 'traditional' focus on aggression (e.g. *Demonic Males* – Wrangham and Peterson, 1996) to considerations of cooperation and reconciliation (e.g. *Peacemaking Among Primates* – de Waal, 1989) among primates. By being cognizant of our biases we become acutely aware that culture is at work in the practice of science (Nader, 2001). (2006: 79; see also Strum and Mitchell, 1987)

As social anthropologist Annette Weiner commented in a feminist critique of her predecessor Malinowski's ethnographic 'knowledge' of the Trobrianders: 'My taking seriously the importance of women's wealth not only brought women as the neglected half of society clearly into the ethnographic picture but also forced me to revise many of Malinowski's assumptions about Trobriand men' (1988: 5).

The ethnographic data produced by primatologists presents important comparative material relating to the 'neglected half' of our species, the nonhuman primates. Social anthropologists can be encouraged to engage with this material via 'liminal' sub-disciplines such as ethnoprimatology. In the process of learning about this formerly muted group, social anthropologists may be forced to revise many of their assumptions about human primates (see Corbey, 2005 and Haraway, 1989 for some excellent examples).

COEXISTING WITH PRIMATES

While cultural primatologists emphasize the need to study primate populations in their 'natural' habitat, free from any 'corrupting' human influence (Riley, 2006: 77) the reality of the situation is that humans and other primates have coexisted, competed with and even learnt from each other for thousands of years. According to Wheatley (1999), for example, many primates live in the same 'natural' habitat as humans. In India, 86–88 percent of the Rhesus macaque (*Mucaca mulatta*) population lives in commensal or semi-commensal settings with humans. Moreover, this perceived need to separate humans from all that is 'natural' completely disregards our shared evolutionary history and is based on the outdated misapprehension that humans, by dint of their 'culture', are no longer a part of nature (see also chapters 2, 3, 13 and 16).

There may well be merit to studying primate behaviour in situations where contact with humans is minimal; to help ensure the success of conservation initiatives for example (i.e. unique cultural behaviours make certain species 'worth saving'). Moreover, anthropogenic activity is so invasive in many parts of the world that without this move to retain 'pristine' habitats, the long-term future of many of the world's primate species looks bleak (Cormier, 2003: 155; McGrew, 2007). However, contact with humans and changing eco-systems can also lead to the emergence of new and innovative cultural behaviours.

In my own research working with Chacma baboons (*Papio ursinis*) on South Africa's Cape Peninsula, the steady encroachment of humans into baboon territory has created numerous opportunities for the baboons, who are now adept at stealing from unwary humans (although admittedly the term 'stealing' erroneously suggests that the baboons themselves have some awareness of human notions of property and ownership). These adaptations to the rapidly changing situations in which the baboons find themselves bring cultural primatology and ethnoprimatology together. As a result of anthropogenic activity baboons' 'cultural evolution' is accelerating at a rate which makes it difficult for researchers to monitor and ultimately to protect the baboons (Hurn, 2011b). Indeed, primatologists often refer to some cultural practices as 'maladaptive', in that they are potentially harmful to the individuals or groups who engage in them.

For the Cape's baboons, and for primates in many other parts of the world, activities such as crop-raiding may appear to be beneficial and certainly yield some short-term gains such as a quick meal. In the long term, however, these practices place animals in often mortal danger from retributive attacks. While in reality primates do less damage to crops and property than other 'pests', it is the perception of these animals and the type of damage they inflict (as opposed to the reality) which has become a prime area of ethnoprimatological concern (Lee and Priston, 2005).

NEGATIVE PERCEPTIONS OF PRIMATES

Human perceptions of primates often play significant roles in the willingness or reluctance of individuals and communities to engage in primate conservation initiatives. Here ethnoprimatology comes to the fore once again. An understanding of human interactions with primates in areas of sympatry can be invaluable when it comes to helping ensure viable futures for all concerned. An ethnoprimato-logical example (although the author does not refer to it as such) comes from anthropologist Paul Richards' (1993, 1995, 2000) ethnographic fieldwork with the Mende of Sierra Leone.

In Sierra Leone, chimpanzee attacks on humans, especially children, are well attested (Richards, 2000: 81). In addition, chimpanzees are linked with political corruption for many Mende, which makes their protection a threat to human society on another level; people who wish to acquire superior political power are thought to disguise themselves as chimpanzees (among other animals) through metamorphosis and attack humans to obtain body parts for the 'bad medicine' necessary for political and economic gain. These beliefs stem from the colonial period when locals, usually children, were captured in the forests and sold into slavery. It was suspected that politically motivated individuals in the villages were in cahoots with the traders and used the money obtained from this activity to further their own political careers. Added into the equation is the fact that domestic slavery persisted in Sierra Leone until 1927, while the communal labour of youth was a 'right' of chiefs until 1955. As a result, what many regard as the betrayal of the young by the powerful is a living memory for the older generations and these memories, coupled with coexistence with politically motivated chimpanzees (de Waal, 1982) sustains folklore and mythology that stigmatizes chimpanzees.

While hostility towards chimpanzees in this particular cultural context can be linked to contemporary problems associated with humans and wild animals living in close proximity and competing for scarce resources, it is also important for conservationists to consider the historical relationships between humans and animals in wider political and economic context. Such a violent history and the mythical power of 'were-chimpanzees' goes a long way towards explaining why their protection is feared and opposed by many Mende. Richards notes that financial compensation offered to Mende leaders to encourage participation in chimpanzee conservation initiatives served, unsurprisingly, to exacerbate the problem.

PRIMATE CONSERVATION

Primatologist Phyllis Lee (2010a) provides a comprehensive review of ethnoprimatological studies concerned with conservation. Some primatologists such as the late Dian Fossey (1983) adopted what Lee refers to as a 'reactive' but which might be better termed an essentially post-humanist approach, whereby the conservation needs of primates were seen as more important than those of their human neighbours (an attitude which earned Fossey many enemies and arguably led to her death in 1985). As Lee observes, contemporary neoliberal research-led interventions are now much more focused on community involvement and integration, as opposed to alienation. Nonetheless, primate conservation projects still have marginal success rates, as exemplified by the rapidly diminishing numbers of primates even in areas where community education and enfranchise- ment of local people has been prioritized (for example, Hockings and Humle, 2009).

For some areas where attitudes have traditionally been benevolent, the forces of globalization and 'development' are altering human perceptions of, and interactions with, other primates. Indeed, in Sulawesi, Indonesia, Riley notes that 'villagers possess folklore that envisions monkeys and humans as interrelated biologically, ecologically, and culturally, and ... this folklore is manifested in taboos against harming macaques, even in areas of human–macaque overlap where Tonkean macaques raid crops' (2006: 81). The power of such folkloric beliefs is sufficiently strong that they are able to transcend the power of market forces (Riley, 2010). In other parts of the world, especially across South Asia where Hinduism is widespread, primates such as Rhesus macaques (*Macaca mulatta*) are revered and provisioned because of their association with the monkey-god Hanuman (see for example Cormier, 2003: 33; Lee and Priston, 2005: 2). Yet contradictions exist in practice; while monkeys are worshipped and fed at temples, they may well be shot should they stray into the fields of farmers in areas where economic pressures make cash or subsistence crops intrinsically more 'valuable' than the lives of sacred but transgressive animals (Eudey, 1994).

Such double standards are not limited to areas of sympatry. Haraway (1989: 1) observes a 'two-way traffic', where primates are snatched from the wild to be used by scientists in the developed world, where, conversely, they are then also the focus of conservation initiatives and animal rights campaigns. Many primates are also threatened because their habitats are being destroyed to meet post-domestic consumer demands for wood and palm oil. Sorenson (2009), for example, discusses at length the devastating impact of the palm oil trade on orangutans in Indonesia (see also Marchal and Hill, 2009). Yet these processes are part of global markets and so, while ethnoprimatological research on the ground can go some way to educating local human communities about the value of biodiversity conservation, these localized instances need to be considered in respect of larger political and economic pressures which may often extend beyond the control of communities or even national governments.

PRIMATE ECO-TOURISM

One area where coexisting with primates can directly benefit local communities is eco-tourism, and there are numerous anthropological accounts of various eco-touristic ventures focused on primate conservation. Anthropologist John Knight, for example, has written extensively on Japanese monkey parks as sites of conservation. Humans can enter the habitat of the monkeys, who are brought into view through provisioning (in contrast to zoos, where denatured animals are brought into human space and kept there in cages). Yet, as Knight observes (2005, 2006, 2011), such purportedly 'natural' attractions in reality radically alter the behaviours of the primates concerned and as a result their 'value' as conservation and educational initiatives is debatable.

Utilizing ethnographic data collected at the Orang-utan Research and Conservation Project in Indonesian Borneo, Constance Russell (1995; Russell and Ankenman, 1996) has explored the inherent hypocrisy of eco-tourists, some of whom engage in anthropomorphic fantasies about orangutans, perceiving them as either 'children' to be saved or as embodiments of pristine nature (also in need of salvation). Many of the eco-tourists studied by Russell were seemingly unable to make the connection between their own desire to 'hold' or photograph these animals, and the circumstances which had led to their predicament and that of many of the world's endangered species (see also chapter 13).

CLOSING THE GAP

Primatology, and anthropology more generally, has come in for some criticism in the past as an area of scholarship which uses other primates as ideological tools either to separate humans from the animal kingdom (by showing how different 'we' are from our closest biological relatives) or to single out and elevate the order of primates (for example, Corbey, 2005; Haraway, 1984; see also chapter 16). In the contemporary world the research aims and findings of cultural primatologists and ethnoprimatologists are helping to reduce the gulf between humans and other primates, showing just how interconnected we are. Indeed, as Riley has noted, recognition of a 'human–nonhuman primate community' challenges boundaries between species and nature/culture, seeing all as members of a 'dynamic ecosystem' (2006: 77).

The work of primatologists is indirectly providing the impetus for researchers investigating other seemingly disparate species. Many ethologists and zoologists use primate models for examining complex issues such as sentience and emotions outside of this order (for example, on dogs, Silva and de Sousa, 2011; on corvids, Bugnyar et al., 2004; Emery and Clayton, 2004). Anthropologists have a very real and important role to play here too – as some of the examples cited above have suggested; while ethnographic detail is imperative for understanding human–primate interactions on the ground, these interactions cannot be divorced from the macro-economic and political processes of globalization.

SUGGESTIONS FOR FURTHER READING

Campbell, C.J., Fuentes, A., MacKinnon, K.C., Panger, M. and Bearder, S.K. 2007. *Primates in perspective*. Oxford: Oxford University Press.

Cheney, D. and Seyfarth, R.M. 2007. *Baboon metaphysics*. Chicago: University of Chicago Press.

Fuentes, A. 2006. Human–nonhuman primate interconnections and their relevance to anthropology. *Ecological and Environmental Anthropology* 2(2): 1–11.

Fuentes, A. 2010. Naturalcultural encounters in Bali: monkeys, temples, tourists and ethnoprimatology. *Cultural Anthropology* 25(4): 600–624.

Knight, J. 1999. Monkeys on the move: the natural symbolism of people–macaque conflict in Japan. *Journal of Asian Studies* 58(3): 622–647.

Loudon, J.E., Howells, M.E. and Fuentes, A. 2006. The importance of integrative anthropology: a preliminary investigation employing primatological and cultural anthropological data collection methods in assessing human–monkey co-existence in Bali, Indonesia. *Ecological and Environmental Anthropology* 2(1): 2–13.

Loudon, J.E., Sauther, M.L. Fish, K.D., Hunter-Ishikawa, M and Ibrahim, Y.J. 2006. One reserve, three primates: applying a holistic approach to understand the interconnections among ring-tailed lemurs (*Lemur catta*), Verreaux's sifaka (*Propithecus verreauxi*), and humans (*Homo sapiens*) at Beza Mahafaly Special Reserve, Madagascar. *Ecological and Environmental Anthropology* 2(2): 54–74.

Patterson, J.D. and Wallis, J. (eds) 2005. *Commensalism and conflict: the human–primate interface*. American Society of Primatologists.

Strum, S. 2000. *Primate encounters: models of science, gender and society*. Chicago: University of Chicago Press.

12
Science and Medicine

Medical anthropology has seemed hitherto to lack in full engagement with phytomedical reality, and the acceptance that the healthcare practices of most people on this planet depend on plants and animals. (Ellen, 2006: S10)

'Science' is often presented in public discourse as a marker of 'progress'. In contemporary academia we are currently experiencing the withdrawal of funding from the arts, humanities and 'social sciences' in favour of STEM subjects ('hard' or 'natural' science, technology, engineering and maths). Driving these funding decisions is the assumption that science provides the key to solving the world's problems. Yet, as anthropologists are only too aware, 'scientific knowledge' is not absolute. There are myriad ways of 'knowing' the world and 'science' is just one of them. The prioritizing of one system of knowledge over others is, to some extent, ethnocentric and can mean that important 'folk' knowledge is overlooked because it is viewed as 'inferior'. Such a view is at odds with the anthropological project in the postcolonial era.

OBJECTIVE DETACHMENT

In some human–animal interactions the pursuit of objectivity (and objectification) is an overt expression of politically motivated power. According to Kalof and Fitzgerald for example, 'the use of animals in science is an objectifying process that has deep ethical implications' (2007: 305). While ethics is an obvious area of interest for anthropologists as value systems vary between and within cultural groups, what is particularly noteworthy is the identification of an 'objectifying process'. There are many circumstances in which humans may objectify animals, such as when working in an animal shelter (for example, Arluke, 1994; Frommer and Arluke, 1999; Palmer, 2006; Taylor, 2010), or when farming livestock (Serpell, 1999b). Commentators often discuss the 'coping mechanisms' or 'distancing devices' individual humans employ when faced with contradictory relationships with other animals. For example, a farmer may spend considerable amounts of time with his or her animals, but the ultimate fate of these animals is to be sold on or killed and eaten and so to get too close would bring emotional dissonance.

The field of laboratory experimentation is a particularly extreme example because while farmers and shelter workers have to deal with the reality that animals in their care will die, often at their hands, their day-to-day interactions typically revolve around 'caring' for, or at very least maintaining, the lives of the majority. In the course of a day's work some scientists conduct invasive, unpleasant and often fatal procedures on animals. This 'fact' becomes significant when considered in relation to the ways in which these researchers think about the processes they perform and their perceptions of the animals who are the subjects of their research.

The attitudes of professionals whose work requires them to conduct experiments on live animals in a laboratory setting have been subjected to some ethnographic scrutiny (for example, Birke, 1994; Lansbury, 2007; Serpell, 1999b). Feminist biologist Lynda Birke found that clear gendered hierarchies existed in the research laboratories where she conducted fieldwork, with female technicians who 'cared' for the animals and male scientists who conducted the experiments. According to Birke all workers were expected to remain 'detached' from their research subjects, and the ability to do so was linked to gender:

> Objective detachment is ... stereotypically masculine in our ['post-domestic'] culture ... while 'not letting your emotions get in the way' is reminiscent of suppressing something feminine. Women in science have to take on board that fundamental contradiction; going through processes of desensitization toward animals is an essential part of attaining the required level of detachment. To identify with your animals (a more 'feminine' position) is to cease to be objective. (1994: 46)

ANTHROPOMORPHISM

This identification with animals has been termed 'anthropomorphism' and for many years was seen as a cardinal sin among scientists (see Daston and Mitman, 2005; Griffin, 2001). Yet anthropomorphism, as Milton (2005) has convincingly argued, does not really involve identifying with animals at all (see also chapters 3 and 16).

There are four issues at stake here. First, the incompatibility between the definition of anthropomorphism and its application; second, the assumption that humans are uniquely capable; third, the suggestion that anthropomorphism (when taken to mean an identification with a nonhuman other) is something which must be overcome; and, fourth, the misapprehension that the pursuit of objective detachment is an achievable goal which makes for better science.

Milton suggests that 'egomorphism' represents a more suitable alternative to anthropomorphism. Egomorphism is the recognition of mutuality between individuals, irrespective of species, and is thus reminiscent of de Castro's 'perspectivism', where animals reveal their personhood through their actions and interactions with humans (see also chapters 4, 9 and 10). Anthropomorphism is an act of anthropocentric projection, while egomorphism is an act of intersubjective empathy. Referring to an identification with animals as anthropomorphism is therefore incorrect. Yet both anthropomorphism and egomorphism present challenges to the pursuit of objective detachment. When the 'personhood' of an animal other is recognized in a laboratory setting for example, researchers are faced with a difficult scenario: how to deal with the reality of inflicting suffering on another sentient being? As a result it is understandable that researchers are deterred from getting close in the first place by a taboo or institutionalized fear of any form of identification.

Anthropomorphism also risks skewing the results of research because projecting human thoughts and feelings onto nonhuman others is anthropocentric and as such will present an inaccurate picture of the animals involved. For example, a cat who has been placed in a cage in a laboratory may be unhappy, but his or her unhappiness will be manifestly different to that which might be felt by, say, a chimpanzee or a human. While many cats do enjoy the company of others, being kept in isolation might be less of an 'issue' for a felid than it would for a highly social primate. Anthropomorphism would be the assumption that the cat was miserable because he or she was lonely on the basis that humans would feel that way in the same situation. An egomorphic response on the other hand would be the recognition that the cat was unhappy, but that unhappiness would be conceived of in feline as opposed to human terms. Anthropomorphism can thus potentially impact on the research process by making inaccurate assumptions about animal subjects. This does not mean, however, that perceiving certain mental, physical or emotional states in other animals is anthropomorphic projection. Rather anthropomorphism can lead to such states being misinterpreted because they are considered from an exclusively human perspective (see Candea, 2010; Rivas and Burghardt, 2002).

'CURING' ANTHROPOMORPHISM

The fact that scientists need to overcome anthropomorphism suggests that identifying with other animals is something which occurs to us as 'natural' or is 'inbuilt'. This argument has been advanced by numerous scholars who have written on anthropomorphism (for example, Kennedy, 1992). The animistic beliefs of many people around the world have been classified as anthropomorphic by anthropologists and there is a school of thought in cognitive psychology (the Piagetian framework) which has suggested that anthropomorphism is an innate human characteristic which is subdued within certain cultural contexts. Kennedy, however, condemns anthropomorphism as a 'disease' which has afflicted 'science' and which therefore needs to be 'treated'.

Other scholars, such as anthropologist Pascal Boyer (1996) argue that anthropomorphism is counter-intuitive. Boyer's argument is difficult to apply to animals because he is referring primarily to religious anthropomorphism, whereby inanimate 'objects' such as statues or mountains are imbued with intentionality. Recognizing the intentionality of animals, however, who are undeniably 'animated' (in the sense that they move unaided) is only counter-intuitive if the anthropomorphic projector does not really believe that animals are also intentional. What is self-evident to some humans however is that animals are indeed intentional (Bekoff and Allen, 1992; Griffin, 2001) and failure to see them as 'persons' is an anthropocentric act of denial (see also chapters 2, 3, 10 and 16).

In a ground-breaking discussion, a group of animal technicians and scientists (Reinhardt et al., 2006) shared accounts of interacting with animals utilized in scientific research. All of the contributors expressed varying levels of discomfort about conventional approaches to laboratory animals. Moreover, the discord between their experiences and what is expected of them and the animals involved suggests a wider schism within a profession whose practitioners have traditionally subscribed to the tenets of anthropocentricity and objectivity, and a 'new wave' of egomorphic individuals for whom both objective detachment and anthropomorphism are problematic. These sentiments were expressed by one participant as follows:

Asking us to share our personal observations is like opening up a can of worms for me! Researchers never decided to get into research because they wanted to work with animals. They are very conceptual in their methods and in their thinking. This alienates them from the creatures they study. What amazes me is that they rarely think about their subjects as sentient beings but focus so much on measurable data. It would benefit the scientific quality of their research greatly if they would take just a bit of extra time to train themselves and their staff in how to properly interact [with], handle and treat their animals. If I were to force you to do something for me that you were absolutely terrified of doing, how long would you take to do it and how well would you do it? If I were to help you learn and not be afraid of what I wanted you to do, how much faster and how much better would you be at it? ... I have watched people grab, forcibly restrain and manipulate a monkey as if they were dealing with an object, and then wonder why the animal showed so much resistance and signs of distress such as defecating, urinating and squealing. I've also watched monkeys pretty much jump at the prospect of cooperating with a person. Needless to say that the objective of the interaction, e.g., collection of a blood sample, was achieved much faster and without aggressive defense reactions. (Down, in Reinhardt et al., 2006: n.p.)

COPING MECHANISMS

Social science commentators such as James Serpell (1999b) have documented the coping mechanisms employed by scientists for whom identification with animals is problematic. Serpell considered the use of the sacrificial metaphor (also observed by Birke, 1994) whereby procedures can be carried out on animals and justified because the results could save the lives of many others. This was certainly the rationale expressed by primatologist and neuroscientist Robert Sapolsky, when reflecting on his time conducting invasive experiments on laboratory rats (2002). Sapolsky's laboratory-based research focused on stress and its impact on brain activity (1992) and he was motivated by a desire to better understand (in the hope of finding a cure) the Alzheimer's disease which was taking hold of his father (2002: 220). This 'higher purpose' made it easier to subject his sacrificial subjects to unpleasant procedures.

For egomorphic individuals such as those who participated in Reinhardt's discussion, an identification with animals can be put to good effect within such a rubric. By perceiving and responding to the specific needs of laboratory animals by way of environmental enrichment, for example, the use of positive reinforcement (see for example Laule et al., 2003; Schapiro, 2003) or, as noted by Down in Reinhardt et al. (2006), by simply taking the time to habituate nervous individuals to human contact, the humans involved in the various stages of experimentation can help to make the process less unpleasant for all concerned (see, for example, Wait and Buchanan-Smith, 2002). Temple Grandin has famously adopted a similar approach and rationale to her work in improving the welfare of livestock at abattoirs across the United States (Grandin and Johnson, 2006).

As with anthropological research and the reflexive turn in the social sciences more generally, a heightened awareness of the interactions between researcher and subjects is key to the acquisition of 'meaningful' data and subsequently the meaningful interpretation of that data. In a laboratory setting, reflexivity means being aware of potentially limiting factors such as gender bias, sexual dimorphism in the animal subjects, stress triggers and responses which will not just be species-specific but also vary from one individual to another. Consequently then (and rather paradoxically) the ability and willingness of scientists to identify with animals in an experimental context, and the move to treat animals as individuals as opposed to objectified 'things', can actually benefit the research process.

BRINGING IN ANIMALS

In his discussion of the relationships between scientists (in this case, field biologists) and meerkats (*Suricata suricatta*) at the Kalahari Meerkat Research Project in South Africa, Matei Candea (2010) raises the possibility that detachment should be regarded as a key aspect of some relationships as opposed to a negation of relations altogether. Candea argues that meerkats themselves are habituated to the presence of the researchers, but treat humans as convenient 'objects' which can be climbed so as to obtain a better vantage point. Researchers are thus tolerated unless they get too close uninvited, whereupon the meerkats themselves object by exhibiting defensive behaviours such as hissing. This leads Candea to suggest that a polite distance has to be cultivated on both sides for the relationship to be acceptable; the meerkats want to be left to their own devices and the researchers want to be 'objective' by minimizing their impact on the meerkats and avoiding any emotional attachment or engagement.

Candea states that objectivity and detachment were pursued by researchers who maintained what could be seen as a 'working relationship' with the meerkats; 'Their studiously polite, inter-patient "being with" the meerkats was carefully set apart from the "being together" of interactions with pets' (2010: 254). Therefore, rather than seeing engagement and detachment as opposing forces, Candea argues that they should be considered as symbiotic; in order to engage with the meerkats and attempt to understand their way of being, researchers had to retain some degree of detachment. In many respects this is what anthropologists themselves do when engaging with human subjects in a reflexive manner; because their reason for being in the field is to conduct an ethnographic study, then, regardless of how involved they become with their informants they still ultimately need to take a step back and engage in the analytical endeavour that is 'writing up', and that requires detachment.

ZOOPHARMACOGNOSY

Most pet owners will be conscious of the fact that their dogs or cats occasionally seek out and eat grass to help dislodge fur-balls, but there is a wealth of systematically documented evidence for much more complicated forms of such behaviours. Zoopharmacognosy or self-medication in animals has received some anthropological attention in recent years, but this attention has been primarily from the biological side of the discipline. The practices were initially documented as animals ingesting plants and other materials of no nutritional value, or in some cases, high levels of toxicity. On closer inspection however, the medicinal or therapeutic properties of these substances were revealed. The most sustained research conducted to date has been in relation to primates; chimpanzees in particular have been found to be prolific self-medicators (see for example Fowler et al., 2007), even combining botanical and geological ingredients to create more potent treatments (Klein et al., 2008).

Huffman (1997) has noted that not only do some animals learn which plants to eat and how to find them by watching parents or elders, they also learn processing techniques to ensure maximum efficacy. One particular example is pith chewing of *Vernonia amygdalina*, which is consumed by chimps and other primates to alleviate gastrointestinal pain, diarrhoea, worm infestation, bacterial infection and weight loss. Another common practice enacted by chimpanzees (*Pan troglodytes*), bonobos (*Pan paniscus*) and gorillas (*Gorilla gorilla*) involves folding and swallowing whole leaves from

Aspilia mossambicensis. These leaves are passed intact, bringing with them large quantities of intestinal worms, and the ingestion of these leaves is linked to times of year when gut parasite populations are at their highest. Huffman (among others) also documents rubbing sores and skin complaints with plants which contain natural antiseptics and the ingestion of plants known to affect hormone levels. The latter is particularly significant as it suggests that the animals in question are attempting to regulate their reproductive cycles (Huffman, 1997). Clearly, there is considerable potential for further investigation into these practices which may also shed light on the cognitive abilities of species who self-medicate, such as their understanding of cause and effect.

CROSS-SPECIES LEARNING

Human societies living in close proximity to self-medicating animals frequently use the same plants and mineral substances themselves. This raises the question: who 'discovered' these phytomedicinal and geophagic benefits in the first place? Did humans observe animals self-medicating? Did animals observe humans? Or did both come to the same conclusions independently? Huffman suggests that the nomenclature of some phytomedicinal treatments implies that humans followed the lead of their nonhuman neighbours. In some cases the learning process is made explicit. For example:

> *L. porteri*, appropriately called 'bear medicine' in parts of Western North America, is used as a topical anaesthetic and antibacterial by native Americans in the southwest ... Navaho folklore states that revered use of the plant was taught to them by the bear. (Huffman, 1997: 190)

There is also contemporary, empirical evidence from ethnographic fieldwork which attests to the direction in which information passes. In relation to the Amazonian Guajá, Cormier (2002: 68) notes that local ethnobotanical knowledge is gleaned from watching monkeys. Gradé et al. (2009) have also ventured, on the basis of an extensive study of selective grazing among domestic ungulates and the folk knowledge of 147 pastoralists and healers in Uganda, that human knowledge of medicinal plants is informed by observations of animal behaviours.

Humans who live alongside chimp populations utilize *Vernonia amygdalina* for themselves and their livestock. Some domesticates however appear to have no knowledge of the plant's toxicity and show no selectivity or aversion to this plant, with often fatal consequences. This has led the Temme of Sierra Leone to refer to the plant as '*a-difwir*' (goat killer). As far as Huffman is concerned such nomenclature demonstrates that this is a long-standing problem for pastoralists, and yet, surprisingly, the goats themselves have not learnt to avoid this poisonous plant. Given the emphasis on learned transmission of phytomedicinal or indeed any 'cultural' knowledge in animals (including humans) such a maladaption needs to be accounted for. Huffman (1997: 193) suggests that the cause might be herding practices which separate mothers and kids during grazing and, as a result, opportunities for intergenerational transmission of this 'cultural' knowledge is lost.

ETHNOVETERINARY MEDICINE

Ethnoveterinary medicine is defined by McCorkle (1986) as the knowledge and skills people have about their animals, the methods they use to treat veterinary conditions and the 'folk' beliefs which relate to the care of animals more generally. While these indigenous approaches to animal health and welfare will often be highly complex, specialized and based on the cumulative experience of generations, they are frequently dismissed by outsiders. For example, sub-Saharan pastoralists such as the Nuer traditionally kept their cattle herds in smoke filled enclosures in a bid to prevent them being bitten by insects. This practice was noted (and dismissed as being 'bad' for the cattle) by Evans-Pritchard (1940). Yet recent research (Torr et al., 2011) has demonstrated that keeping cattle in this manner reduces their chances of being bitten by tsetse flies (*Glossina sp.*) by up to 90 percent.

In the contemporary world, where parasite and pathogen resistance to pharmaceutical drugs is a very real and escalating problem, zoopharmacognosy and human folk remedies represent potential alternatives to synthetic preparations (Huffman, 2003). In addition, while allopathic medicine is often typified by (and criticized for) treating symptoms as opposed to causes, many folk systems are more holistic in approach and application. For example according to Mathias-Mundy and McCorkle (1989) 'farmers in West Java, Indonesia, raise their goats and sheep in sheds on stilts with a slatted floor, and feed them with cut fodder. As a result the animals have few intestinal worms'.

In many parts of post-domestic Europe and north America one of the reasons that intestinal worms have become resistant to anthelmintics (chemical treatments) is because owners or carers treat animals such as horses, then turn them back out onto infected pasture and so they become reinfected almost immediately. The holism of many ethno-veterinary approaches is very much in keeping with wider 'cultural' ways of being in, and therefore perceiving and interacting with, the world, exemplified in the so-called 'hunter-gatherer ontology' (de Castro, 1998; see also chapters 4 and 9). In socio-cultural and environmental contexts where humans recognize their 'place' within a complex ecosystem, it is easier to see how the different elements of that ecosystem work and interrelate. In post-domesticity, where connections between individuals and the systems which sustain them are severed, some humans and human institutions (such as allopathic medicine) have apparently lost that sense of the bigger picture.

ANIMAL-ASSISTED THERAPY

James Serpell (2000: 127) has suggested that animals can act as mediators between humans, their 'inner animality' and the 'natural world' from which post-domestic society has disengaged. There has been a real explosion of academic interest in the effects of human–animal relationships which consistently suggests that close, positive relationships with animals can have manifold therapeutic benefits to human health and well-being.

Animals used in animal-assisted therapy programmes have also been empirically proven to benefit withdrawn or anti-social individuals such as the physically or mentally disabled, victims of abuse and young offenders through the provision of 'a form of non-threatening, non-judgemental, reassuring non-verbal communication and tactile comfort' which can help 'to break the vicious cycle of loneliness, helplessness and social withdrawal' (Corson and O'Leary Corson, 1980: 107 in Serpell, 2000: 109). Further:

AAIs [animal-assisted interventions] have been widely implemented in a variety of mental health settings for adolescents, and preliminary evidence indicates a range of potential benefits including anxiety reduction; improved rapport and communication between patients and therapists; enhanced attendance at, compliance with, and retention in therapy; and improved behavior outside the context of therapy. Animals also appear to serve as catalysts for learning, as sources of contact comfort, as outlets for nurturance, as models of positive social behavior, and as bolsterers of staff morale. (Kruger et al., 2004: 3)

ZOONOSES

While close physical contact with animals can be beneficial to human health, it can also bring with it some significant risks. Biological continuity between humans and other animals means that we can often play host to parasites and pathogens which invade our bodies during some cross-species interactions. These are referred to as zoonoses. When discussing measles, a virus which has made the jump from cattle to humans, Jared Diamond comments 'transfer is not at all surprising, considering that many peasant farmers live and sleep close to cows and their faeces, urine, breath, sores and blood' (1998: 206–7). Indeed, animal management practices have frequently been identified as significant factors in the emergence and transmission of zoonotic disease. The case of Bovine Spongiform Encephalopathy (BSE), which occurred in cattle herds across the UK in the 1980s, is a particularly interesting case in point.

BSE is a zoonotic disease, but one which cannot spread through physical contact. Rather, animals must eat the tissue of another animal already infected with a transmissible spongiform encephalopathy (TSE). It is thought that the disease became prolific in British cattle because some animals were fed on the remains of sheep infected with the TSE 'scrapie'. Feeding herbivorous animals such as cows and sheep on meat-based proteins and ground up bone-meal was commonplace until it was banned in 1990 in the wake of the BSE outbreak (Hoinville, 1994).

Historian Harriet Ritvo (2004) notes that because cattle were seen as markers of 'British' identity, people were encouraged to continue to eat beef during the 'crisis' as a form of patriotism. Yet this did not necessarily translate in practice. Indeed, anthropologist Pat Caplan (2000) conducted a multi-sited study in England and Wales exploring consumer responses to BSE. Her findings are important for several reasons. First, each study locale generated quite different results, demonstrating the heterogeneity of 'the British' (see also Rapport, 2002) and the need to consider this intra-cultural variation in context. Second, while she approached the issue from the perspective of risk-taking, Caplan's findings actually reveal a great deal about human–animal interactions.

Caplan's two research locations were in south-east London and west Wales. In London, she encountered four categories of respondents; those who stopped eating beef long term, those who stopped eating beef temporarily, those who switched to organic beef and those for whom the scare had no direct consequences. In Wales, she encountered three categories; those who stopped eating beef, those who ate beef under certain conditions and those who continued to eat beef as before. Proportionately far fewer consumers in Wales were affected by the scare than in London. This could be partially attributed to the knowledge that consumers had about where their meat had come from and their trust in the producers to have fed and cared for their animals responsibly. In London, where most consumers shopped at supermarkets and therefore had virtually no knowledge of the 'life history' of the meat on the shelves, there was a marked shift in attitudes in favour of cutting out beef or shifting to organic meat because of what were perceived to be stricter controls on animal welfare and management. In west Wales, on the other hand, consumers frequented local butchers with whom they could build a close relationship based on trust.

The use of the term 'trust' is significant given Ingold's observation that, in the shift to agriculture, the relationship between humans and other animals changes from one based on trust to one based on domination (see also chapter 5). It has been widely noted that the industrialized farming practices which arguably led to the BSE outbreak are exploitative and represent an aberration of trust (McKay, 2006), and also that the livestock industry is now a major economic and political force which exists and profits frequently at the expense of the animals upon whom its success depends.

TRANS-BIOPOLITICS

In their recent article outlining the complexity of power relationships with particular reference to the use of animals in medical research and prevailing attitudes towards zoonotic disease, Gwendolyn Blue and Melanie Rock (2010) coin the term 'trans-biopolitics' to demonstrate the politically motivated and economically driven nature of many institutionalized human–animal interactions. Interestingly, in comparing BSE and FSE (Feline Spongiform Encephalopathy), they suggest that the lives of humans and livestock (who are susceptible to BSE) are prioritized over the lives of pets and other 'captive' but economically insignificant animals affected by FSE.

Anthropological commentators on zoonotic disease have often found that the attitudes towards the threats posed by zoonotic disease have what Ritvo (2004) has termed a 'blame the victim' mentality. In other words, while animals are often victims of contemporary dietary preferences and the industrialized farming practices upon which meeting these consumer demands rests, the animals themselves are frequently blamed or punished in human responses to zoonotic outbreaks; for example, some research implicates badgers in the transmission of bovine TB and culling has been proposed in a bid to prevent potential outbreaks (Caplan, 2010).

The political and economic underpinning of many human–animal interactions in the post-domestic world is also revealed in the hidden dangers of eco-tourism, an activity which is widely touted as a benign and sustainable activity (for example Badalamenti et al., 2000). Like the European colonialists of the 15th to the 19th centuries, who brought with them infectious diseases and viruses against which the immune systems of indigenous populations didn't stand a chance, contemporary eco-tourists present significant health risks for endangered wildlife (Muehlenbein and Ancrenaz, 2009: 230). The risks are particularly high in primate eco-tourism because of the close genetic relatedness between members of the same order (see also Muehlenbein et al., 2010).

SUGGESTIONS FOR FURTHER READING

Arluke, A.B. 1988. Sacrificial symbolism in animal experimentation: object or pet? *Anthrozoös* 2(2): 98–117.

Bolton, M. and Dengen, C. (eds) 2010. *Animals and science: from colonial encounters to the biotech industry*. Cambridge: Cambridge Scholars.

Cassidy, R. 2001. On the human–animal boundary. *Anthrozoös* 14(4): 194–203.

Fine, A.H. (ed.) 2006. *Handbook on animal-assisted therapy: theoretical foundations and guidelines for practice*, 2nd edn. New York: Academic Press.

Fouts, R.S., Fouts, D.H. and Waters, G.S. 2002. The ethics and efficacy of biomedical research in chimpanzees with special regard to HIV research. In: in Fuentes, A. and Wolfe, L. (eds) *Primates face to face: the conservation implications of human–nonhuman primate interconnections*. Cambridge: Cambridge University Press.

Franklin, S. 2007. *Dolly mixtures: the remaking of genealogy*. Durham, NC: Duke University Press.

Franklin, S. 1995. Science as culture, cultures of science. *Annual Review of Anthropology* 24: 163–184.

Gigliotti, C. 2009. *Leonardo's choice: genetic technologies and animals*. Vancouver: Springer.

Hatley, J. 2011. Blood intimacies and biodicy: keeping faith with ticks. *Australian Humanities Review* 50: 63–75.

Heatherington, T. 2008. Cloning the wild mouflon. *Anthropology Today* 24(1): 9–14.

Holmberg, T. 2008. A feeling for the animal: on becoming an experimentalist. *Society & Animals* 16(4): 316–335.

Lefkowitz, C., Paharia, I., Prout, M., Debiak, D. and Bleiberg, J. 2005. Animal-assisted prolonged exposure: a treatment for survivors of sexual assault suffering posttraumatic stress disorder. *Society & Animals* 13(4): 275–295.

Lowe, C. 2010. Viral clouds: Becoming H5N1 in Indonesia. *Cultural Anthropology* 25(4): 625–649.

Lynch, M.E. 1988. Sacrifice and the transformation of the animal body into a scientific object: laboratory culture and ritual practice in the neurosciences. *Social Studies of Science* 18(2): 265–289.

Mahaney W.C. and Krishnamani R. (2003) Understanding geophagy in animals: standard procedures for sampling soil. *Journal of Chemical Ecology* 29(7): 1503–1523

McCardle, P., McCune, S., Griffin, J.A. and Maholmes, V. (eds) 2010. *How animals affect us: examining the influences of human–animal interaction on child development and human health*. Washington, DC: American Psychological Association.

McCorkle, C.M., Mathias, E. and Schillhorn van Veen, T. (eds) 1996. *Ethnoveterinary research and development*. London: Intermediate Technology Publications.

McKay, R. 2006. BSE, hysteria, and the representation of animal death: Deborah Levy's *Diary of a Steak*. In: Animal Studies Group, *Killing Animals*. Urbana: University of Illinois Press.

Serpell, J.A. 1991. Beneficial effects of pet ownership on some aspects of human health and behaviour. *Journal of the Royal Society of Medicine* 84: 717–720.

Servais, V. 2005. Enchanting dolphins: an analysis of human–dolphin encounters. In: J. Knight (ed.) *Animals in person: cultural perspectives on human–animal intimacies*. Oxford: Berg.

Smith, J.A. and Boyd, K.M. 2002. *The Boyd Group papers on the use of nonhuman primates in research and testing*. Leicester: British Psychological Society.

Smuts, B. 2006. Between species: science and subjectivity. *Configurations* 14: 115–126.

Villbala, J.J., Provenza, F.D., Hall, J.O. and Lisonbee, L.D. 2010. Selection of tannins by sheep in response to gastrointestinal nematode infection. *Journal of Animal Science* 88: 2189–2198.

13
Conservation

People destroy their environment and then worship nature. (Rosaldo, 1989: 108)

The Anthropocene as an epoch in the Earth's history began some 200 years ago, marked by a widespread technological shift to industrialization and the associated impact of anthropogenic activity on the planet's geological and environmental stability (Crutzen and Stoermer, 2000). Conservation is such a prominent issue for anthropologists therefore because the anthropogenic activities which threaten other species also have negative impacts on human communities globally. However, there is no general consensus regarding sustainable human–animal–environmental relations. Disparate attitudes towards the fate of the natural world and the importance ascribed to wildlife conservation can result in conflicts between human groups because of the contrasting ways in which animals and other 'natural' phenomena are perceived, represented, valued and 'consumed'. This becomes particularly problematic when the animals in question are endangered and therefore protected by law. Anthropology can play a vital role in helping people understand the ways in which others perceive animals, and how these perceptions determine subsequent interactions. As Mullin notes, indigenous groups and Western environmental or animal rights campaigners don't always see eye to eye:

Since the end of the colonial era, cultural anthropologists have often taken on the role of advocates for the communities they study, and with respect to transnational conflicts over animals, that has increasingly meant opposing conservationists and animal rights activists, whose campaigns have imposed hardships on communities dependent on hunting and fishing or on agriculture that conflicts with efforts to protect endangered species (or species such as African elephants and some cetaceans), considered in the West to be particularly worthy of protection even though not facing extinction. (1999: 218)

APPLYING ANTHROPOLOGY

The relationship between anthropologists and their informants is seldom straightforward, and, when environmental issues are thrown into the mix, anthropologists often find themselves with some difficult decisions to make. These decisions lie at the heart of debates concerning the role of anthropology in a postcolonial world. Should anthropologists document the cultural beliefs and practices of their human informants as a purely academic endeavour? Or should they adopt a more active role and 'take sides', becoming advocates for particular causes (see for example Lee, 2010a, 2010b; chapter 16)?

In debates over environmental issues, many anthropological subjects are cast as perpetrators of environmental crimes when their traditional subsistence or recreational activities are seen as unsustainable or environmentally unsound. Indeed, while anthropologists have discussed the question of indigenous 'environmental wisdom' at length (see chapter 4), many contemporary environmental organizations such as Greenpeace have seized on the notion of the 'ecological indian' [sic] as a corrective to all that is wrong with the industrialized or post-domestic world. When the 'natives' fail to conform to such an ideal, they face strong criticisms from individuals and organizations who conveniently forget that their own actions are not always beyond reproach (see for example Erikson, 1999; Martello, 2004). Einarsson's ethnography presents whaling as a case in point:

> it is one thing to postulate that whales [or indeed any other animal species] are special and that animals should have rights, and another thing to condemn the cultural practices of people relating to the use of animals and attempt to force them to give up these practices. Animal rights transformed into practice easily turn into what might be called ethnocentric cultural imperialism. (1993: 80)

As Lindquist has observed (2000: 174), whales, like wolves, are popular 'power animals' among New Age neo-shamans, and they are also regarded in positive, often anthropomorphized terms within post-domestic societies more generally (see also Peace, 2005). Whales are seen as large, gentle, intelligent mammals who form complex social groups and possess their own language. As a result of these apparent similarities to humans they are accorded a greater degree of respect than many other animals (see also Batt, 2009):

> whales above ... most other animals, are worth saving because of their similarity to ourselves, and thus no expense is to be spared in conservation efforts devoted to them. But it is difficult to imagine, in effect, an assumption which runs more contrary to an environmentalist position than this, shot through as it is with the belief that human populations and their qualities are what determines the worth and value of everything else on the planet. (Peace, 2005: 206; cf. Mullin, 1999: 216)

Consequently for many members of many post-domestic societies (with the obvious exceptions of whaling nations), the practice of whaling is considered both unnecessary and cruel. Because of the whales' size, the methods employed to catch and kill them cannot be guaranteed to be humane, and this is also a major cause for concern among environmental and welfare organizations such as Greenpeace, the Whale and Dolphin Conservation Society and WSPA (World Society for the Protection of Animals), as well as for the general public.

From an etic 'conservationist' perspective then, the value of whaling in economic terms appears to be greatly outweighed by moral and ecological concerns, but the practice is of considerable cultural as well as economic importance to those who participate. The reflexively aware, comparative approach which anthropologists can bring to such situations can help to highlight all perspectives.

SMALL-TYPE COASTAL WHALING

Anthropological researchers looking at a traditional form of commercial whaling in Japan (Small-Type Coastal Whaling – henceforth referred to as STCW) found that STCW differs from other forms of commercial whaling on several levels (Iwasaki-Goodman and Freeman, 1996). The most important distinction made was that every part of the whale was utilized, in line with the 'conservation ethic' characteristic of a traditional hunter-gatherer ontology elsewhere in the world. The research, which placed and attempted to explain whaling in relation to culturally and historically specific circumstances, found that not only was STCW of socio-economic importance for localized whaling communities (through the provision of employment, income from the sale of meat and through tourism generated by the local availability of whale-based cuisine), but it also fulfilled important symbolic cultural functions. The symbolic importance of whaling to the cultural identity of these communities was so significant that the researchers coined the term 'Japanese whaling cultural complex' to describe it (Iwasaki-Goodman and Freeman, 1996: 379).

The importance of whaling in this context rests on the centrality of whale meat in Japanese customary diet, and the construction of regional identities through local preferences for specific cuts of whale meat or blubber, which are transformed into local culinary specialties. Another key function of whaling products obtained through STCW lies in the institutionalized practice of gift exchange for which Japan is renowned. Whale meat and blubber form the basis of exchange networks both within the whaling communities and beyond them. These exchanges serve to create alliances and reinforce individual and community identities, as members of whaling communities maintain social networks based on the desirability of the whale products they are able to supply. While the whaling industry nationally (and in other whaling nations, see Kalland, 2009) is important in terms of the employment it provides, STCW is unique in Japan in that the crews of its vessels are tied by kinship bonds (this is also the case outside Japan, however, among the Makah of the north-west United States for example; see Erikson, 1999; Martello, 2004). Whaling boats tend to be run as family businesses and, for most participants, there is a long tradition of family involvement in the industry.

From 1987 onwards, the International Whaling Commission imposed a moratorium which drastically reduced the quota of whales that STCW fisheries were allowed to 'harvest'. Because of the local importance of whaling for small coastal communities, the effects of the moratorium have been significant. The supply of whale meat became insufficient to meet local, let alone national, demand (indeed, Peace notes that very few contemporary Japanese regularly consume whale meat; 2010: 7), to the extent that whale dishes are referred to as '*natsukashii tabemono*' or nostalgic food (Iwasaki-Goodman and Freeman, 1996: 397). Because of the localized nature of whale-based cuisine, the tourist industry has also suffered.

In addition to the obvious negative impact of job losses and the subsequent economic decline of STCW communities, there are also other significant effects relating to the social and cultural importance of whaling. The fact that gift-giving forms the basis of most social relationships in Japan has caused serious problems for members of STCW communities for whom whaling products were their staple exchange commodity. As a result the social status of individuals, families, businesses and even whole communities has been undermined as they are no longer able to fulfil reciprocal exchange obligations. This has had a detrimental effect not only on social relationships, but also on business relationships which are also maintained through the exchange of gifts, and has served to heighten the economic and psychological distress of whalers and threaten the future integrity of whaling communities.

PERCEIVING WHALES

Aside from the interest anthropologists have had in whaling as a socio-cultural institution, the ways in which these animals are *perceived* by whalers and those who oppose whaling is also an area of significant concern. Peace's ethnographic research aboard whale-watching vessels in Australian waters demonstrates that whales have become important icons in Australia (since the country stopped commercial whaling itself in 1978), uniting all segments of society (both indigenous and those of non-native descent).

The encroachment of Japanese whalers upon the oceans surrounding Australia has thus become a source of protracted political debate which stirs up racist resentment towards the 'Japanese' in general. Yet the strength of international feeling about whaling, and the recrimination directed at Japan (and other countries that engage in whaling) also causes resentment not just among whalers themselves but also their fellow countrymen and women, for whom whaling is part of their history and national identity, regardless of its limited range and economic viability in the present. As a result 'the Japanese' (or 'the Norwegians' or 'the Makah') feel passionately that sovereignty should extend to their nation's cultural traditions (Peace, 2010). There are also important differences of opinion about whale classification, which appear to be incompatible across the cultural divide.

'Australians' (and these nationalities are placed in inverted commas here in recognition of the fact that not all Australians will subscribe to this 'dominant' discourse, and not all Japanese will support whaling) on the other hand, recognize whales as mammals, and consequently attribute to them characteristics which they commonly associate with this 'higher' order of animals. Whales are deemed worthy of 'saving' from inhumane and ignoble deaths at the hands of 'cruel and barbaric' whalers. For the 'Japanese' on the other hand, whales are 'mere' fish (Peace, 2010). Nonetheless, on occasion practices occur which reveal a certain inconsistency between whaling and the Buddhist recognition of human–animal continuity. These are reminiscent of traditional 'indigenous' hunting practices (see also chapters 4 and 14). As Peace notes; 'Even when killing whales is considered problematic, traditional Buddhist rituals carried out by the whalers aim to appease the deceased creature's spirit...' (2010: 7).

On the Japan Whaling Association (JWA) website a discussion of the brain size and behavioural complexity of whales concludes that 'whales betray little evidence of behavioural complexity beyond that of a herd of cows'. Regardless of the strength of the evidence on which this claim is being made, the point is anthropologically significant because in comparing whales, creatures whom many outsiders regard with awe and fascination with a species of 'livestock' which forms the basis of most post-domestic diets (see chapter 7), the JWA is ultimately highlighting the inherent hypocrisy in the arguments of their critics.

EXPERIENCING WHALES

Einarsson's (1993) ethnographic study of Icelandic whaling, and Kalland's (2009) recent monograph on whaling in Japan and Norway reveal that for whalers in post-domestic societies whaling remains an important cultural tradition as well as a marker of national identity and a way of life. What is particularly instructive about Einarsson's account are the narratives which detail whalers' experiences of whales. These stand in sharp contrast to etic images of whales: 'While environmentalists tell stories about cetaceans rescuing people, Icelandic small-scale fishermen tell stories about whales sinking boats and causing deaths, apart from destroying gear and eating scarce fish otherwise caught by fishermen' (Einarsson, 1993: 76).

This observation led Einarsson to conclude that on one side of the debate are individuals ('the whalers') who, out of necessity, construct a 'utilitarian and anthropocentric' view of animals. Such a view is informed partly in relation to the 'cultural' significance of whaling, but also as a result of their own (sometimes negative) first-hand experiences. On the other side are individuals removed from the 'reality' of whaling as a way of life, who regard whales in anthropomorphic terms (Peace, 2005, 2010) and appear to view 'nature' (including whales) from an 'ecocentric' perspective

(Einarsson, 1993: 77). But this ecocentricity is relative, conditional on the species in question and the activity being enacted.

While environmental organizations actively campaign against the keeping of cetaceans in captivity, European and North American theme parks and aquaria draw in large visitor numbers annually. While no cetaceans have been kept in captivity in the UK since 1993, there are two marine parks in Europe, one in France and one in Tenerife, which exhibit live Orcas (*Orcinus orca*), not to mention the numerous facilities in the United States and Canada. According to Miami Seaquarium's website for example, the park attracts upwards of 600,000 visitors per year. These paying tourists come to see the Seaquarium's main attraction, a lone female Orca named Lolita who has lived in her small tank for nearly 40 years

The practice of keeping 'intelligent' cetaceans in captivity is often justified on the grounds of 'education', that visitors will be encouraged to care about the conservation of these endangered animals in the wild once they have encountered them first hand (see for example White, 2007: 201). However, much like the Australian whale-watching tours described by Peace, live cetacean exhibits risk presenting an anthropomorphic image of the animals, one which also removes them from their ecological context, despite increasing attempts at 'simulating' natural environments (Franklin, 1999: 80):

> This relentless attribution of human qualities necessarily separates – and indeed extracts – the whales from the complex ecological systems of which they are an integral part ... it is their superficial similarities to human populations which is focused upon in whale tour discourse [and in environmental discourse, and in Oceanariums], this has the inevitable consequence of leaving quite unexplored the place of the whale population in this vast macro-ecology, a system which is itself in the process of significant transformation due to global meteorological changes. Crudely put, a sustained concern with how 'similar' whales are to humans renders impossible the informed comprehension of their place in the ecological system of the southern hemisphere [or anywhere else]; and that may be a high price to pay for an afternoon's entertainment. (Peace, 2005: 206)

THE COST OF ECO-TOURISM

So, while whale-watching or keeping whales in captivity in the name of education might be perceived as more 'sustainable' or ethically sound ways of interacting with these animals than whaling, there are some important factors at work which are frequently overlooked by those who would condemn STCW but not think twice about visiting Sea World. Indeed, whale-watching or the more recent development, swimming with wild cetaceans, is portrayed as an ecologically benign activity which actually benefits the animals being observed or interacted with because the revenues generated go back into wildlife conservation. Whale-watching is also often presented as an alternative to traditional whaling activities which could provide commensurate employment opportunities and potentially an even greater income for communities than the lethal practice of commercial whaling (Papastavrou, 1996). A similar argument is made for eco-tourism activities elsewhere in the world where local peoples are dissuaded from poaching through their employment as tour guides or rangers for the multitude of tourists who come to shoot wildlife with cameras as opposed to guns. Peace (2005: 206) convincingly argues that 'non-consumptive' practices such as whale-watching are forms of symbolic consumption which are symptomatic of post-domestic capitalist over-consumption and postcolonial cultural imperialism, arguably also the root cause of the current global environmental crisis.

The environmental abuses of many Europeans in the colonial past are often conveniently overlooked by contemporary environmentalists, or, if they are acknowledged, they are used as neocolonial justification for the zealous manner in which the environmental cause is pursued (see Mullin, 1999: 206–7). This hypocrisy is certainly not lost on indigenous populations, who are frequently subjected to nationally or internationally enforced restrictions on their activities. As Lee and Priston note in relation to the failure of conservation initiatives aimed at protecting primate populations around the world; 'European attitudes, which have no tradition of coexistence with primates ... have been *imposed* on reluctant farmers' (2005: 2, emphasis added). While the sentiment could be construed as well-meaning (a paternalistic bid to ensure non-Western others don't make the same mistakes), the reality may be that the humans in question do not have a choice. In the case of the bush meat trade for example, individuals are often forced to hunt endangered species in order to survive, and in areas where crop damage or scarce resources make certain animal species unwelcome neighbours, human communities on the poverty line have to choose to act (typically with violence directed at the animals in question) or starve (Peterson and Ammann, 2003). The practice is thus another example of postcolonial cultural imperialism which undermines traditional knowledge and denies indigenous groups autonomy when it comes to 'managing' not just 'their' wildlife (or rather the wildlife with whom they coexist) but their own 'right to life'.

Such behaviour is a cause of confusion for many indigenous peoples, who are often on the receiving end of conservation policies and initiatives and who, in some cases, have always striven to maintain animal populations through the cultivation of a respectful relationship based on nurturance and 'trust' (Ingold, 1994a [1988]; see also chapters 4 and 5). What separates hunter-gatherers from the majority of conservationists is the belief that by hunting members of a particular animal species they are actually helping to maintain the population by releasing individuals from their current existence so that they may be re-born to strengthen the 'herd'. A similar line of argument is adopted by many recreational hunters and anglers who see themselves as grassroots conservationists (see for example Washabaugh and Washabaugh, 2000).

Most native peoples have witnessed the carnage and devastation which colonial hunters inflicted on game animal populations and therefore take umbrage at what they regard as the double standards of environmentalist rhetoric, which 'inverts' the common indigenous totemic premise that animals made the world for humans and are ultimately responsible for its continuation, and replaces it with the post-Enlightenment premise that all animal life should be under human stewardship and control (see Ingold, 1994a [1988]: 12).

HUMANS AS PART OF NATURE

Some native peoples, and hunter-gatherers in particular, are additionally problematic for conservationists because they are 'anomalous' or even in certain instances, 'transgressive' – they do not conform to the dominant conceptualization of conservation. As Ingold points out, contact with humans is regarded as polluting and destructive for the 'environment':

scientific conservation works ... by sealing off portions of the environment and their animal inhabitants, and by restricting intervention so as to exclude any possibility of direct participation. However, many areas designated for conservation are also home to indigenous peoples – most often to hunter-gatherers who are not thought to have altered the environment to any significant extent. For conservationists, their presence can be a source of acute embarrassment, since there is no way of accommodating them within schemes of scientific conservation *except as part of the wildlife*. Yet again, we find a double standard being applied for humanity: one for the scientist as conserver of nature, the other for the hunter-gatherer as a species of nature conserved. But hunter-gatherers too regard themselves as the conservers of their environments, entrusted with the responsibility for 'looking after' it. Not for them, however, the detached, hands-off approach of the scientist. On the contrary, they see themselves as caring for the plants and animals in the environment with the same close and affectionate involvement that they bring to caring for other people. Hence they find no contradiction between conservation and participation. (Ingold, 2000: 68)

Perhaps of most anthropological significance, however, is the failure of many conservation initiatives to consider the complex histories of specific human interactions with specific animals in specific environments when it comes to devising and implementing conservation strategies. These histories are often inextricably linked with European colonial activities, and are influenced or even driven by external forces and global markets (such as poaching of rhino in Africa to supply a desire for powdered rhino horn in Asia). As Lee and Priston note: 'In the past, attempts to deal with problems have run into difficulties through lack of local consultation ... The appropriate management strategy depends on the prevailing economic and cultural context, as well as conservation objectives' (2005: 2).

SUGGESTIONS FOR FURTHER READING

Chrulew, M. 2011. Managing love and death at the zoo: the biopolitics of endangered species preservation. *Australian Humanities Review* 50: 137–157.

Fuentes, A. and Wolfe, L.D. (eds) 2002. *Primates face to face: the conservation implications of human-nonhuman primate interconnections*. Cambridge: Cambridge University Press.

Knight, J. 2006. *Waiting for wolves in Japan: an anthropological study of people–wildlife relations*. Hawai'i: University of Hawaii Press.

Lee, P.C. 2010a. Sharing space: can ethnoprimatology contribute to the survival of nonhuman primates in human-dominated globalized landscapes? *American Journal of Primatology* 72: 925–931.

Lee, P.C. 2010b. Problem animals or problem people? Ethics, politics and practice or conflict between community perspectives and fieldwork on conservation. In: J. MacClancy and A. Fuentes (eds) *Centralizing fieldwork: critical perspectives from primatology, biological and social anthropology*. Oxford: Berghahn.

Lowe, C. 2006. *Wild profusion: biodiversity conservation in an Indonesian archipelago*. Princeton, NJ: Princeton University Press.

Malamud, R. 1998. *Reading zoos: representations of animals and captivity*. New York: New York University Press.

Milton, K. (ed.) 1993. *Environmentalism: the view from anthropology*. London: Routledge.

Milton, K. 1996. *Environmentalism and cultural theory: exploring the role of anthropology in environmental discourse*. New York: Routledge.

Milton, K. 2002. *Loving nature: towards an ecology of emotion*. London: Routledge.

Russell, C.L. 1995. The social construction of orangutans: an ecotourist experience. *Society & Animals* 3(2): 151–170.

Russell, C.L. and Ankenman, M.J. 1996. Orangutans as photographic collectibles: ecotourism and the commodification of nature. *Tourism Recreation Research* 21(1): 71–78.

Theodossopoulos, D. 1997. Turtles, farmers and 'ecologists': the cultural reason behind a community's resistance to environmental conservation. *Journal of Mediterranean Studies* 7(2): 250–267.

Theodossopoulos, D. 2000. The land people work and the land the ecologists want: indigenous land valorisation in a Greek island community threatened by conservation law. In: A. Abramson and D. Theodossopoulos (eds) *Land, law and environment: mythical land, legal boundaries*. London: Pluto Press.

Theodossopoulos, D. 2002. Environmental conservation and indigenous culture in a Greek island community. the dispute over the sea turtles. In: M. Colchester (ed.) *Conservation and mobile indigenous peoples: displacement, forced settlement, and sustainable development*. Oxford: Berghahn Books.

Theodossopoulos, D. 2005. *Troubles with turtles: cultural understandings of the environment on a Greek island*. Oxford: Berghahn Books.

van Dooren, T. (2010) Pain of extinction: the death of a vulture. *Cultural Studies Review* 16(2): 271–289.

14
Hunting and Blood Sports

[H]unting is not a unified category reducible to predation but should incorporate culturally specific representations of predation. (Kwon, 1998: 116)

Anthropologists have adopted several interpretive frameworks when attempting to account for acts of violence in human societies. These include an 'operational approach' which considers the external or etic factors thought to influence human behaviour (such as competition over resources leading to conflict), the 'cognitive approach' which considers cultural systems and how they influence the behaviour of members, and what might be termed a phenomenological or 'experiential approach' whereby the experiences of individuals lead them to behave and respond in a highly subjective manner (Schmidt and Schröder, 2001: 1). Violence towards animals has been interpreted by anthropologists according to what, to all intents and purposes, also constitute operational, cognitive and experiential approaches.

While anthropological interest has tended to focus on 'hunting' and, in particular, the heavily ritualized subsistence hunting practices found in some domestic or pre-domestic contexts (see chapter 4), other activities which fall within the general categories 'hunting' and 'blood sports' have also been accorded some anthropological attention. However, there exists an interesting contradiction within the anthropological literature suggestive of a postcolonial propensity to regard some traditions and cultural practices involving violence from a relativistic perspective; indigenous hunting is acceptable, even 'noble', while similar activities conducted in post-domestic contexts are condemned as 'barbaric' and 'immoral'. Consequently this chapter is primarily concerned with acknowledging the diversity of activities which are traditionally subsumed under the headings 'hunting' and 'blood sports', and with interrogating the inconsistency in anthropological attitudes towards acts of human–animal (or human instigated animal–animal) violence in domestic and post-domestic societies.

DIVERSITY WITHIN THE CATEGORIES 'HUNTING' AND 'BLOOD SPORTS'

Despite the obvious differences between, say, bullfighting on the one hand (Marvin, 1988; Pink, 1996), and game-bird shooting on the other (Dahles, 1993), human ritual activities that culminate in the death of an animal are often portrayed in essentialist terms by academic commentators (for example, Yates, 2009). Sociologist Adrian Franklin states for example that:

> hunting in Britain is considerably less popular than angling, and aside from the continuation of small game hunting by a rural working class, it has remained an upper-class sport and a central feature of their domination of the British countryside. (1999: 114)

Franklin lumps both 'hunting' and 'angling' together in the category of 'hunting sports' (1999: 106). Such classification is too vague, however, failing to accommodate the vast range of hunting practices which occur in Britain. These include game-bird shooting, 'lamping' (shooting foxes at night), hunting rabbits (with dogs and/or guns), hunting foxes with hounds on foot, on horseback or in a vehicle, stag hunting with hounds and/or guns, hunting hare with lurchers or greyhounds, shooting pigeons or hunting them with birds of prey, hunting rats with terriers, baiting badgers with dogs and hunting mink with hounds. Although some of these practices are currently illegal in the UK, they all still occur in some form or another, either openly or covertly, attracting different followings, employing different methodologies, requiring different skill-sets and resources, occurring in different 'hunt countries' and being practised for many different reasons.

'Hunting' is a highly subjective activity and hunt followers experience the 'hunt' in a myriad of ways, all equally real and authentic, but their embodied experiences are governed by different (and at times conflicting) needs and emotions; the operational and cognitive approaches respectively. These are influenced and shaped by participants' individual circumstances, including (but by no means limited to) their personal life history, their livelihood, their socio-economic status, their level of immersion in the 'hunting community' (where relevant, as some forms of hunting are solitary affairs), their means of following or participating in the action, their experiences with animals, and their motivation for attending in the first place. Local 'cultural' norms and practices, national or even international attitudes and legislation also influence the hunting experience for participants in different ways. Then there are the intangibles which lead to 'hunts' being unique as opposed to predictably mundane events; the weather, time of year, and the behaviour of fellow participants, both human and animal, which all affect the outcome of a particular hunt and the experiences of individuals.

THE 'HUNTING HYPOTHESIS'

In his historical overview of Euro-American ideas about 'hunting', biological anthropologist Matt Cartmill (1993) demonstrates the diversity of this category. However, Cartmill also defines hunting as an act which separates humans as a species from other animals: humans hunt, animals predate. Thus even acts of subsistence hunting raise humans above the rest of the natural world because for us, hunting has become 'cultural' (although chimpanzees [*Pan trogolodytes*] and other species also hunt in a ritualized manner). More significant however is the belief that hunting is what made us cultural beings in the first place.

Hunting and the consumption of meat has long been thought a critical aspect of our evolutionary heritage. According to proponents of the 'hunting hypothesis' (for example, Dart, 1926, 1940) anatomically modern humans came into being when our prehistoric ancestors, *Australopithecus africanus*, relinquished their arboreal, ostensibly vegetarian existence and paved the way for bipedalism and terrestrial living by developing tools and becoming proficient hunters. Cartmill, following Dart's thesis, refers to *Australopithecus* as the 'killer ape' whose 'blood lust' set humans apart from other animals and set the scene for humanity's eternal battle with the natural world.

According to the 'hunting hypothesis', humans evolved to hunt and, in the process, adopted an antagonistic approach to interactions with animals. But there are alternative interpretations which contradict the assumption that humans have a violent heritage; it is also argued that humans were scavengers who acquired their meat not through hunting, but by relying on the predatory prowess of large carnivores (Binford, 1981). The fact of the matter is that a great deal of what we 'know' about the early years of the human species is open to debate. Indeed, Dart (1926) himself initially thought, on the basis of the bone remains in the Taung site in South Africa where the first *Australopithecus* skull was found, that the Australopithecenes 'did not live to kill large animals, but killed small animals in order to eat', surviving mainly on the 'exploitation of every accessible food source' (1940). This is much like the subsistence strategies of contemporary Chacma baboons in the region (Hurn, 2011b).

Tentative conclusions drawn from the analysis of scant and often contradictory archaeological remains mean that today neither the hunting hypothesis nor the scavenging hypothesis provide a convincing interpretive framework (Domínguez-Rodrigo, 2007). What is more likely is that our early hominid ancestors were jacks of all trades: opportunistic foragers, hunters *and* scavengers. That the hunting hypothesis captured academic and popular imaginations when it was published in the 1950s, and that it has held sway for so long, was largely an accident of timing. The atrocities of the Second World War revealed deep flaws in the human species and the racism of early theorists, whose unerring belief in human 'progress' had enabled them to position Europeans above other peoples in a hierarchical evolutionary schema, was seriously challenged as these ideas were taken to the extreme by the Third Reich.

After the war, rather than differentiating 'Europeans' from a range of human others, anthropologists and archaeologists utilized the hunting hypothesis to differentiate humans from their closest nonhuman relatives. In pursuing hunting as a mode of subsistence humans could be seen to have separated themselves from the other primates and from 'nature' more generally. Thus 'hunting' came to be viewed as a marker of 'culture' and eventually 'civilization' (see, for example Ortega y Gasset, 1972). Yet such a view runs contrary to the similarly long-held position that it is the shift away from hunting to domestication that marks the first step towards civilization (see chapter 5). Moreover in the contemporary, post-domestic world, hunting outside of subsistence or survival conditions has become something of an anachronism which, in the eyes of the mainstream majority including some anthropologists, has no place among 'civilized' people.

HUNTING IN THE ANTHROPOLOGICAL IMAGINATION

Edmund Leach's digression on foxhunting provides a good starting place. Within a discussion of the linguistic expressions of cultural and ritual taboos Leach asserted:

in England the hunting and killing of foxes is a *barbarous ritual* surrounded by extraordinary and fantastic taboos. The intensity of feeling aroused by these performances almost baffles the imagination. All attempts to interfere with such customs on the grounds of 'cruelty' have failed miserably. (1964: 52–3, emphasis added)

The 'extraordinary and fantastic taboos' referred to include the linguistic inversions of terms specific to hunting (for example, the fox is called a 'dog' while the dogs who hunt it are referred to as 'hounds': see Marvin, 2000: 200), but what is of particular relevance is that Leach dismissed mounted foxhunting as a 'barbarous ritual' without looking for more meaningful explanations for its practitioners' determined continuation of the ritual in the face of mounting opposition.

Another similarly judgemental digression comes from Yi-Fu Tuan (1984) who provided the following condemnation of 'hunting':

Among *so-called civilized peoples*, hunting is the traditional sport of kings and of the nobility ... Hunting is a blood sport. Notwithstanding its modern-age aesthetic of red coats and of brass bugles flashing in the morning sun, it retains its flavor of violence in mud, sweat, blood and death cries. (1984: 95, emphasis added)

Such cursory observations do not really do justice to the body of ethnographic material relating to 'hunting' among 'so-called civilized peoples' which is empirically grounded and rich in distinguishing detail (for example, Bell, 1994; Dahles, 1993; Fukuda, 1997; Hufford, 1992; Hurn, 2009, forthcoming; Marvin, 2000, 2001, 2002, 2003, 2005a, 2005b, 2006; Pardo and Prato, 2005). In comparison to studies of traditional hunting practices, the ethnography of hunting in non-subsistence cases is thin on the ground. Anthropologist Garry Marvin speculates as to why this might be the case, suggesting:

Perhaps this is because they [recreational hunting rituals] have been seen as trivial and insignificant events unworthy of elevated academic attention; perhaps because it has been thought that they can easily be explained away as anachronistic; or perhaps, more likely, because they have been regarded as morally unacceptable practices. (2000: 139)

Yet other potentially 'morally unacceptable practices' involving animals which persist in more 'traditional' ethnographic locales (such as cock-fighting in South East Asia and bullfighting in the Mediterranean) are well attested and have long been accorded balanced anthropological consideration (for example, Brandes, 2009; Dundes, 1994; Geertz, 1973; Lindquist, 2006; Marvin, 1984, 1988; Pink, 1996, 1997).

RITUAL ASPECTS

Ethnographic studies concerned with hunting practices suggest that very few people 'enjoy' the kill. They may enjoy the ritual elements, or the sociality of participating in a communal act (Hufford, 1992). They may also find the competitive aspects challenging and fulfilling (for example, Dahles, 1993). Another key attraction for many aficionados is the interactions which transpire between the animals, such as fox and hounds (Hufford, 1992; Marvin, 2003, 2005a). In these instances, success is judged on the basis of the performances of the different animal actors involved. As essentially domesticated animals (cf. Marvin, 2005a), the abilities of the hounds are linked to the humans who bred and trained them.

Many dismissals of 'hunting' (and especially ritualized practices such as mounted foxhunting), are based on its perceived sporting qualities; that participants ride to hounds for the thrill of the chase. However, the reality is far more complex. Some anthropological commentators have suggested that mounted foxhunting with hounds, for example, is not a sport because the aim is always for the fox to die. It must, therefore, constitute a *sacrifice* in a manner reminiscent of those found in subsistence contexts (cf. Bell, 1994: 182; Holt, 1989: 44, 50; Hurn, forthcoming; Marvin, 2000: 108). Such an assertion may appear paradoxical given that, according to certain schools of thought, sacrifices are ultimately concerned with *negating* violence (Bouroncle, 2000: 55; Girard, 1977 [1972]: 36), and reconciling hunters and herd animals (Ingold, 1987: 243, 254, 258, 2000: 69). Indeed, it is widely accepted anthropologically that the collective ritualization inherent in the hunting practices of traditional hunter-gatherer communities governed by animistic beliefs serve to alleviate the guilt associated with killing another living thing, as well as to appease the animal spirits.

Marvin (2000) asserts that the ritual is important in the context of the English foxhunt because the fox is anomalous – or, as Douglas would say, 'matter out of place' (1966) and therefore needs to be dealt with under the auspices of ritual activity. Ritual serves to safeguard the community, to protect members from the residual pollution that remains following contact with symbolic 'dirt'.

LIMINALITY

Marvin's belief that foxes are anomalous because they kill animals destined for human consumption has support in other ethnographic contexts (for example, Ólafsson, 1995 on foxhunting in Iceland). He suggests that the fox is problematic and therefore killed in a ritual manner '[a]s a result of the relationships which the fox has with *animals* in its world' (Marvin, 2002: 154, emphasis added).

Anthropologists Fukuda (1997), Hurn (2009, forthcoming) and Marvin have all noted that there is a strong farming contingent within the subscriber and membership base of mounted foxhunts across the UK. Serpell also notes that:

> because they live together in what is, to some extent, a combined social group, it is not unusual for farmers and herdsmen to establish social bonds with their animals and vice versa. The moral dilemma is, therefore, far more intense for the farmer than the [subsistence] hunter, because killing or harming the animal in this context effectively constitutes a gross betrayal of trust ... (Serpell, 1999a: 42; cf. Theodossopoulos, 2005a)

Such betrayal therefore necessitates some form of coping mechanism to deal with the contradiction of caring for animals raised as commodities destined for human consumption. The most obvious of these is the use of nomenclature such as 'livestock', and the anonymity of intensive agricultural production, but the ritualistic nature of foxhunting may have some role in the appeasement of guilt in an agricultural system where there is no other opportunity to 'propitiate' the sacrificial animals.

This is certainly how many indigenous reindeer herders conceive of their comparable desire to engage in the retributive hunting of wolves (Lindquist, 2000; Vitebsky, 2005); while the reindeer (like the sheep and chickens kept by British farmers and smallholders) are ultimately kept and killed for human consumption, in life they are afforded the 'care' of human protection. When that protection is undermined via the predation of another animal the hunt can provide a means of restoring human paternalistic authority.

For others, hunting might, as Ortega y Gasset (1972: 139) suggested, permit 'the greatest luxury of all, the ability to enjoy a vacation from the human condition' through the 'humbling of man [sic] which limits his superiority and lowers him towards the animal' (1972: 59). In other words, the act of foxhunting might be viewed as a competition with humans at the mercy of their nonhuman quarry; a romantic notion of the hunt facilitating a return to nature. This is how folklorist Mary Hufford (1992) also accounted for the foxhunting enacted by a group of working-class men who followed their hounds in pick-up trucks as they pursued foxes through the New Jersey Pine Barrens in the USA. For the participants in what Hufford refers to as 'Chaseworld', the hunt represents a 'rite of sociality' between humans and their hounds. In the music (vocalizations) of their hounds the men were able to construct a narrative of events which constitutes a 'secular ritual' (Turner, 1977: 43–5), binding them together in a liminal activity as a collective with a shared purpose and sense of identity.

ANIMALS AS SYMBOLS

While some anthropologists are now rightly critical of considering animals exclusively as metaphors, the reality remains that for many anthropologists and their informants animals are still good to think (see also chapter 6). Certainly for Moore's Greek shepherds the wolves (*Canis lupus*) they hunted to extinction were convenient symbols for the corrupt politicians and urban dwellers who, it was felt, did not care about the plight of the farming community and therefore could be re-classified as two-legged wolves. Because these human 'predators' could not be held accountable, shepherds took out their frustrations on the four-legged variety. For my own farming informants in west Wales, red foxes (*Vulpes vulpes*) became symbolically representative of the large numbers of English incomers who were perceived as 'destroying' the local way of life. While vulpine incomers threatened life and livelihood through acts of predation, human incomers were seen as equally threatening in their actions which included refusing to speak the Welsh language, and putting property prices out of reach of local youngsters who in turn left to find work in the cities (see Hurn, 2009, forthcoming).

Aside from 'hunting' there are numerous other 'recreational' or sporting activities which fall into the category 'blood sports'. These too are seen as controversial, and anthropologists have traditionally perceived the animals involved in metaphorical terms. In one of the most famous ethnographic examples, Clifford Geertz's (1973) study of cock-fighting in Bali, the fight was classified as a 'status bloodbath', not between the birds themselves but between their human owners, for whom the fighting cocks became unambiguous metaphors. Subsequent revisions, for example Johan Lindquist's (2006) overview of the contemporary situation in Indonesia, have responded to criticisms of Geertz's construction of a coherent 'Balinese culture' which the cock-fight itself was supposed to represent in microcosm. For Geertz, the cock-fight was a '*Balinese* reading of *Balinese* experience, a *story* they *tell themselves* about *themselves*' (1973: 448).

While the criticisms that not all Balinese think or see themselves in a homogeneous manner are certainly valid, Lindquist suggests that in many respects, the contemporary cock-fights which he witnessed in Indonesia also presented a convenient window into the state of affairs in the country more generally. Gamblers from Singapore and prostitutes from West Java mixed with itinerant workers from Malaysia in what Lindquist calls a 'contact zone'. They were united not by their shared culture, but by their collective engagement in illicit activities. The cock-fight then became 'a place where meaning is being produced (or at least communication is taking place) between individuals, but in a context structured by emergent forms of inequality, and facilitated by a transnational border regime that has no clear geographical boundaries' (2006: 42).

In comparison to cock-fighting there have been few ethnographic studies of dog-fighting, partly, no doubt, because the underground nature of the fighting scene makes it nigh-on impossible for outsiders to gain access. Despite these difficulties, Saffron Burley (2008) conducted a short period of fieldwork in north London with the aid of a pit bull terrier called Biscuit, who acted as gatekeeper between Burley and the young owners of similarly stigmatized dog breeds. While Burley's informants discussed dog-fighting with her, she did not witness it herself. She nonetheless provides some interesting insights into the complexity of human–dog relationships in this particular context, relationships which have often been dismissed in the past as rather one-dimensional. Instead, Burley suggests that the relationships between her individual informants and their individual dogs are extremely varied and complex.

While some youths kept the dogs to make money from fighting them, others developed genuinely 'loving' relationships with their dogs to the extent that they refused to pit them against another dog. In most cases, though, the breeds of dog involved were chosen because they looked and had the potential to act the part, to give an air of menace, to protect their owners or, if it came to it, put up a good fight with another similarly bred dog. They were status symbols in a manner reminiscent of Caglar's (1997) equally disenfranchised informants (see also chapter 8), and in this respect could be viewed as metaphors for their human owners; stigmatized breeds owned by excluded and maligned young men. However, when discussing the reasons her informants kept these dogs, especially among those who were emotionally attached to their pets, Burley and her informants acknowledged that the non-judgemental support offered by a dog can be invaluable for self esteem, but also for diffusing potential conflict. For example, according to one of Burley's informants:

> You could get some kid who's a real prick, but he's got this dog with him, so you can't teach him the lesson he deserves 'cos you'll get your throat ripped out. The thing is, the dog doesn't think he's a prick, the dog thinks he's the coolest guy in the world. That's the thing about dogs. (2008: 8)

DEVIANCE AND NORMALCY

There is a body of qualitative data relating to illegal dog-fighting in the southern United States (Evans et al., 1998; Evans and Forsyth, 1998; Forsyth and Evans, 1998). 'Dogmen', as they are termed by these researchers, engage in what are widely regarded as 'deviant' activities in the sense that they breed and keep pit bull terriers who will then be used for fighting, often to the death. The Dogmen interviewed for these studies saw themselves as good, honest, respectable people most of the time. Moreover, they believed that they were enabling their dogs to indulge in an activity which came naturally to them and which they enjoyed. According to Forsyth and Evans (1998) this was part of the rationalization of their activity, but, interestingly, they suggest that such 'neutralization' is only necessary when individuals concerned feel the need to uphold 'conventional' morality (see also Hurn, forthcoming; Sykes and Matza, 1957). While Burley's study suggested a link between dog-fighting and other illegal activities such as drug pushing, many of the Dogmen interviewed in the US eschewed such associations, asserting that they were not criminals, but their interest and participation in dog-fighting was part of their cultural heritage and therefore something over which they had no real control.

BULLFIGHTING

Recourse to 'culture' and 'tradition' is a common defence of hunting and blood sports by aficionados and this is certainly the case with bullfighting, a national pastime throughout much of south-western Europe (see Vale de Almeida, 1997, for a comparison between Spanish and Portuguese practices). Bullfights also occur in many former Spanish and Portuguese colonies. In Latin America bullfights serve for many as politically important events at a local level. In her study of bullfighting in Colombia, for example, Christina Escobar (2000) describes how bullfighting festivals provide the setting for complex political battles in the form of patron–client relationships to be played out in the arena, but also around it. Unlike illegal dog or cock-fights, bullfights are publicly performed rituals which also draw in large numbers of tourists.

Several anthropologists have conducted extended ethnographic studies of 'bullfighting culture' in Spain. Drawing on the wider ethnographic literature concerned with the 'Mediterranean' and 'Andalusia' as ethnographic regions, Garry Marvin (1988) presented the 'bullfight' as an expression of what it means to be human. The matador, in his suit of lights, represents the epitome of (urban, male) culture and civilization, while the essentially 'wild' bull is iconic of the realm of (rural, female) nature. The bullfight plays out human control and subjugation of nature, and restores the balance between human and animal, man and woman, nature and culture, rural and urban. Such binary oppositions are called into question, however, by Sarah Pink's (1997) study of female bullfighters. While female matadors are a contradiction in terms, the presence of women in this man's world has led to the reinvention of traditional practices in line with wider contemporary societal changes.

The traditional importance ascribed to the maintenance of clear gender divisions in much of the Mediterranean led anthropologists to conclude that cultural values were governed by the notions of 'honour' and 'shame' (see also chapter 15). Indeed, in many ethnographic engagements with hunting and blood sports there is a recurring emphasis on the assertion of masculinity (bound up with notions of honour) over femininity (associated with shame; for example Evans et al., 1998; Marvin, 1984, 1986, 1988). Pink's study does an excellent job of challenging such representations. By focusing on the younger generations of 'Andalusians', and in particular young female bullfighters, Pink demonstrates that the notions of honour and shame which may have had some currency in the past are no longer dominant organizing principles. Nonetheless, while traditional beliefs about sex and gender may be waning, the reality of being a female matador is extremely difficult because many of those who call the shots (the trainers, managers, promoters, etc.) still do subscribe to traditional beliefs.

Aside from the physical form of female bullfighters being regarded as inappropriate in the bullring (they must bind their breasts and adopt masculine attire) there is also the issue of 'femaleness' and its association with nature. The belief that matadors must be male because the taking of life is 'unnatural' for women who, 'by their nature' give life, is reminiscent of many traditional views of gender roles (for example, Hurn, 2008a). However, the women in Pink's ethnography are illustrative of many modern women for whom gender constructs can be challenged and redefined in accordance with their own individual needs, desires and experiences.

The rise of global media has also played a role in challenging both perspectives of gender and of the bullfight more generally. Pink discusses the ways in which bullfighting is now a commodity consumed by an audience no longer located in a geographic locale, and therefore beyond the reach of local cultural expectations. So while in the past there might have been some merit to considering bullfighting as an expression of masculinity, and a 'ritual of dominionism' (Yates, 2009), in a postmodern, global context there are innumerable ways of experiencing the bullfight, or, indeed, any hunting or violent ritual. As a result, it becomes increasingly difficult, if not impossible, to generalize about 'blood sports'.

One theme which consistently recurs in all of the literature, however, is 'belonging'. The participation in a collective act provides comfort in a world of alienation (for example, Bronner, 2004, 2008), while the ability to 'outwit' or out-perform a nonhuman opponent provides some sense of control (as per the large body of anthropological and sociological material on risk-taking more generally, see, for example, Douglas and Wildavsky, 1983; Lupton, 2006; Lyng, 2005).

Stanley Brandes' (2009) recent article on the reception of bullfighting in contemporary Spain reveals numerous tensions around the place of bulls and bullfighting in relation to the Spanish citizenry. First, there is the symbolism of the bull, which is widely regarded as synonymous with Spain by many tourists, Spaniards and the ethno-nationalist opposition in Catalonia. It is thus hardly surprising that in July 2010 the Catalan parliament banned bullfighting as a symbolic act of resistance. There is also a growing animal rights movement in Spain more generally, which interrogates the morality surrounding the use of animals in public, violent spectacles.

According to Fuentes (2006), while humans have the potential for cruelty, violence is not innately human. It is not part of our biological make-up to inflict unnecessary suffering on other living things. In fact, according to de Waal (2009), the opposite is true, and humans along with many other animals are 'hard-wired' towards altruism. This 'fact' is significant for it means that 'culture' and individual persons become 'responsible' for behaviours which 'harm' others. Sponsel (2009) has also persuasively argued that, far from being innate, wanton killing is actually anathema to most primates, including humans. In light of these observations the prevalence of acts of violence demands explanation. Yet there is a difference between acts of violence, cruelty and wanton killing. Certainly the centrality of ritual to many 'blood sports' is suggestive of some continued need for atonement, and it is this feeling of 'guilt' which the ritualized nature of activities such as 'hunting' and 'bullfighting' serve to propitiate.

SUGGESTIONS FOR FURTHER READING

Animal Studies Group. 2006. *Killing animals*. Urbana: University of Illinois Press.

Howe, J. 1981. Fox hunting as ritual. *American Ethnologist* 8(2): 278–300.

Newton-Fisher, N.E. 2007. Chimpanzee hunting behaviour. In: Henke, W. and Tattersall, I. (eds) *Handbook of paleoanthropology*. Berlin: Springer Verlag.

Twining, H., Arluke, A. and Patronek, G. 2000. Managing the stigma of outlaw breeds: a case study of pit bull owners. *Society & Animals* 8(1): 25–52.

Woods, M. 2000. Fantastic Mr Fox? Representing animals in the hunting debate. In: C. Philo and C. Wilbert (eds) *Animal spaces, beastly places: new geographies of human–animal relations*, pp. 185–204. London: Routledge.

15
Animal Rights and Wrongs

Arguments for the acceptance of animals as kin do not support their recasting as sexual partners. (Cassidy, 2007c: 87)

Individuals may ... be extremely distressed if the habitual object of their sexual arousal is widely viewed as at variance with common or traditional arousal patterns. (Davis and Whitten, 1987: 76)

This chapter is not explicitly concerned with animal rights, at least not in the sense of the history of the animal rights movement (for a historical overview see Kean, 1998). Nor is it directly concerned with the morality of human interactions with animals *per se*, although some basic moral arguments will be advanced (see Rowlands, 2009, for an engaging discussion, and Singer's classic work, 1975, 2006). Rather the focus is on the ways in which conflicting positions vis-a-vis a particularly controversial issue – interactions of a sexual nature between humans and animals – reveal fundamental inconsistencies in our thinking about, and treatment of animals. These contradictions oscillate between recognizing animal personhood (a key component of the animal rights movement) on the one hand, and the persistence of a hierarchical distinction between 'them' and 'us', human and nonhuman on the other. Inconsistencies emerge in the stark contrast between the paternalistic need to 'protect' some animals and the institutionalized 'harming' of others for economic and material ends.

Traditionally, sexual activity between humans and animals has been referred to as 'bestiality' (Dekkers, 2000), but in light of recent anthropological engagement (for example, Cassidy, 2007c, 2009b), and disciplinary advances in our understandings of both human sexuality and human–animal interactions in general, anthropologists, along with scholars from cognate disciplines now recognize that the sheer diversity of ideologies, identities and practices which exist in reality render 'bestiality' an unsatisfactory catch-all.

HUMAN SEXUALITY

Sexuality in many post-domestic contexts is closely associated with 'animality' (see chapter 2). Our ability to control sexual urges becomes another distinguishing marker of difference between 'humans' and 'animals', 'culture' and 'nature'. In many parts of the world sexuality has long been seen as something to be collectively controlled (see Foucault, 1990, 1992, 1998 [1976]). For example, a large body of ethnography concerned with the rural Mediterranean, plus much of north Africa, Latin America and the Arab world has focused on the socio-cultural regulation of sexual behaviour. Many of these ethnographic regions are purportedly governed by a gender-based system of 'honour' and 'shame' (for example, Brandes, 1980, 1981; Dubisch, 1993; Marvin, 1986, 1988; Pink, 1997).

What has come to be referred to as the 'honour and shame' model has been interpreted by anthropologists as a means of maintaining patriarchal dominance because responsibility for upholding the honour of the household falls to women and, by association, their male relatives. Men are tasked with controlling female sexuality which would otherwise bring shame on the family. This desire to control female sex and sexual reproduction at the societal level, and the overt assertion of masculinity is grounded in dominant theologically derived ideologies regarding 'normal' or accepted sexual practices. In much of Europe for example, this traditionally equated to procreative heterosexual sex within marriage. In reality, however, dominant ideologies are often subverted (for example, Kirtsoglou, 2005; Pink, 1997) but not all non-normative sexualities are accorded the same degree of tolerance and, even among those whose sexual identities differ from the mainstream, some ways of being sexual are more acceptable than others.

ANIMAL RIGHTS AND FEMINISM

Sarah Green (1997) in her ethnographic research with lesbian feminist communities in London observed considerable heterogeneity and fragmentation within the 'gay' scene (see Weston, 1993 and Boellstorff, 2007 for synthesizing reviews of anthropological approaches to 'lesbian and gay studies' and 'queer studies' respectively). According to Green, 'lesbian feminists never mixed socially with women who identified themselves as S/M dykes [sadomasochists], and it was not uncommon for lesbian feminists to campaign to have S/M dykes excluded from venues, meetings or even marches and demonstrations' (1997: 15). In a sense, Green's informants viewed the sadomasochists as dishonouring to the cause in the same way (though for different reasons) as patriarchal societies claim that promiscuous women 'dishonour' their families. However, the widely accepted reason for this particular separatist hostility was the belief that lesbian women who engaged in sadomasochistic practices were legitimating dominance-based hierarchies and perpetuating violence against women; societal evils against which, so it was thought, all feminists should unite.

The shared condemnation of violence against muted or vulnerable groups often brings feminists and the animal rights movement together (see also Benthall, 2007; Fuentes, 2006). The 'Brown Dog Riots' of 1907, for example, saw a collective of minority interest political activists (the suffragettes, trade unionists and anti-vivisectionists) join forces against the oppressive patriarchal system, epitomized by the 'scientists' at whose hands the eponymous 'Brown dog' and countless others had died (Lansbury, 2007).

VIOLENCE AGAINST ANIMALS

In the contemporary world, animals are subjected to innumerable acts of culturally and legally sanctioned violence (see also chapter 14). These 'harms' range from the enrolment of millions of animals in intensive agricultural systems (see chapters 5 and 7) and vivisection (see chapter 12), to mass extinctions as a result of anthropogenic activities. Many animals (human and nonhuman alike) are also harmed or become victims of violence illegally, as a result of neglect or the wanton cruelty of individuals or groups.

The root causes of cruelty towards animals in particular are difficult to identify (although there is a recognized link between cruelty to animals and cruelty to humans, for example, Arluke et al., 1999). However, acts of abuse, cruelty or violence are often the result of psychological dissonance. Acts of violence towards animals are also recognized as responses of individuals who have themselves been victims of abuse and/or alienation (Ascione and Shapiro, 2009). Harmful sexual violations of animals are widely documented and discussed by psychologists and criminologists as aberrant, pathological behaviours (for example, Yates et al., 2001), but there are many other ways in which humans obtain sexual gratification from animals which do not involve deliberate or psychotically driven acts of violence, and which are not typically regarded by psychologists as mental disorders (unless they result in mental distress for the protagonist; Bering, 2010). However, in the minds of the anthroposexual mainstream these acts, when consciously solicited and performed, are no less controversial and, for many, constitute worse crimes because there is no recourse to diminished responsibility. As a result, and despite their significant differences, all acts of a sexual nature involving animals have traditionally been subsumed under the category 'bestiality'.

BESTIALITY

In their cross-cultural review of anthropological approaches to human sexuality, Davis and Whitten (1987: 77–8) devoted a tiny paragraph to the topic of 'bestiality' on the grounds that it had received very little anthropological attention. At the time they were writing that was certainly the case. However, lack of academic focus is not necessarily a reliable indicator of prevalence.

In his book *Dearest pet: on bestiality*, naturalist Midas Dekkers (2000) concludes that humans have a long association with practices which might constitute bestiality. One account comes from proto-anthropologist Herodotus (2003, Bk II: 46) who reported; 'In my lifetime a monstrous thing happened in this province [Mendes, Egypt], a woman having open intercourse with a he-goat. This came to be publicly known.' As a Greek (or rather adopted Athenian) Herodotus found the blurring of the species barrier between mortals particularly shocking (see chapter 2; see also Cartledge, 1997). In the classical Athens of Herodotus' day the most acceptable and appropriate sexual relations occurred between free males, while sex with women was a necessary evil to ensure the continuance of the family line (for a more nuanced discussion see Cartledge, 1997; Dover, 1989). As 'naturally servile' beings, animals would have constituted inappropriate sexual partners, although it is interesting that the protagonist in Herodotus' example was a woman, a member of another naturally inferior category (see chapter 2).

Classical Greek ideas have had a significant influence through the ages. Similar revulsion towards bestiality can be found in biblical proscriptions: 'You shall not lie with any beast and defile yourself with it, neither shall any woman give herself to a beast to lie with it: it is a perversion' (18: 23). In the event of such abominations occurring, both human and animal were condemned to death (Leviticus 20: 15–16; see also Cassidy, 2009b: 97). In a paper on zoosex Cassidy also recounts a particularly tragic example from 17th-century France involving a girl accused of bestiality with her pet dog:

> Apparently uncertain as to whether such an act was anatomically possible, the judge appointed a number of female assistants in order to put the dog and the girl to the test. As the women

undressed Claudine [the accused], the dog leaped upon her. On the basis of this evidence both the dog and the young woman were strangled, their bodies burned and scattered to the four winds, 'that as little trace as possible might remain to remind mankind of their monstrous deeds'. (2009b: 95)

While in 17th-century Europe the hegemonic discourse of human superiority to animals can be held partly accountable, in other cultural contexts where Christianity did not and does not hold sway, we might expect things to be different. Elsewhere, while bestiality still appears to be a taboo, the objections are reflective of the cultures in question. In relation to the ethnographic record, Davis and Whitten (citing Beidelman, 1961 on the Mohave of north America, and Devereux, 1948, on the Kuguru of Nigeria) focused on the functional inappropriateness of bestiality in these contexts: that it blurs the boundaries between human and animal (Devereux, 1948) and that it constitutes a misappropriation of someone's property (Beidelman, 1961), but not on its morality *per se*.

ZOOPHILIA

The reasons why sexual relations between humans and animals are culturally taboo and legally prohibited in many cultural contexts are multifarious, but the association of bestiality with cruelty, abuse and violent domination of vulnerable creatures who are legal 'incompetents' in need of human protection undeniably (albeit paradoxically) influences many contemporary attitudes. Yet certain proponents of intimate, sexual relationships between humans and other animals also claim to be passionate animal rights activists who care deeply about animal welfare (see Cassidy, 2009b: 109). So-called 'zoosexuals' or 'zoos', are people for whom sex with an animal is part and parcel of a loving inter-species relationship. Zoosexuality therefore should be differentiated from other forms of sexual contact with animals.

Recognizing the fluidity of identity psychologist Jesse Bering (2010) made an interesting observation in his column for *Scientific American*: that there is a difference between bestiality as a *behaviour* and 'zoophilia' as a distinct *sexual orientation*. Indeed, the traditional approach has been to consider sex with a nonhuman a behavioural abnormality, either a psychological deviance or a functional surrogate for sex with a member of one's own species in a manner reminiscent of 'Western' rationalizations of homosexuality until comparatively recently. However, as Cassidy notes, there are many ways in which the human–animal relationship is afforded a non-normative meaning, expressed in a sexual as opposed to a purely functional manner, for example:

> [the term] 'Furries' can be used to refer to fans of cartoons featuring anthropomorphic animals, or to people who dress up in fur suits. 'Plushies' love and/or are sexually attracted to stuffed animals. 'Therians' range from people who identify with a particular species of animal to those who consider themselves to be animals of a particular species trapped in a human body. Individuals who refer to themselves using these terms may or may not choose to engage in zoosex. (2009b: 108; see also Gerbasi et al., 2008, and Nast, 2006, on 'Furries' specifically)

SEMANTICS AND INTENTIONALITY

Cassidy questioned the place of other seemingly uncontroversial human–animal intimacies when thinking about 'bestiality', stating:

> Bolliger and Goetschel ... explicitly exclude the 'petting and hugging of animals, riding and any conscious or unconscious fantasies of zoophilic acts [...] or the mere observation of intercourse between animals' (2005: 24) from their definition. To exclude these activities from any consideration of zoophilia seems a little premature to me. (Cassidy, 2007c: 90)

However, to include them is perhaps overly 'suspicious' in that it suggests zoophilia might be lurking behind what, for many, are explicitly non-sexual acts. Such semantics calls for a re-analysis of different types of love, attraction and sex between humans and other animals. For example, some individuals experience sexual arousal while horse riding as a result of close genital contact with the saddle and the rhythmic motion of the horse's gait (Dekkers, 2000; Scruton, 2006: 17). Nonetheless horse riding is a socially acceptable activity because it is widely assumed, or rather taken for granted, that the remote possibility of genital stimulation is not the motivating factor behind most people's desire to get in the saddle. And what of 'aesthetics'? Those same individuals may find horses aesthetically pleasing but their sexual arousal and gratification is unrelated to their appreciation of the equine form; any sexual stimulation they may receive is an unconscious side-effect as opposed to an overt sexual orientation. Cassidy's thoroughbred aficionados (2002,

2004, 2007b) and my own Welsh cob enthusiasts (Hurn, 2008a, 2008b) also found the look of certain horses 'attractive' in the sense that they were aesthetically pleasing (see also Patton, 2003), but there is no reason to assume a link between that visual appreciation and any sexual attraction.

Many pet owners will openly confess to loving their pets, just as many humans may love certain of their human friends. Indeed, love does not always equate to sex, and 'falling in love' can be rooted in a Platonic, emotional as well as an erotic connection. For example, some of Cassidy's (2004) racing informants admitted that 'falling in love' was a prerequisite for purchasing a particular animal, while Birke (2008) discussed falling in love as a result of heightened inter-species communication courtesy of 'Natural Horsemanship' (see also chapter 9). Donna Haraway has also described her relationship with companion dog Cayenne Pepper as love and recounted the following intimate exchange as an example of their complex and mutual shared bond: 'Her red merle Australian shepherd's quick and lithe tongue has swabbed the tissues of my tonsils, with all their eager immune system receptors' (2008: 16). Does such 'intimacy' constitute a zoophilic or zoosexual act? Haraway herself describes it as a 'forbidden conversation ... oral intercourse' but there is no suggestion in the text that there is anything sexual about this exchange. The taboo Haraway refers to is inter-species intimacy in general, epitomized in Sartre's condemnation of pet keeping; 'if you love children and animals too much, you love them instead of adults' (1966: 249).

Other 'intimate' acts between humans and other animals, such as stroking, hugging, scratching and tickling have no overt sexual connotations, but could have depending on the intentions or motivations of the humans involved, not to mention the reactions of the animal recipients, some of whom may become sexually aroused themselves as a result of asexual physical contact. Further, as Anthony Storr notes in his study of human cruelty, in human and nonhuman species 'sexual behaviour patterns are habitually used for nonsexual, social purposes ranging from friendly greeting and the inhibition of threat and aggression to the establishment or affirmation of dominance–submission relationships' (1991: 76).

ANTHROPOZOOMETRICITY AGAIN

Philosopher Peter Singer made a similar point when discussing the reaction of primatologist Biruté Galdikas to the seemingly sexual advances of a male orangutan (*Pongo pygmaeus*):

While walking through the camp with Galdikas, my informant was suddenly seized by a large male orangutan, his intentions made obvious by his erect penis. Fighting off so powerful an animal was not an option, but Galdikas called to her companion not to be concerned, because the orangutan would not harm her, and adding, as further reassurance, that 'they have a very small penis.'

As it happened, the orangutan lost interest before penetration took place, but the aspect of the story that struck me most forcefully was that in the eyes of someone who has lived much of her life with orangutans, to be seen by one of them as an object of sexual interest is not a cause for shock or horror. The potential violence of the orangutan's come-on may have been disturbing, but the fact that it was an orangutan making the advances was not. That may be because Galdikas understands very well that we are animals, indeed more specifically, we are great apes. *This does not make sex across the species barrier normal, or natural, whatever those much-misused words may mean, but it does imply that it ceases to be an offence to our status and dignity as human being.* (Singer, 2001: n.p., emphasis added)

Singer's final sentence is italicized here because he has received innumerable criticisms from scholars and animal rights organizations who have accused him of supporting bestiality (see Cassidy, 2009b), including a call for him to resign from his position as President of the Great Ape Project (Cormier, 2003: 153). What Singer actually did here was highlight the hypocrisy of human attitudes and behaviours towards animals. However, in the process, Singer also fell victim to a similar anthropocentricity (or anthropozoometricity); judging the orangutan from a human perspective by assuming that such an attack was 'sexual' in nature. Indeed, it is important to note the fact that the orang quickly 'lost interest', suggesting that his intention might have been other than sexual, a dominance display perhaps when faced with a newcomer.

MORALITY

In terms of the morality of zoophilia, Cassidy's (2007c, 2009b) research on zoosex has suggested a clear demarcation between individuals who force their sexual urges onto (or into) 'animal objects' (see also Singer, 2001), and those individuals ('zoos') for whom the sexual act is a requited physical expression of the mutual emotional love between two individual people, one of whom just happens to be, say, a dog or a horse. This recognition of personhood which 'zoos' claim is the basis of their relationship with their animal 'partner', and which, to all intents and purposes constitutes a physical intersubjectivity of sorts (see chapters 9, 10 and 16), makes it difficult for those who also recognize personhood and intentionality in animals to challenge their position (even though they may strongly disagree with it).

This is the point Singer was making; not that 'sex with animals is good' as his detractors have claimed, but that it may well be that some animals do feel 'comfortable' or even 'happy' with humans as their sexual partners. After all, for animals in captivity (pets in particular), and especially if they are kept in isolation, humans take on most of the roles that would otherwise be fulfilled by conspecifics (such as grooming, companionship, protection and food provision). Nonetheless, some of the criticisms of Singer's argument are based on the potential for an increase of animal sexual *abuse* (which denotes violence and harm) if 'zoosexuality' becomes more socially acceptable. This criticism demonstrates a lack of understanding of the issue however; that zoosexuality is not a 'choice' but a sexual orientation, and in this respect critics of Singer's argument are expressing prejudices reminiscent of those which have been (and in some contexts still are) expressed towards other non-normative, but now 'mainstream' sexualities such as homosexuality. The use of the term 'partner' by zoosexuals (as per Cassidy, 2009b: 91, 109) is key. However, such a relativistic argument is inherently problematic.

Regardless of how 'respectful' a zoo is with his or her lover, or how much the latter enjoys their union, the relationship is based on a fundamental inequality between them. Unlike sexual relationships between consenting adults who (in theory at least) choose to engage with each other in such a manner, animals (and other vulnerable groups such as children) cannot give their informed consent to participate in an act, the consequences of which they do not or cannot fully comprehend (see Donnan and McGowan, 2010, for a recent discussion of anthropological thinking on sexual matters, including consent). Nonetheless, this is a culturally specific approach to the issue, and in many other cultural contexts 'consent' and 'childhood' and the 'appropriateness' of sexual relationships between adults and children are conceived of differently (Montgomery, 2008: 183). This is illustrated in Herdt's (2006) ethnographic study of the Sambia of Papua New Guinea for example, where sexual contact between young boys and adult men was seen as an important aspect of initiation into adulthood.

In our day-to-day (non-sexual) interactions with companion and domestic animals (and indeed other dependants) post-domestic humans habitually make decisions on their behalf; whether to take them to the vet, where to take them for a walk, what to feed them and so on. The assumption is that in some instances, usually when the dependant is incapable (either through lack of knowledge, experience or cognitive ability) of making an informed decision, these decisions are made for the dependant but with their best interests at heart. It follows, therefore, that if the outcome of a decision might not be in the dependant's best interest, a particular action should be avoided altogether or an alternative course of action taken. Having sex with a human may not be in an animal's best interests, nor the human's for that matter. Certainly in the historical examples cited both parties were executed, and in a recent case of a convicted zoosexual documented by psychologists Christopher Earls and Martin Lalumiere (2002), the individual in question had killed the mare with whom he had been intimate out of jealousy (for an interesting related discussion see Yates et al., 2001). There is also the very real issue of zoonotic disease (see also chapter 12).

Inter-species sex may also be problematic for many because of the paternalistic ways in which we think about animals, epitomized in conservationist propaganda (see chapter 13); animals need to be protected from humans and from anthropogenic activities. Both positions are plausible, but as the post-humanist movement stresses the agency and intentionality of animals we must also be aware that in some cases, as with Galdikas' orangutan, animals may be capable of asserting themselves. However, as Tuan (1984) has convincingly argued, in many contexts affection between humans and domestic animals is inextricably connected with domination (see chapter 8 and also Washabaugh and Washabaugh, 2000, for a similar point).

In relation to human expectations of animals, and widespread anthropomorphic misrecognition of animal needs and desires, Haraway argues that the commonly held belief and subsequent expectation that dogs love unconditionally (for example, Masson, 1998) means that many owners base their relationships 'on mistakes, if not lies [which] ... are in themselves abusive – to dogs and to humans' (2003: 33). Such 'mistakes' have serious implications for animal welfare, even when the underlying motivation for action is 'love'. To introduce another example, 'hoarding' is classified as the 'pathological collecting of animals' (Patronek, 2008: 200) where the numbers of animals in a hoarder's possession exceed the means and ability of that individual to adequately attend to their basic needs. According to veterinary surgeon Patronek's study of hoarding cases dealt with by animal welfare organizations in the USA, hoarders often cited their love for the animals when asked by welfare or law-enforcement officers why they were in such (often mutually) damaging situations; they 'loved' their animals too much to part with them.

HUMAN ADAPTATION

Geographers Barbara Ching and Gerald Creed assert that, regardless of their basis in fact, 'accusations of bestiality are common in derogatory jokes about rustic males in many cultures' (1997: 23). The similarities with another controversial 'taboo', cannibalism, are significant. Cannibalism was often something which other people were accused of by Europeans at the height of the colonial period. Arens' (1979) assertion that he found no compelling evidence in support of institutionalized cannibalism has been rejected as ethnocentricity (Ekholm Friedman, 1991; Obeyesekere, 2005) – for Arens, as a 'Westerner' the idea that humans could eat the flesh of a fellow human being was unthinkable. Just as the prospect of eating human flesh is abhorrent to many post-domestic sensibilities so too is the notion of sex with animals, thus making it an appropriate term of abuse (Leach, 1964). The disgust that both of these taboo acts invoke shares a common root cause: the belief that humans are special. Thus to engage in anthropophagy or to favour 'excessive' intimacy with nonhuman others is a rejection of that hierarchical classificatory system.

When considering the conflicting ways in which humans use (and also abuse) animals, biological anthropologist Augustin Fuentes suggests:

> that the viewing of the complex array of relationships between humans and other animals is enlightened by an understanding of niche construction as a human adaptive pattern. That is, part of our evolutionary success is tied to manipulation of the environment and the organisms in it, with a greater degree of impact than other animals. (2006: 129)

Zoosexuality might be interpreted from such a position in one of two ways. First, that zoosexuality is an evolutionary dead-end. Indeed, even with the most high-tech new reproductive technologies a zoosexual and his or her nonhuman partner cannot create a viable hybrid offspring (although whether or not humans and the other Great Apes could is open to debate). Moreover, in wild and domestic animals where some inter-species pairings have occurred, such as lions and tigers to produce ligers and tions, the resultant offspring are typically sterile. Second, that zoosexuality is a response to a lack of readily available human partners. In respect of the latter there is (admittedly dated and methodologically problematic) statistical support for the widespread derogatory association between 'farmers' and sex with animals in the form of the Kinsey Report (Kinsey et al., 1998 [1948]). Zoologist Alfred Kinsey and colleagues found that 50 percent of males raised in a farming environment in the United States had had some form of sexual encounter with animals, as opposed to 8 percent of males and 3.5 percent of females nationally. The researchers concluded that this was perhaps to be expected in an environment where access to available human females was limited, or where, because of the strength of religious belief, girls were less likely to have sex before marriage.

The Kinsey report has been subjected to widespread criticism on grounds of the methodologies, statistical analysis and definitions the team employed (for example, Cochran et al., 1953) and, from a contemporary perspective, their essentially functionalist interpretations of sexual encounters between humans and animals are reminiscent of similarly over-simplistic discussions of homo-eroticism (Poiani and Dixson, 2010). Therefore, in spite of its flaws, the Kinsey report becomes useful as a marker of attitudes towards sexuality at the time the study was conducted, and the need to differentiate between functional sexual behaviour, aberrant sexual behaviour, accidental sexual contact and sexual preference or orientation becomes glaringly apparent.

Anthropologists now recognize and discuss the plasticity of human sexual identity and practice. Just because a woman has sex with a woman, or several women, doesn't necessarily mean she is a lesbian, just as being married to a man with whom she has children doesn't automatically make her heterosexual (Kirtsoglou, 2005). The same applies to intra-species relationships between animals who have been classified as 'bi-sexual'.

In his treatise *In defense of dolphins*, for example, philosopher Thomas White (2007) synthesizes a range of published literature on the behavioural characteristics of dolphins and concludes that dolphins are inherently sexual beings to the extent that sex constitutes a 'social glue' (see also Norris, 1991). White also asserts that dolphins are 'bi-sexual'. While dolphins' social idiom may well be sexual, classifying them as 'bi-sexual' is problematic because it is essentially anthropomorphic. In other words, it attributes human categories to animals who do not share them. Dolphins, like many other animals, do not have the same cultural baggage about sex that many human groups have constructed; they are not 'heterosexual' or 'homosexual' or 'bi-sexual': they just 'are'. In many respects, the recent contributions in the field of 'queer theory' which argue for the plasticity of human sexuality are moving our understanding of human sexuality away from constructivist categorizing (see chapter 16).

SUGGESTIONS FOR FURTHER READING

Beetz, A. 2010. Bestiality and zoophilia: a discussion of sexual contact with animals. In: F. Ascione (ed.) *The international handbook of animal abuse and cruelty: theory, research, and application*. West Lafayette, IN: Purdue University Press.

Podberscek, A.L. and Beetz, A.M. (eds) 2005. *Bestiality and zoophilia: sexual relations with animals*. West Lafayette, IN: Purdue University Press.

16
From Anthropocentricity to Multi-species Ethnography

There is no animal in the general singular, separated from man by a single indivisible limit. We have to envisage the existence of 'living creatures' whose plurality cannot be assembled within the single figure of an animality that is simply opposed to humanity. (Derrida, 2008: 47)

CHALLENGING ANTHROPOCENTRICITY

In 1989 anthropologist Barbara Noske issued a clarion call urging anthropologists to acknowledge and challenge the anthropocentricity of the anthropological endeavour. While this echoed the positions of similarly inclined post-humanists such as feminist philosopher Donna Haraway (2000) and sociologist Ken Shapiro (1993), in mainstream anthropology Noske's call went largely unheeded for quite some time. The primary reason for such a slow response was, as noted in earlier chapters, the simple fact that etymologically and historically anthropology has been concerned with humans. However, while many traditionalists staunchly defend their species-specific focus, the recognition of continuity (that humans are themselves animals), coupled with the fall-out from the reflexive turn, which has raised for discursive analysis the alienation of muted groups, including nonhumans, means that the 'animal turn' is rapidly gaining momentum.

There are several important issues which arise out of the accusation of anthropocentricity. First, it forces us to confront the widely held notion that *Homo sapiens* are special. Human exceptionalism enables us to justify the utilization and exploitation of other species who are deemed different and, in many important respects, 'inferior' (see chapter 2). In a discipline renowned for considering the predicament of the 'underdog' (Nader, 1972) such an imbalance needs acknowledgement and redress, a process which the 'animal turn' has slowly but surely instigated. Second, but still relating to human exceptionalism, is the anthropological emphasis on 'culture' as an exclusively human preserve. Part of the reflexive reconsideration of the place of humans vis-a-vis other animals more generally, which the accusation of anthropocentricity has facilitated, is a more appreciative understanding of the cultural practices of nonhuman others. Third, even though humans engage with other animals in myriad ways during their day-to-day lives, and despite the fact that many of our human informants recognize other animals as active subjects or 'persons' there is still a tendency for anthropologists to objectify nonhumans or regard them as irrelevant to the anthropological endeavour. The animal turn has encouraged a more balanced consideration of the multifarious and often unacknowledged roles that animals play in human societies. Lastly, the post-humanist recognition that other animals are indeed integral actors within human social lives and are therefore worthy of anthropological attention in their own right has led to a move to 'bring in' the animal; to consider human–animal interactions from the perspective of the nonhuman as well as the human.

'Bringing in' animals to ethnographic fieldwork and anthropological theory raises several complex issues. If anthropologists consider both the human and nonhuman aspects of human–animal interactions, interactions which are frequently based on inequalities, whose 'voice' or experience should take priority? And what should be done in situations where animals might be 'suffering' unduly as a result of their enrolment in human social lives? Aside from these pressing questions of loyalties and advocacy, there are other more practical issues concerning the appropriate methodological and theoretical approaches to adopt when conducting what has come to be referred to as 'multi-species ethnography' (Kirksey and Helmreich, 2010a).

HUMAN EXCEPTIONALISM RECONSIDERED

Primatologist Richard Wrangham sums up the flaws of human exceptionalism by considering how the situation might appear to a delegation of Martian biologists sent to assess the state of human, but especially anthropological knowledge at the start of the 21st century:

> They might congratulate us on recognizing our morphological and evolutionary proximity to the apes, but wouldn't they wonder at the persisting anthropocentricity that so often causes a false dichotomy between us and our cousins? As interplanetary biologists, they would puzzle at the widespread notion that

behavior which varies across human populations can't have been influenced by genes, unlike other animals; or at the fact that even though primatology's raison d'être is to shed light on humanity, most comparative primate studies exclude data on humans. Looking at the range of earth's species and their many differences, they would surely be startled that conventional anthropological wisdom often deems human social structure infinitely variable, whereas all other species are granted their typical social forms. Noting the human pervasiveness of fission-fusion grouping and male-bonded communities, patriarchy and war – a combination strikingly similar to traits among chimpanzees – they would be surprised that we don't yet have a unified theory of ape and human social evolution. And surely, they would lament a species that allows its nearest relatives to slide to extinction without a determined howl at the tragedy of the loss. (1987: 445)

As a primatologist Wrangham is particularly well positioned to comment on the falsity of many anthropological notions of human–nonhuman differences. Indeed, as Milton notes:

The question of what distinguishes us from nonhumans ... cannot be addressed without a thorough knowledge of the nonhuman as well as the human. Thus most social and cultural anthropologists are probably not qualified to comment on human uniqueness however inclined they might be to make pronouncements about it. (2003: 19)

Many anthrozoologists or scholars who consider humans and other animals are indeed making concerted efforts to learn as much as they can about the ethology of these nonhuman species, or build upon their pre-existing knowledge. In many instances it was a long-standing interest in particular nonhuman species which informed their research focus in the first place.

INTERSPECIES INTERCONNECTIONS

Humans are amazingly effective adaptors and, as individuals and as a species, we have made some truly exceptional achievements. However, the sort of human exceptionalism on which anthropology and many other human ontologies are based can no longer be justified. It is, according to Haraway, 'foolish' to think otherwise (2008: 244). Just as postcolonialism forced anthropologists to see the error of their (or rather their forebears') ethnocentricity, so post-humanism has enabled us to see that humans are just one species among many whose lives are inextricably linked and mutually dependent. Human exceptionalism or 'species solipsism' (Midgley, 1994a, 1994b) becomes exposed when we are confronted with the equally exceptional, but exceptionally different lives of other animals. Such other-than-human creatures tend to be considered within the ecosystems where they play specific roles or have carved out particular niches. The humanist approach has been guilty of taking humans out of context and putting them on a pedestal. In reality humans exist within multi-species communities, and the existences and survivals of these multiple species are interrelated.

As conservationists are well aware, when one species declines or becomes extinct, the knock-on effects for all other organisms within the ecosystem they leave behind are often considerable. Anthropogenic activity in particular has innumerable ramifications for the other species with whom we share this planet. As Thom van Dooren (2010) demonstrates in relation to the plight of White-backed (*Gyps bengalensis*) and Long-billed (*Gyps indicus*) vultures in India, every action has many unforeseen and on occasion irrevocable consequences.

Across India vultures are dying because the cattle carcasses they consume are contaminated with high residual levels of anti-inflamatory drugs. Anti-inflammatories are routinely administered to cattle to ensure they remain as productive as they can be for as long as possible. This makes treated cattle more comfortable, and ensures that humans on the poverty line are able to get every last drop of milk or labour out of their invaluable animals. For the vultures, however, it means a lingering and unpleasant death, and, as vulture numbers decline, there is a proportionate increase in the population of feral dogs. Dogs are less efficient at cleaning carcasses than vultures. While vultures strip a carcass clean, dogs leave putrefying flesh behind where pathogens such as Anthrax can spore. Growing dog populations also lead to a higher incidence of attacks against humans and domestic animals.

There are economic and cultural implications too. For example, fewer vultures mean that Parsi communities, who practise a form of sky burial, are left with extreme difficulty in disposing of the bodies of their dead, resulting in considerable cognitive and social dissonance, not to mention public health risks. In describing such an array of consequences arising from the death of vultures van

Dooren draws us into the holistic 'biosocial world of entangled lives and deaths' of which we are all a part.

'CULTURE' AND CONSCIOUSNESS REVISITED

The question of culture was discussed in chapter 3, but is returned to here for consideration in the specific light and shadow cast by the animal turn. While the recognition of continuity between humans and other animals is an important part of addressing anthropocentricity, and while there is considerable merit to interrogating the narrow anthropological definitions of 'culture' and acknowledging the abilities and achievements of other animals, the emphasis on culture is problematic nonetheless. As primatologist Barbara King notes:

> the anthropological relationship with great apes has become not about what makes them great apes – not humans – but just how much like us they are. Or, more properly, just how much like us we can construct them to be. And constructing them like us increasingly has come to mean emphasizing that great apes have culture. (2001: 1, in Mullin, 2002)

King's point is an important one; that human characteristics are what makes other animals 'worthy' of consideration and conservation (see also chapter 13). This anthropozoometric approach is not only misguided however, but also harmful. Rather than recognizing nonhumans as 'special' in their own right, the emphasis on humans as the marker against which other species are measured means that, more often than not, they are found wanting.

The emergence of 'panthropology' (Whiten et al., 2003; see chapters 3 and 11) is a case in point, as primatologists attempt to secure 'rights' and recognition for 'their people', and the species deemed most 'like us' (see for example Batt, 2009). Admittedly, however, the approach set out by Whiten et al. is much more inclusive than any existing anthropological model, and they also acknowledge the potential for continuity and culture outside of the primate order, asserting that:

> rather than fruitlessly debating which species do or do not have culture (just our own, according to some definitions; many, according to others), we can begin to dissect more systematically the phenomenon of human culture into a number of components

and assess the extent to which each of these may be manifested to different degrees in various other species.

While the question of culture remains an ongoing source of debate, there is much less controversy over the question of consciousness, or rather self-consciousness, in other animals. As Milton (2003: 20 drawing on Damasio, 1999) suggests, even what are regarded as 'lower animals' are now recognized as having emotions, where these are defined as 'a collection of physical responses which produce a visible or measurable result (tears, a blush, a quickening heartbeat)'.

A 'feeling' is an individual's own perception of the emotion, and an animal can only be conscious (at least in Damasio's and Milton's model) if they are aware of their emotional state, and can draw on those feelings and past experiences in order to avoid pain and pursue pleasure. That many other nonhumans are self-conscious is self-evident in our day-to-day interactions with them, but is also verified scientifically by experiments where animals are subjected to unpleasant stimuli such as electric shocks. In the vast majority of cases, most animals consistently seek to avoid these noxious experiences at all cost (see Griffin, 2001; Griffin and Speck, 2004).

If other animals are conscious beings, who may exhibit some form of (albeit rudimentary) culture, then the move to incorporate them as actors in ethnographic research and anthropological theory appears plausible at least. In response to a spate of publications in *Anthropology Today* concerned with humans and animals but focused almost exclusively on the human perspective Milton wondered whether an anthropology of nonhuman others was possible: 'If there is continuity between human and nonhuman animals, then some of the assumptions we make about humans should be valid for nonhumans, making it possible, at least in theory, to study their lives using a broadly anthropological approach' (2003: 19). This leads to the question of methodology, but nonhuman personhood and the tangential issue of 'what animals are really like' also require consideration (see also Knight, 2005: 10).

WAYS OF 'BRINGING IN' THE ANIMAL

How can anthropologists whose disciplinary identity is grounded in the methodology of participant observation engage in practice with nonhuman as well as human others? There is considerable precedent here however, and numerous primatologists (for example, Fossey, 1983; Goodall, 1986; Marais, 1990; Sapolsky, 2002; Weber and

Vedder, 2002), zoologists (Moss, 1988; see also Candea, 2010), sociologists (Alger and Alger, 2003; Marshall-Thomas, 2010) and wildlife film-makers (King, 2010; see also Milton, 2003: 20) have employed participant observation to infiltrate nonhuman communities, becoming if not accepted 'members' then tolerated visitors. A discussion of the extent to which anthropologists can truly become 'members' of the human communities they study falls beyond the scope of this volume, but suffice to say that in human as in nonhuman associations, levels of integration and acceptance of the researcher vary. A great deal is contingent on the ability and inclination of the individual to understand what is expected of them, and respond accordingly, and this is true regardless of the species under investigation. For example, in her account of over a decade spent living and working with orangutans in Borneo, primatologist Biruté Galdikas explains that what she had 'taken as indifference and rejection was the orangutan expression of acceptance' (1995: 16), revealed to her when she was presented with a newborn baby for inspection by its orangutan mother.

In a recent ground-breaking volume, social anthropologist Jeremy MacClancy and biological anthropologist and primatologist Augustin Fuentes (2010) have sought to engage scholars from their respective fields in reflexive discussion about methods and the potential for truly interdisciplinary collaboration. According to one contributor, primatologist Pamela Asquith (2010), unlike the emphasis on participation in social anthropology, primatologists try to err more on the side of observation, to limit their impact on the natural behaviours they seek to document. However, such an approach is not really so different from that employed in the ethnographic fieldwork of social anthropologists. In their adoption of reflexivity in lieu of unattainable objectivity social anthropologists are also arguably pursuing an unadulterated fieldwork experience.

While the 'scientific' pursuit of 'objectivity' has led many primatologists to avoid direct contact or involvement in their subjects' social and political lives, for others, understanding their subjects makes or made physical contact acceptable and desirable (see MacClancy, 2010; Schaller, 2007). Again the parallel with social anthropology emerges, where the question of how far anthropologists should go in the pursuit of understanding is an ongoing source of debate. Nonetheless, the emulation of ethnography in terms of method and reflexive appraisal, and the personal engagement between individuals, human and animal, is clearly visible and often explicitly articulated in the work of primatologists (for example,

Smuts, 1985; see also Asquith, 2010; MacClancy, 2010; Rees, 2007).

The preceding discussion has related primarily to the use of ethnographic methods to study other primates, and it is certainly easier to make a case for 'bringing in' our closest relatives or indeed other gregarious terrestrial mammals than it would be to conduct ethnographic studies involving marine creatures, insects or migratory birds. That is not to say that such studies are impossible, just that they would present hitherto unexplored logistical, interpretive and analytical challenges. Yet these challenges might be mitigated in some respects if the nonhuman others under investigation are accepted as 'persons'.

WHAT ARE ANIMALS 'REALLY LIKE'?

There has been some discussion among anthropologists over how the nonhuman other should feature in ethnographic encounter and text, and the general consensus has been that anthropologists need not concern themselves with what other animals are 'really like', but rather should focus on what our human informants think about them (Ingold, 2000; Milton, 2000; Tapper, 1994).

In a discussion of the interactions between Inuit hunters and caribou during the hunt, Ingold *described* the behaviour of the caribou, who turn and stare at the hunter. He then explained that the Inuit believe the caribou are persons who 'give' themselves in an act of sacrifice, before offering the 'scientific' explanation for the behaviour (see chapter 2). Ingold then drew the section to a close by stating that 'explaining the behaviour of caribou is none of their [anthropologists'] business' (2000: 14). Such a position resonates with wider anthropological concerns regarding the 'reality' of the behaviours exhibited by our human informants (see for example Rabinow, 1986).

In her discussion of the plight of the transgressive ruddy duck (*Oxyura jamaicensis*) population in the UK and the construction of culturally defined boundaries or classificatory systems Kay Milton states 'none of this is intended to imply that the boundaries are not "real" – I do not consider it part of an anthropologist's role to judge the truth of the ideas they analyse. But like all ideas they can be contested' (2000: 234–5, see also 236). However, a few pages later in the same article Milton asserts:

it would be easy to see the ruddy duck campaign as precisely this kind of activity: an attempt to restore order by eliminating a transgressor of boundaries. But would this be *a realistic characterization of the campaign or of conservation in general? Is this what conservationists are 'really' doing?* (2000: 238, emphasis added)

Placing 'really' in inverted commas suggests that Milton is aware of the irony here, but the point remains that there is often inconsistency in anthropological attitudes towards 'truth' or 'social realities' (for example, Marcus and Fischer, 1999); it is recognized that these are fluid and contingent, but anthropologists still attempt to understand what our human informants are 'really like', or ascertain what they are 'really doing'.

ANTHROPOMORPHISM AND EGOMORPHISM

As a result of fieldwork in the Ecuadorian Amazon Eduardo Kohn asserts that 'some notion of the motivations of others is necessary to get by in a world inhabited by volitional beings'. He continues with the caveat that 'we can never know what other selves – human or nonhuman – are "really" thinking, just as we can never be so sure of what we ourselves are really thinking' (Kohn, 2007: 9). This last remark is crucial. As noted in chapter 10 we can never 'really' know, but we can make reasonable deductions. However, in relation to animals this is made additionally challenging because of the persistent tendency among some social scientists towards anthropomorphism, that is *attributing* characteristics to nonhuman others rather than perceiving in them characteristics which we share. This, on the face of it, semantic difference is actually incredibly significant because if self-consciousness and intentionality are merely attributed as opposed to recognized, then the resulting interaction cannot be truly intersubjective.

Milton (2005: 266) suggests that anthropomorphism is in fact a distancing device employed by people who believe that the characteristics they attribute to animals are in fact the unique preserve of humans. As an alternative, Milton proposes 'egomorphism', or the *recognition* of personhood in other animals on the basis of our ability to *understand* things by *perceiving* characteristics *in* them. This perceptive ability is contingent on our own experiences and world view. So, for example, farmers who make their living from raising large numbers of sheep for slaughter have no desire to understand how an individual sheep 'really' feels, because the act of perceiving emotions and consciousness in sheep would result in serious cognitive dissonance for the farmer. Amazonian hunters on the other hand recognize jaguars (*Panthera onca*) as intentional persons and seek to understand them because they have a great deal to lose if they misjudge these physically and spiritually powerful individuals (Fausto, 1999, 2008; Kohn, 2007).

Milton's concept 'egomorphism' shares many similarities with de Castro's 'perspectivism' (1998), and it is worth emphasizing again the fact that many human persons have no difficulty in recognizing an 'egomorphic' connection with nonhuman persons. However, many others do not and, in the process of making and analysing that connection, anthropologists who focus on human–animal interactions are often placed in the difficult position of potentially conflicting loyalties.

WHO SPEAKS FOR WOLF? ADVOCACY AND ANIMALS

In a recent article in the multi-disciplinary journal *Humanimalia* Linda Birke (2009) also asked what social-science based studies of human–animal relationships tell us about what animals are 'really like'. However, rather than being concerned with the practicalities of grasping a nonhuman perspective, Birke wonders what animals themselves get out of the burgeoning academic interest in their predicaments. While anthropologists have been active in discussing advocacy in relation to their human subjects, very little attention has been given to considering where loyalties should lie in these multi-species interactions (see Petto and Russell, 1998 for a notable exception). The Association of Social Anthropologists of the UK and the Commonwealth makes no mention of animals in their ethical guidelines (ASA, 1999) and, while the American Anthropological Association's guidelines do include responsibilities towards animals (AAA, 1998: section III, A1, 2 and 6), this is a product of the broad-based approach to anthropology in the United States, which includes primatologists within the association's membership. While the harming or exploitation of 'animals' by researchers is expressly forbidden, there is no mention of advocating on their behalf if they are seen to be abused by others (AAA, 1998: section III, A1, 2 and 6).

Arjun Appadurai has noted that 'anthropology survives by its claim to capture other places (and other voices) through its special brand of ventriloquism. It is this claim that needs constant examination' (1988: 20; see also Kirksey and Helmreich, 2010a) because, in 'speaking for' others, anthropologists run the risk of establishing or perpetuating hierarchies and inequalities. For example, in their detailed and convincing explanation for why they chose not to advocate on behalf of their informants, the Colombian Arhuacos, Kirsten Hastrup and Peter Elsass asked 'in what sense could we "speak for" them without possibly inflicting romantic postcolonial views upon them to the exclusion of a thorough understanding of the complex Colombian context?' (1990: 304). They went on to note that to 'speak for' someone 'presupposes that one knows who he [or she] is'. As a result of such dilemmas many anthropologists give their informants voice by incorporating them into the research process, or by providing them with the tools to speak for themselves (for example, Turner, 1992).

Veronica Strang (2000a, 2000b, 2003) is an example of an anthropologist who has successfully advocated on behalf of her informants, while simultaneously empowering them to speak for themselves as a result of her involvement in indigenous land claim cases. Elsewhere, James Clifford and George Marcus (1986) have emphasized polyphony, or the inclusion of diverse voices in preference to the authoritative narrative of the anthropologist within the ethnographic text. Polyphony or polyvocality is now a taken-for-granted aspect of postmodern ethnographic writing, and yet the voices are predominantly human.

According to Robert Layton, 'advocacy derives naturally from the practice of anthropology ... it is an integral part of the process of representing other people's views' (1996: 40) while for Nancy Scheper-Hughes (1995) 'speaking for' others who cannot speak for themselves for whatever reason is a moral duty for anthropologists who work in situations where there is oppression and exploitation. Such a stance is not only morally correct, but, it might be argued, also theoretically and methodologically beneficial (see also Kellett, 2009).

As Laura Nader has famously commented, anthropologists tend to 'value studying what they like and liking what they study and, in general, we prefer the underdog' (1972: 303). If we consider other living beings and their relations to most humans in post-domestic societies we cannot help but surmise that there is a considerable imbalance of power between 'them' and 'us'; they are both metaphorical and literal 'underdogs'. However, even in so-called 'domestic' societies, humans can exert considerable influence over the lives of other animals. For example, there is a well-known traditional story relating to the ancestors of the Oneida nation of upstate New York which tells of human–wolf conflict and its resolution. The Oneida population grew to such an extent that they had to move from their ancestral lands, but the location of their new settlement was right in the middle of wolf territory. After numerous wolf attacks the Oneida council met and discussed their options; they could either hunt the wolves to extinction to resolve the problem, or move. They opted for the latter and nominated someone to always 'speak for wolf' during council meetings to ensure that in future the interests of nonhuman others would be considered and such conflict could therefore be avoided (Underwood, 1994).

Contemporary anthropogenic activities impact on the lives and futures of other species to unprecedented levels and, while other living things, mosquitoes for example, or viruses wreak their own havoc, there is a certain moral dimension, a knowledge of potential impacts and ramifications attached to human actions which make them all the more reprehensible. As a result, advocacy appears to segue from the anthropological study of human–animal interactions, in some cases at least, and as the training and expertise which anthropologists acquire during their careers makes them well positioned to act as mediators, there is no reason why this ability to mediate cannot extend across the species barrier (Petto and Russell, 1998), provided the mediators are sufficiently knowledgeable to take on such a role.

While well-meaning, such a movement nonetheless resembles a return to the postcolonial critiques of advocacy and it is here that the animal turn differs from preceding revisionist approaches to anthropological knowledge and practice. While they have been 'muted', alienated and oppressed in many respects, groups including women, children, the elderly, indigenous people, 'gay' people or people 'of colour' can speak for themselves when given the chance. Notwithstanding the few apes who have mastered human sign language (but who still then rely on humans to interpret what they are saying), there is always going to be a need for someone to 'speak for' animal persons on a political or legal stage.

In an exceptional case, primatologist Sue Savage-Rumbaugh, whose renowned work with bonobos (*Pan paniscus*), particularly one individual named Kanzi (Savage-Rumbaugh and Lewin, 1994), is concerned with understanding their cultural complexity and linguistic abilities, recently included her nonhuman informants as co-authors of a paper which considered the welfare of captive primates (Savage-Rumbaugh et al., 2007). Because these individual bonobos can communicate using sign language and lexigrams,

Savage-Rumbaugh was able to discuss their experiences with them and use this information to challenge existing perceptions of the needs of nonhuman primates in captivity. For other researchers, whose nonhuman informants cannot communicate with such clarity, there remains a great deal of ground to be broken.

TRANS- OR MULTI-SPECIES ENGAGEMENTS

Anthropologist Eduardo Kohn (2007) has recently called for the boundaries of the discipline to be expanded. While he doesn't cite her work, in making this call Kohn is taking up the gauntlet laid down by Noske before him. Kohn proposes an 'anthropology of life' (2007: 6) which situates human worlds within the macro, holistic processes of which they are a part: 'An anthropology of life questions the privileged ontological status of humans as knowers' and represents 'an anthropology that is not just confined to the human but is concerned with the *effects of our entanglements* with other kinds of living selves' (2007: 4, emphasis added). This suggests (as per van Dooren, 2010) that the effects on both 'us' and 'them' need to be considered, and in the process what 'they are like' and how they might see the world become legitimate anthropological concerns. This does raise theoretical and methodological issues as noted above, but these do not need to be insurmountable.

Interestingly, many of Kohn's ideas resonate with those expressed by Tim Ingold, in particular his most recent move to 'bring anthropology back to life' (2010: 4; see also 2011b) by recognizing human life as a 'movement of opening, not of closure'. Bringing other living beings into our studies opens up new opportunities for anthropologists as they pursue their goal of a 'generous, comparative but critical understanding of human life' (Ingold, 2010: 1). By engaging with other ways of being, be they human or nonhuman, our own ontological security is challenged and we confront and reassess our prejudices.

In his discussion of Runa interactions with their dogs and other animals (for example, jaguar) Kohn reveals 'the kind of anthropology that is possible when we allow the exigencies of a transspecies ethnography to break us out of the loop that traps humans as analytical objects within a framework of analysis that is exclusively human' (2007: 18). Kohn's ethnography of Runa *and* their dogs *and both* human and canine interactions with jaguar was developed within what he terms an 'Amazonian multinaturalist framework', a response to de Castro's 'perspectivism'. In other words, humans and 'culture' cease to become the markers of difference and the arbiters of experience. By recognizing other animals as persons, and conversing with them both obliquely (through the spirit realm) and directly (using verbal and non-verbal communication) Runa notions and experiences of being in the world are placed on a continuum which incorporates nonhumans as equal players, or, in the case of spirits, as superiors deserving respect. While insightful, Kohn's ethnography nonetheless presents the experiences and understandings of the dogs and jaguar involved from a human (albeit Runa) as opposed to a canine or feline perspective. Elsewhere Mattei Candea (2010) has engaged in a comparable trans-species ethnography which juxtaposes the perspectives of various human groups (zoologists, volunteers, TV producers, TV audiences) while also attempting to consider the perspectives of the meerkats themselves (see also chapter 12).

A recent special issue of the journal *Cultural Anthropology* devoted to 'Multi-species ethnography' (Kirksey and Helmreich, 2010b) has moved the discussion further forward still, by truly attempting to 'see' the world through, for example, the sensuously tactile forms of marine organisms (Hayward, 2010), with whom it is incredibly difficult to engage in any 'conventional' fashion. These engagements are no less meaningful for their unconventionality, and the contributors cover an impressive range of theoretically complex issues. Eva Hayward (2010), for example, in her multi-species ethnography of marine biologists and cup corals (*Balanophyllia elegans*) argues against a programmatic approach to such encounters, emphasizing instead the value of embodied knowledge grounded in phenomenology and feminist/queer theory.

THEORIZING MULTI-SPECIES ENGAGEMENTS

Emerging from the postmodernist tradition, and heavily influenced by the work of feminist theorists such as Judith Butler (for example, 1990, 1993, 2004), queer theory or 'queering' is concerned with challenging dominant discourses concerning human sexuality (termed 'heterosexual normativity'), and asserting that identities are not fixed. While predominantly the theoretical territory of LGBT (lesbian, gay, bi-sexual and transgender) scholars for considering sexuality, there is much to be gained from utilizing the movement's underlying tenets, namely challenging normative relationships of power in relation to, for example, race, class and gender, and recognizing the plasticity of identity in general.

In the study of multi-species interactions, queer theory provides a reflexive discursive framework within which various (and often imbalanced) embodied experiences can be analysed. For example, Barad's (2008) paper in the edited volume 'Queering the non/human' (Giffney and Hind, 2008) focused on scientific realizations about the echnioderms 'brittlestars' (*Ophiura ophiura*), notably that they do not have brains, but despite this are able to respond, act (interact) and survive. Barad suggested that 'the excitement surrounding this finding ... has more to do with its potential applications than pure amazement at the ingenuity of this creature's bodily know-how' (2008: 322). Nonetheless, increased awareness of and engagement with such alternative embodied knowledge also forces us to once again confront taken-for-granted assumptions about classificatory boundaries and ways of being in the world.

Barad's paper is part of a volume which seeks to challenge 'human' and 'nonhuman' by re-examining both queer theory and our accepted interactions and associations with animals (see also Ruffolo, 2009). Given their respective concerns with challenging dyads – animals as objects/animals as subjects on the one hand, and queer/heteronormative on the other – queer theory, or rather 'post-queer' presents a synergistic framework for post-humanists or anthrozoologists, irrespective of their sexual orientations. As Ruffolo notes 'post-queer' 'challenges the territorializations of stratification by offering a politics of becoming that is not hierarchically structured but is instead a complex multiplicity of flows' (2009: 56–7).

Post-queer becomes even more pertinent to post-humanist anthropology and multi-species ethnography in light of Colebrook's (2008) suggestion that, unlike post-queer, post-humanism is in fact implicated in perpetuating hierarchies, subjectivities and 'normative ethics'; in many respects, post-humanism, with its emphasis on the nonhuman, is more in line with dominant ideas and practices of the mainstream than is post-queer, simply by virtue of the numbers of humans who (overtly) engage in interactions with other animals as opposed to (openly) engaging in sexual activity with members of the same sex (Poiani and Dixson, 2010: 6). A more detailed consideration of queer theory and the fluid, highly politicized nature of human sexuality is beyond the scope of the current endeavour, but several points might be drawn out for further consideration to highlight the potential for utilizing queer insights in the investigation of trans- or multi-species interactions (and vice versa). Following Hayward (2010), this is not a 'hostile conflation of queers and animals' but rather a recognition of shared, muted histories, prejudiced receptions and discriminations.

For many years critics of homosexuality have claimed that same-sex acts are 'unnatural' because homosexuality does not exist in 'nature', that is, outside of the human species (Corvino, 1997: 5, 141). Such assertions have been convincingly overturned however by the vast body of recent material which documents same-sex sexual activity in numerous animal species (see, for example, Bagemihil, 1999; Poiani, 2010; Sommer and Vasey, 2006). Admittedly sexual activity does not equal sexuality (see chapter 15), nonetheless these empirical developments support the notion of human–animal continuity; perhaps more importantly they highlight the importance of reflexive inter- and multi-disciplinary theoretical exchange when considering human–animal interactions. It is important to acknowledge these developments, as well as to bear in mind that the essentialist rendering 'that animals are queer so then queerness is natural' (Hayward, 2010) oversimplifies things. What is perhaps more significant is the fact that ethological material about the 'polymorphous' sexual lives of other species presents valuable opportunities to interrogate and re-envision dominant, culturally rooted ideas about 'normality' more generally. Given that 'normative' ideas about humans and other animals in many post-domestic contexts revolve around the humanist notion of human exceptionalism, 'queering' the nonhuman as well as the human allows for other ways of being to be acknowledged as exceptional in their own right, as collectives (species) and as *individuals*.

THE INDIVIDUAL

In his account of the pain of vultures, van Dooren (2010) highlights the importance of recognizing individuality. More often than not conservationist rhetoric and practice is concerned with ensuring the survival of the collective, and this allows for the rights and well-being of individuals to be disregarded (see also Hurn, 2011b). By considering the pain of individual vultures, van Dooren makes it apparent that the species-centred approach of wildlife management alienates us from their plight. Highlighting the suffering of individuals draws us in, facilitating empathic or egomorphic engagement and connecting the fate of vultures with our own.

The so-called 'cosmopolitan turn' in philosophical anthropology, as debated by Nigel Rapport and Roland Stade (2007) among others, has also emphasized the interconnected nature of contemporary existence and the need for mutual respect of and for individuals (see also Appiah, 2006; Rapport, 2007). Nonetheless these cosmopolitan theorists tend to focus exclusively on the human. According to Pnina Werbner: 'Cosmopolitanism is about reaching out across cultural differences through dialogue, aesthetic enjoyment, and respect; of living together with difference' (2008: 2). But such a utopian ethic is seldom extended beyond the human species, and therein lies the problem.

As conservationists and anthropologists working in war-torn or impoverished areas are only too aware, until there is respect for human life there is little hope of securing the futures of nonhuman species. Perhaps an alternative approach is needed, and multi-species engagements might hold the key. As many multi-species ethnographers have demonstrated, embodied interactions with members of other species can open our eyes to different ways of being-in-the-world, make clear to us the interconnectivity between all life forms, and enable us to re-evaluate culture-centric and anthropocentric ontologies (see also Wolfe, 2003).

WHAT'S IN A NAME?

Nomenclature can serve to oppress or to empower, and as such is highly revealing of the attitudes of those who use particular terms (albeit sometimes without conscious awareness of the signified meaning). From 'Eskimo' to 'Inuit', 'Indians' to 'First Nations', 'homosexual' to 'queer' the names people are given or choose to adopt for themselves tell a story. In relation to humans and other animals, the terminology often adopted is 'nonhuman' or 'other-than-human'. While the intention is to demonstrate that humans are themselves animals, the prefix in both cases is suggestive of inferiority; the animals are being measured in relation to humans again and found wanting (see also Kirksey and Helmreich, 2010a). In the current context the term 'nonhuman animal' has been employed not as an indication of inferiority, but as a recognition of continuity (Birke, 2009: fn 1).

Terms like 'multi-species ethnography' are starting to crop up with increasing regularity in anthropological parlance, and yet species are also cultural constructs, the result of Linnaean taxonomic classification (see also chapters 1 and 6). Given the importance of the phenomenological tradition in understanding multi-species engagements, perhaps 'beings' or 'living beings' represents a suitable alternative? Then again, maybe the naming is irrelevant, and what is most important in this 'animal turn' is the embodied knowledge or 'sensorial-ontology' which arises when species meet and interact (Barad, 2008; Hayward, 2010). It remains to be seen how this field develops and what methodological and theoretical innovations multi-species ethnographers will devise to enable them to adequately understand and represent all of their informants.

ZOONTOLOGIES

One final point to be made ties together many of the themes raised in the preceding chapters. Kohn uses the term 'cosmological autism' to refer to the occasional loss of Runa 'souls' which otherwise enable them to see the subjectivity of other 'persons' in the forest. Autism as a medical term 'refers to a state of isolation that is a result of cognitive difficulties in treating other people as intentional beings' (Kohn, 2007: 9), and so following Kohn I would suggest that many anthropologists and indeed post-domestic individuals to date have exhibited 'zoological autism' in their inability to recognize the 'personhood' of some nonhuman others. 'Bringing in' the animal does not equate to 'putting out' the human (Wolfe, 2009). On the contrary, post-humanism encapsulated in the emergent flow of a holistic multi-species ethnography might present a way to 'save the human'.

SUGGESTIONS FOR FURTHER READING

Bird-Rose, D. 2011. Flying fox: kin, keystone, kontaminant. *Australian Humanities Review* 50: 119–136.

Grimshaw, A. 2011. The bellwether ewe: recent developments in ethnographic filmmaking and the aesthetics of anthropological inquiry. *Cultural Anthropology* 26(2): 247–262.

Irvine, L. 2007. The question of animal selves: implications for sociological knowledge and practice. *Qualitative Sociology Review* 3(1): 5–22.

Kosek, J. 2010. Ecologies of empire: on the new uses of the honey bee. *Cultural Anthropology* 25(4): 650–678.

Matthews, F. 2011. Planet beehive. *Australian Humanities Review* 50: 159–178.

Pandian, A. 2008. Pastoral power in the postcolony: on the biopolitics of the criminal animal in South India. *Cultural Anthropology* 23: 85–117.

Raffles, H. 2001. The uses of butterflies. *American Ethnologist* 28(3): 513–548.

Raffles, H. 2010. *Insectopedia*. New York: Pantheon.

Rees, A. 2001. Anthropomorphism, anthropocentrism, and anecdote: primatologists on primatology. *Science, Technology, & Human Values* 26(2): 227–247.

Rose, D. and van Dooren, T. 2011. Introduction: unloved others: death of the disregarded in the time of extinction. *Australian Humanities Review* 50: 1–4.

Smith, M. 2011. Dis(appearance): earth, ethics and apparently (in)significant others. *Australian Humanities Review* 50: 23–44.

Tsing, A. 2011. Arts of inclusion, or, how to love a mushroom. *Australian Humanities Review* 50: 5–21.

References

AAA. 1998. *American Anthropological Association Code of Ethics*. Available at: http://www.aaanet.org/committees/ethics/ethcode.htm

Abu-Lughod, L. 1991. Writing against culture. In: R. Fox (ed.) *Recapturing anthropology*, pp. 137–162. Santa Fe, NM: School of American Research Press.

Adams, C.J. 1990. *The sexual politics of meat: a feminist-vegetarian critical theory*. Oxford: Polity Press.

Adams, C.K. 1892. *Christopher Columbus: his life and his work*. New York: Dodd, Mead and Co.

Ahearn, L.M. 2001. Language and agency. *Annual Review of Anthropology* 30: 109–137.

Aikio, A. 2006. On Germanic–Saami contacts and Saami prehistory. Suomalais-Ugrilaisen Seuran Aikakauskirja. *Journal de la Société Finno-Ougrienne* 91: 9–55.

Alger, J.M. and Alger, S.F. 2003. *Cat culture: the social world of a cat shelter*. Philadelphia, PA: Temple University Press.

Allen, C. and Bekoff, M. 2005. Animal play and the evolution of morality: an ethological approach. *Topoi* 24(2): 125–135.

Alves, R.R.N., Barboza, R.R.D. and Souto, M.S.W. 2010. Primates in traditional folk medicine: a world overview. *Mammal Review* 40(2): 155–180.

Anderson, K. 1995. Culture and nature at the Adelaide Zoo: at the frontiers of 'human' geography. *Transactions of the Institute of British Geographers* 20(3): 275–294.

Anderson, K. 1997. A walk on the wild side: a critical geography of domestication. *Progress in Human Geography* 21: 463–485.

Anderson, K. 1998. Animal domestication in geographic perspective. *Society & Animals* 6(2): 119–136.

Anderson, M. 1986. From predator to pet: social relationships of the Saami reindeer-herding dog. *Central Issues in Anthropology* 6(2): 3–11.

Appadurai, A. (ed.) 1986. *The social life of things: commodities in cultural perspective*. Cambridge: Cambridge University Press.

Appadurai, A. 1988. Introduction: place and voice in anthropological theory. *Cultural Anthropology* 3(1): 16–20.

Appiah, K.A. 2006. *Cosmopolitanism: ethics in a world of strangers*. New York: W.W. Norton and Co.

Ardener, S. (ed.) 1975. *Perceiving women*. London: Malaby Press.

Arens, W. 1979. *The man-eating myth*. Oxford: Oxford University Press.

Aristotle. 2004. *History of animals*. London: Kessinger Publishing.

Aristotle. 2005. *The Politics*, trans. B. Jowett. Digireads.com

Arluke, A. 1994. Managing emotions in an animal shelter. In: A. Manning and J. Serpell (eds) *Animals and Human Society: Changing Perspectives*. London: Routledge.

Arluke, A., Levin, J., Luke, C. and Ascione, F. 1999. The relationship of animal abuse to violence and other forms of deviant behavior. *Journal of Interpersonal Violence* 9: 963–975.

ASA. 1999. *Association of Social Anthropologists of the UK and the Commonwealth Ethical Guidelines for Good Research Practice*. Available at: http://www.theasa.org/ethics/guidelines.shtml

Ascione, F.R. 1993. Children who are cruel to animals: a review of research and implications for developmental psychopathology. *Anthrozoös: A Multidisciplinary Journal of the Interactions of People and Animals* 6(4): 226–247.

Ascione, F.R. and Arkow, P. 1999. *Child abuse, domestic violence, and animal abuse: linking the circles of compassion for prevention and intervention*. West Lafayette, IN: Purdue University Press.

Ascione, F.R. and Shapiro, K. 2009. People and animals, kindness and cruelty: research directions and policy implications. *Journal of Social Issues* 65(3): 569–587.

Asquith, P.J. 2010. Natural homes: primate fieldwork and the anthropological method. In: J. MacClancy and A. Fuentes (eds) *Centralizing fieldwork: critical perspectives from primatology, biological and social anthropology*. Oxford: Berghahn.

Badalamenti, F., Ramos, A.A., Voultsiadou, E., Sanchez Lizaso, J.L., D'anna, G. Pipitone, C. et al. 2000. Cultural and socio-economic impacts of Mediterranean marine protected areas. *Environmental Conservation* 27(2): 110–125.

Bagemihl, B. 1999. *Biological exuberance: animal homosexuality and natural diversity*. New York: St Martin's Press.

Barad, K. 2008. Queer causation and the ethics of mattering. In: N. Giffney and M.J. Hird (eds) *Queering the non-human*, pp. 311–338. Aldershot: Ashgate.

Barnard, A. 2007. *Anthropology and the bushman*. Oxford: Berg.

Barron, C. 2003. A strong distinction between humans and non-humans is no longer required for research purposes: a debate between Bruno Latour and Steven Fuller. *History of the Human Sciences* 16(2): 77–100.

Barton, R.A. 2006. Animal communication: do dolphins have names? *Current Biology* 16(15): 598–599.

Batt, S. 2009. Human attitudes towards animals in relation to species similarity to humans: a multivariate approach. *Bioscience Horizons* 2(2): 180–190.

Beidelman, T.O. 1961. Kuguru justice and the concept of legal fiction. *Journal of African Law* 5(1): 5–20.

Bekoff, M. 2007. *The emotional lives of animals: a leading scientist explores animal joy, sorrow, and empathy – and why they matter*. Novato: New World Library.

Bekoff, M. and Allen, C. 1992. Intentional icons: towards an evolutionary cognitive ethology. *Ethology* 91: 1–16.

Belk, R.W. 1996. Metaphoric relationships with pets. *Society & Animals* 4(2): 121–146.

Bell, M.M. 1994. *Childerley: nature and morality in a country village*. London: University of Chicago Press.

Benthall, J. 2007. Animal liberation and rights. *Anthropology Today* 23(2): 1–3.

Bentley-Condit, V.K. and Smith, E.O. 2010. Animal tool use: current definitions and an updated comprehensive catalog. *Behaviour* 147(2): 185–32A(–152).

Benzaquén, A.S. 2006. *Encounters with wild children: temptation and disappointment in the study of human nature*. Montreal: McGill-Queen's University Press.

Bering, J. 2010. Animal lovers: zoophiles make scientists rethink human sexuality. *Scientific American*. Available at: http://www.scientificamerican.com/blog/post.cfm?id=animal-lovers-zoophiles-make-scient-2010-03-24

Bermúdez, J.L. 2003. *Thinking without words*. Oxford: Oxford University Press.

Bettany, S. and Daly, R. 2008. Figuring companion-species consumption: a multi-site ethnography of the post-canine Afghan hound. *Journal of Business Research* 61(5): 408–418.

Binford, L. 1981. *Bones: ancient man and modern myths – studies in archaeology.* New York: Academic Press.

Bird-David, N. 1990. The giving environment: another perspective on the economic system of gatherer-hunters. *Current Anthropology* 31(2): 189–196.

Bird-David, N. 1992. Beyond 'the original affluent society': a culturalist reformulation. *Current Anthropology* 33(1): 25–47.

Bird-David, N. 1999. Animism revisited: personhood, environment, and relational epistemology. *Special Issue: Culture – a second chance? Current Anthropology* 40(S): S67–S91.

Bird-David, N. (2006) Animistic epistemology: why some hunter-gatherers do not depict animals. *Ethnos* 71(1): 33–50.

Birke, L. 1994. *Feminism, animals and science: the naming of the shrew.* Milton Keynes: Open University Press.

Birke, L. 2007. 'Learning to speak horse': the culture of 'natural horsemanship'. *Society & Animals* 15(3): 217–239.

Birke, L. 2008. Talking about horses: control and freedom in the world of 'natural horsemanship'. *Society & Animals* 16(2): 107–126.

Birke, L. 2009. Naming names – or, what's in it for the animals? *Humanimalia* 1(1): n.p.

Blackmore, S.J. 2000. *The meme machine.* Oxford: Oxford University Press.

Blue, G. and Rock, M. 2010. Trans-biopolitics: complexity in interspecies relations. *Health: An Interdisciplinary Journal for the Social Study of Health, Illness and Medicine.* e-publication ahead of print.

Blumstein, D.T. and Armitage, K.B. 1997. Alarm calling in yellow-bellied marmots: I. The meaning of situationally variable alarm calls. *Animal Behaviour* 53(1): 143–171.

Boas, F. 1966. *Kwakiutl ethnography.* Chicago: University of Chicago Press.

Boellstorff, T. 2007. *A coincidence of desires: anthropology, queer studies, Indonesia.* Durham, NC: Duke University Press.

Boesch, C. 1996. Three approaches for assessing chimpanzee culture. In A.E. Russon, K.A. Bard and S.T. Parker (eds) *Reaching into thought: the minds of the great apes*, pp. 404–429. Cambridge: Cambridge University Press.

Boesch, C. and Boesch, H. 1982. Optimisation of nut-cracking with natural hammers by wild chimpanzees. *Behaviour* 83(3/4): 265–286.

Bolt, L.M. 2010. Applying human interactive and communicative theories to ringtailed lemur (*Lemur catta*) communication. *Explorations in Anthropology* 10(1): 3–20.

Bouroncle, A. 2000. Ritual, violence and social order: an approach to Spanish Bullfighting. In G. Aijmer and J. Abbink (eds) *Meanings of violence: a cross-cultural perspective.* Oxford: Berg

Boyer, P. 1996. What makes anthropomorphism natural: intuitive ontology and cultural representations. *Journal of the Royal Anthropological Institute* 2(1): 83–97.

Braidwood, R.J. 1957. *Prehistoric men*, 3rd edn. Chicago: Natural History Museum Popular Series, Anthropology, Number 37.

Brandes, S. 1980. *Metaphors of masculinity: sex and status in Andalusian folklore.* Philadelphia: University of Pennsylvania Press.

Brandes, S. 1981. Like wounded stags: male sexual ideology in an Andalusian town. In: S. Ortner and H. Whitehead (eds) *Sexual meanings: the cultural construction of gender and sexuality*. Cambridge: Cambridge University Press.

Brandes, S. 2009. Torophiles and torophobes: the politics of bulls and bullfights in contemporary Spain. *Anthropological Quarterly* 82(3): 779–794.

Brandt, K. 2004. A language of their own: an interactionist approach to human–horse communication. *Society & Animals* 4: 299–316.

Brandt, K. 2005. *Intelligent bodies: women's embodiment and subjectivity in the human–horse communication process*. Boulder: University of Colorado Press.

Brightman, R.A. 1993. *Grateful prey: Rock Cree human–animal relationships*. Berkeley: University of California Press.

Brightman, R.A. 2007. *Traditional narratives of the Rock Cree Indians*. Canadian Plains Research Centre: University of Regina Press.

Bronner, S.J. 2004. 'This is why we hunt': social-psychological meanings of the traditions and rituals of deer camp. *Western Folklore* 63(1/2): 11–50.

Bronner, S.J. 2008. *Killing tradition: inside hunting and animal rights controversies*. Lexington: University of Kentucky Press.

Brothwell, D.R. and Brothwell, P. 1998 [1969]. *Food in antiquity: a survey of the diet of early peoples*. New York: Praeger.

Brumann, C. 1999. Writing for culture: why a successful concept should not be discarded. *Current Anthropology* 40(S1): S1–S27.

Budiansky, S. 1999. *The covenant of the wild: why animals chose domestication*. London: Yale University Press.

Bugnyar, T., Stöwe, M. and Heinrich, B. 2004. Ravens, *Corvus corax*, follow gaze direction of humans around obstacles. *Proceedings of the Royal Society of London B* 271(1546): 1331–1336.

Bulliet, R.W. 2005. *Hunters, herders, and hamburgers: the past and future of human–animal relationships*. New York: Columbia University Press.

Bulmer, R. 1967. Why is the cassowary not a bird? A problem of zoological taxonomy among the Karam of the New Guinea Highlands. *Man* 2(1): 5–25.

Burkert, W. 1983. *Homo necans: the anthropology of ancient Greek sacrificial ritual and myth*. London: University of California Press.

Burley, S. 2008. My dog's the champ: an analysis of young people in urban settings and fighting dog breeds. *Anthropology Matters* 10(1): 1–18.

Butler, J. 1990. *Gender trouble: feminism and the subversion of identity*. London: Routledge.

Butler, J. 1993. *Bodies that matter: on the discursive limits of 'sex'*. London: Routledge.

Butler, J. 2004. *Undoing gender*. London: Routledge.

Caglar, A.S. 1997. 'Go go dog!' and German Turks' demand for pet dogs. *Journal of Material Culture* 2(1): 77–94.

Call, J. 2011. How artificial communication affects the communication and cognition of the great apes. *Mind & Language* 26(1): 1–20.

Candea, M. 2010. 'I fell in love with Carlos the Meerkat': engagement and detachment in human–animal relations. *American Ethnologist* 37(2): 241–258.

Caplan, P. 2000. 'Eating British beef with confidence': a consideration of consumers' responses to BSE in Britain. In: P. Caplan (ed.) *Risk revisited*, pp. 184–203. London: Pluto.

Caplan, P. 2010. Death on the farm: culling badgers in north Pembrokeshire. *Anthropology Today* 26(2): 14–18.

Carrier, J.G. 1992. Occidentalism: the world turned upside-down. *American Ethnologist* 19(2): 195–212.

Carruthers, P. 1989. Brute experience. *Journal of Philosophy* 86: 258–269.

Cartledge, P. 1997. *The Greeks: a portrait of self and others.* Oxford: Oxford University Press.

Cartmill, M. 1993. *A view to a death in the morning: hunting and nature through history.* Cambridge, MA: Harvard University Press.

Cassidy, R. 2002. *The sport of kings: kinship, class and thoroughbred breeding in Newmarket.* Cambridge: Cambridge University Press.

Cassidy, R. 2004. Falling in love with horses: the international thoroughbred auction. *Society & Animals* 13(1): 51–68.

Cassidy, R. 2007a. Introduction: domestication reconsidered. In: R. Cassidy and M. Mullin (eds) *Where the wild things are now: domestication reconsidered,* pp. 1–25. New York: Berg.

Cassidy, R. 2007b. *Horse people: thoroughbred culture in Lexington and Newmarket.* Baltimore, MD: Johns Hopkins University Press.

Cassidy, R. 2007c. Zoosex. *Stimulus/Respond for the Urban Anthropologist: ANIMAL* 18: 83–90.

Cassidy, R. 2009a. The horse, the Kyrgyz horse and the 'Kyrgyz horse'. *Anthropology Today* 25(1): 12–15.

Cassidy, R. 2009b. Zoosex and other relationships with animals. In: H. Donnan and F. Magowan (eds) *Transgressive sex: subversion and control in erotic encounters,* pp. 91–112. Oxford: Berghahn.

Cavalieri, P. and Singer, P. (eds) 1996. *The Great Ape Project: equality beyond humanity.* New York: St Martin's Griffin.

Cheney, D.L. and Seyfarth, R.M. 2007. *Baboon metaphysics: the evolution of a social mind.* London: University of Chicago Press.

Chigateri, S. 2011. Negotiating the 'sacred' cow: cow slaughter and the regulation of difference in India. *Studies in Global Justice* 7(2): 137–159.

Childe, V.G. 1928. *The most ancient East: the Oriental prelude to European prehistory.* London: Kegan Paul.

Ching, B. and Creed, G. W. 1997. *Knowing your place: rural identity and cultural hierarchy.* London: Routledge.

Clark, N. 2007. Animal interface: the generosity of domestication. In: R. Cassidy and M. Mullin (eds) *Where the wild things are now: domestication reconsidered,* pp. 49–70. New York: Berg.

Clifford, J. and Marcus, G. (eds) 1986. *Writing culture: the poetics and politics of ethnography.* Berkeley: University of California Press.

Clottes, J. 2003a. *Return to Chauvet cave: excavating the birthplace of art – the first full report.* London: Thames & Hudson.

Clottes, J. 2003b. *Chauvet cave: the art of earliest times.* Salt Lake City: University of Utah Press.

Clutton-Brock, J. (ed.) 1989. *The walking larder.* London: Unwin Hyman.

Cochran, W.G., Mosteller, F. and Tuckey, J.W. 1953. Statistical problems with the Kinsey Report. *Journal of the American Statistical Association* 264(48): 673–716.

Cohen, A.P. and Rapport, N. 1995. *Questions of consciousness.* ASA Monographs 33. London: Routledge.

Cohen, E. 1986. Law, folklore and animal lore. *Past & Present* 110: 6–37.

Cohen, M.N. and Armelagos, G.J. (eds) 1984. *Paleopathology at the origins of agriculture.* New York: Academic Press.

Colebrook, C. 2008. How queer can you go? Theory, normality and normativity. In: N. Giffney and M.J. Hird (eds) *Queering the non-human*, pp. 17–35. Aldershot: Ashgate.

Coppinger, R. and Coppinger, L. 2001. *Dogs: a new understanding of canine origin, behavior and evolution*. Chicago: University of Chicago Press.

Corbey, R. 2005. *The metaphysics of apes: negotiating the animal–human boundary*. Cambridge: Cambridge University Press.

Cormier, L.A. 2002. Monkey as food, monkey as child: Guajá symbolic cannibalism. In: A. Fuentes and L.D. Wolfe (eds) *Primates face to face: the conservation implications of human–nonhuman primate interconnections*, pp. 63–84. Cambridge: Cambridge University Press.

Cormier, L.A. 2003. *Kinship with monkeys: the Guajá foragers of Eastern Amazonia*. New York: University of Columbia Press.

Cormier, L. 2006. A preliminary review of neotropical primates in the subsistence and symbolism of indigenous lowland South American peoples. *Ecological and Environmental Anthropology* 2: 14–32.

Corvino, J. (ed.) 1997. *Same sex: debating the ethics, science, and culture of homosexuality*. Lanham, MD: Rowman and Littlefield.

Crocker, J.C. 1985. *Vital souls: Bororo cosmology, natural symbolism, and shamanism*. Tucson: University of Arizona Press.

Crutzen, P.J. and Stoermer, E.F. 2000. The Anthropocene. *Global Change Newsletter* 41: 17–18.

Cutt, H., Giles-Corti, B., Knuiman, M. and Burke, V. 2007. Dog ownership, health and physical activity: a critical review of literature. *Health & Place* 13: 261–272.

Cutt, H., Giles-Corti, B., Knuiman, M., Timperio, A. and Bull, F. 2008. Understanding dog owners' increased levels of physical activity: results from RESIDE. *American Journal of Public Health* 98(1): 66–69.

Dahles, H. 1993. Game killing and killing games: an anthropologist looking at hunting in a modern society. *Society & Animals* 1(2): 169–184.

Damasio, A.R. 1999. *The feeling of what happens: body and emotion in the making of consciousness*. London: Heinemann.

D'Anglure, B.S. 1994. Nanook, super-male: the polar bear in the imaginary space and social time of the Inuit of the Canadian Arctic. In: R. Willis (ed.) *Signifying animals: human meaning in the natural world*, pp. 178–195. London: Routledge.

Dant, T. 1999. *Material culture in the social world: values, activities, lifestyles*. Philadelphia: Open University Press.

Dart, R. 1926. Taungs and its significance. *Natural History* 26: 315–327.

Dart, R. 1940. The status of *Australopithecus*. *American Journal of Physical Anthropology* 26: 167–186.

Daston, L. and Mitman, G. (eds) 2005. *Thinking with animals: new perspectives on anthropomorphism*. New York: Columbia University Press.

Davis, D.L. and Whitten, R.G. 1987. The cross-cultural study of human sexuality. *Annual Review of Anthropology* 16: 69–98.

Davis, S.E. and DeMello, M. 2003. *Stories rabbits tell: a natural and cultural history of a misunderstood creature*. New York: Lantern.

Dawkins, M.S. and Bonney, R. (eds) 2008. *The future of animal farming: renewing the ancient contract*. Malden, MA: Blackwell.

Dean, R.J.W., Siegfried, W.R. and MacDonald, I.A.W. 1990. The fallacy, fact, and fate of guiding behavior in the Greater Honeyguide. *Conservation Biology* 4(1): 99–101.

de Castro, E.V. 1996. Images of nature and society in Amazonian ethnology. *Annual Review of Anthropology* 25: 179–200.

de Castro, E.V. 1998. Cosmological deixis and Amerindian perspectivism. *Journal of the Royal Anthropological Institute* 4(3): 469–488.

Dekkers, M. 2000. *Dearest pet: on bestiality*. New York: Verso.

de Malefijt, A.M. 1968. *Homo monstrosus. Scientific American* 219(4): 113–118.

Derrida, J. 2008. *The animal that therefore I am*. New York: Fordham University Press.

de Saint-Exupéry, A. 1995 [1943]. The little prince (*Le Petit Prince*), trans. I. Testot-Ferry. Ware: Wordsworth Editions Ltd.

Descartes, R. 2007 [1649]. From the letters of 1646 and 1649. In: L. Kalof and A. Fitzgerald (eds) *The animals reader: the essential classic and contemporary writings*, pp. 59–62. Oxford: Berg.

Descola, P. 1992. Societies of nature and the nature of society. In: A. Kuper (ed.) *Conceptualizing society*, pp. 107–126. London: Routledge.

Descola, P. 1994. *In the society of nature: a native ecology in Amazonia*. Cambridge: Cambridge University Press.

Devereux, G. 1948. Mohave zoophilia. *Journal of the Indian Psychoanalytic Society* 2: 227–245.

de Waal, F.B.M. 1982. *Chimpanzee politics: power and sex among apes*. London: Cape.

de Waal, F.B.M. 1989. *Peacemaking among primates*. Cambridge, MA: Harvard University Press.

de Waal, F.B.M. 2001. *The ape and the sushi master: cultural reflections of a primatologist*. New York: Basic Books.

de Waal, F.B.M. 2009. *The age of empathy: nature's lessons for a kinder society*. New York: Harmony Books.

de Waal, F.B.M., Boesch, C., Horner, V. and Whiten, A. 2008. Comparing social skills of children and apes. *Science* 317(5843): 1360–1366.

Diamond, J. 1998. *Guns, germs, and steel: the fates of human societies*. New York: W.W. Norton & Co.

Diamond, J. 2002. Evolution, consequences and future of plant and animal domestication. *Nature* 418: 700–707.

Domínguez-Rodrigo, M. 2007. Hunting and scavenging by early humans: the state of the debate. *Journal of World Prehistory* 16(1): 1–54.

Donald, D. 2006. Pangs watched in perpetuity: Sir Edward Landseer's pictures of dying deer and the ethos of Victorian sportsmanship. In: Animal Studies Group, *Killing animals*, pp. 50–68. Chicago: University of Illinois Press.

Donnan, H. and McGowan, F. 2010. *The anthropology of sex*. Oxford: Berg.

Douglas, M. 1966. *Purity and danger: an analysis of concepts of pollution and taboo*. London: Routledge.

Douglas, M. and Wildavsky, A. 1983. *Risk and culture: an essay on the selection of technical and environmental dangers*. Los Angeles: University of California Press.

Douglas-Hamilton, I. and Douglas-Hamilton, O. 1975. *Among the elephants*. New York: Viking Press.

Douglas-Hamilton, I., Bhalla, S., Whittemyer, G. and Vollrath, F. 2006. Behavioural reactions of elephants towards a dying and deceased matriarch. *Applied Animal Behaviour Science* 100(1): 87–102.

Dover, J.K. 1989. *Greek homosexuality*. London: Harvard University Press.

Dubisch, J. 1993. 'Foreign chickens' and other outsiders: gender and community in Greece. *American Ethnologist* 20(2): 272–287.

du Bois, W.E.B. 2005 [1915]. *The negro*. Baltimore, MD: Black Classic Press.

du Bois, S. 2007. Feral children in fiction and fact. *Erbzine* 2105. Available at: http://www.erblist.com/erbmania/dubois-feralchildren-all.pdf

Dunbar, R. 1996. *Grooming, gossip, and the evolution of language*. Cambridge, MA: Harvard University Press.

Dundes, A. 1994. *The cockfight: a casebook*. Madison: University of Wisconsin Press.

Dupre, J. 2006. *Humans and other animals*. Oxford: Oxford University Press.

Duranti, A. 2010. Husserl, intersubjectivity and anthropology. *Anthropological Theory* 10(1–2): 16–35.

Durkheim, E. 1976 [1915]. *The elementary forms of the religious life*. London: George Allen & Unwin.

Durkheim, E. and Mauss, M. 1963. *Primitive classification*. Chicago: University of Chicago Press.

Dwyer, P.D. and Minnegal, M. 2005. Person, place or pig: animal attachments and human transactions in New Guinea. In: J. Knight (ed.) *Animals in person: cultural perspectives on human–animal intimacies*, pp. 37–60. Oxford: Berg.

Earls, C. and Lalumiere, M. 2002. A case study of preferential bestiality (zoophilia). *Sexual Abuse* 14(1): 83–88.

Edelman, B. 2002. 'Rats are people, too!' Rat–human relations re-rated. *Anthropology Today* 18(3): 3–8.

Einarsson, N. 1993. All animals are equal but some are cetaceans: conservation and culture conflict. In: K. Milton (ed.) *Environmentalism: the view from anthropology*. London: Routledge.

Ekholm Friedman, K. 1991. *Catastrophe and creation: the transformation of an African culture*. Philadelphia, PA: Harwood Academic Publishers.

Ellen, R.F. 1986. What Black Elk left unsaid: on the illusory images of Green primitivism. *Anthropology Today* 2(6): 8–12.

Ellen, R.F. 2006. Introduction. *Journal of the Royal Anthropological Institute* 12: S1–S22.

Ellen, R.F. and Fukui, K. 1996. *Redefining nature: ecology, culture, and domestication*. Oxford: Berg.

Emery, N.J. and Clayton, N.S. 2004. The mentality of crows: convergent evolution of intelligence in corvids and apes. *Science* 306: 1903–1907.

Engels, F. 1972 [1884]. *Origins of the family, private property and the state*. New York: International Publishers.

Ereira, A. 1990. *From the heat of the world: the elder brother's warning*. Documentary show on the BBC, December.

Eriksen, T.H. 2001. *Small places, large issues: an introduction to social and cultural anthropology*. London: Pluto Press.

Erikson, P.P. 1999. A-whaling we will go: encounters of knowledge and memory at the Makah Cultural and Research Center. *Cultural Anthropology* 14: 556–583.

Escobar, C. 2000. Bullfighting, fiestas, clientelism and political identities in Northern Columbia. In: L. Romiger and T. Herzog (eds) *The collective and the public in Latin America: cultural identities and political order*, pp. 174–191. Brighton: Academic Press.

Eudey, A.A. 1994. Temple and pet primates in Thailand. *Revue d'Ecologie – La Terre et la Vie* 49(3): 273–280.

Evans, C.S. 1997. Referential signals. In: D.H. Owings, M.D. Beecher and N.S. Thompson (eds) *Perspectives in ethology: communication*, pp. 99–144. New York: Plenum Press.

Evans, R.D. and Forsyth, C.J. 1998. The social milieu of dogmen and dogfights. *Deviant Behavior* 19(1): 51–71.

Evans, R.D., Gauthier, D.K. and Forsyth, C.J. 1998. Dogfighting: symbolic expression and validation of masculinity. *Sex Roles* 39(11/12): 825–832.

Evans-Pritchard, E.E. 1940. *The Nuer*. Oxford: Oxford University Press.

Fausto, C. 1999. Of enemies and pets: warfare and shamanism in Amazonia. *American Ethnologist* 26(4): 933–956.

Fausto, C. 2008. Donos demais: maestria e domínio na Amazônia (Too many owners: mastery and ownership in Amazonia). *Mana* 14(2): 329–366.

Fernández, J. 1991. *Beyond metaphor: the theory of tropes in anthropology*. Stanford, CA: Stanford University Press.

Fiddes, N. 1991. *Meat: a natural symbol*. London: Routledge.

Fifield, S.J. and Forsyth, D.K. 1999. A pet for the children: factors related to family pet ownership. *Anthrozoös: A Multidisciplinary Journal of the Interactions of People and Animals* 12(1): 24–32.

Fitzsimmons, M. and Goodman, D. 1998. Incorporating nature: environmental narratives and the reproduction of food. In: B. Braun and N. Castree (eds) *Remaking reality: nature at the millennium*, pp. 194–220. London: Routledge.

Flannery, K.V., Marcus, J. and Reynolds, R.G. 2008. *The flocks of the Wanami: a study of llama herder on the punas of Ayacucho, Peru*. San Diego, CA: Academic Press.

Foley, J.P. 1940. The 'Baboon Boy' of South Africa. *American Journal of Psychology* 53(1): 128–133.

Forsyth, C.J. and Evans, R.D. 1998. Dogmen: the rationalization of deviance. *Society & Animals* 6(3): 203–218.

Fortis, P. 2010. The birth of design: a Kuna theory of body and personhood. *Journal of the Royal Anthropological Institute* 16(3): 480–495.

Fossey, D. 1983. *Gorillas in the mist*. London: Hodder & Stoughton.

Foucault, M. 1990. *The history of sexuality*, vol. 3: *The care of self*. London: Vintage.

Foucault, M. 1992. *The history of sexuality*, vol. 2: *The use of pleasure*. London: Penguin.

Foucault, M. 1998 [1976]. *The history of sexuality*, vol. 1: *The will to knowledge*. London: Penguin.

Fowler, A., Koutsioni, Y. and Sommer, V. 2007. Leaf-swallowing in Nigerian chimpanzees: evidence for assumed self-medication. *Primates* 48(1): 73–76.

Franklin, A. 1999. *Animals and modern cultures: a sociology of human–animal relations in modernity*. London: Sage Publications.

Franklin, S. 1995. Science as culture, cultures of science. *Annual Review of Anthropology* 24: 163–184.

Franklin, S. 2001. Sheepwatching. *Anthropology Today* 17(3): 3–9.

Franklin, S. 2007. *Dolly mixtures: the remaking of genealogy*. Durham, NC: Duke University Press.

Frazer, J.G. 1922. *The golden bough*. New York: Macmillan.

Frommer, S. and Arluke, A. 1999. Loving them to death: blame-displacing strategies of animal shelter workers and surrenderers. *Society & Animals* 7(1): 1–16.

Fuentes, A. 2006. The humanity of animals and the animality of humans: a view from biological anthropology inspired by J.M. Coetzee's Elizabeth Costello. *American Anthropologist* 108(1): 124–132.

Fuentes, A. 2010. Naturalcultural encounters in Bali: monkeys, temples, tourists and ethnoprimatology. *Cultural Anthropology* 25(4): 600–624.

Fukuda, K. 1997. Different views of animals and cruelty to animals: cases in fox-hunting and pet-keeping in Britain. *Anthropology Today* 13(5): 2–6.

Gaita, R. 2004. *The philosopher's dog: friendships with animals.* New York: Random House.

Galdikas, B.M.F. 1995. *Reflections of Eden: my years with the orangutans of Borneo.* Boston, MA: Little, Brown.

Geertz, C. 1973. Deep play: notes on the Balinese cockfight. In: *The Interpretation of Cultures*, pp. 412–453. New York: Basic Books.

Gerbasi, K.C., Paolone, N., Higner, J., Scaletta, L.L., Bernstein, P.L., Conway, S. et al. 2008. Furries A to Z (anthropomorphism to zoomorphism). *Society & Animals* 16: 197–222.

Giffney, N. and Hird, M.J. 2008. *Queering the non/human.* Aldershot: Ashgate.

Girard, R. 1977 [1972] *Violence and the sacred.* Baltimore, MD: Johns Hopkins University Press.

Goddard, V.A., Llobera, K.P. and Shore, C. 1994. *The anthropology of Europe: identity and boundaries in conflict.* Oxford: Berg.

Goodall, J. 1986. *The chimpanzees of Gombe: patterns of behavior.* London: Harvard University Press.

Goodall, J. 1990. *Through a window: thirty years with the chimpanzees of Gombe.* London: Weidenfeld & Nicolson.

Goode, D. 2006. *Playing with my dog Katie: an ethnomethodological study of dog–human interaction.* West Lafayette, IN: Purdue University Press.

Goodman, M.J., Griffin, P.B., Estioko-Griffin, A.A. and Grove, J.S. 1985. The compatibility of hunting and mothering among the Agta hunter-gatherers of the Philippines. *Sex Roles* 12(11–12): 1199–1209.

Gradé, J.T., Tabuti, J.R.S. and Van Damme, P. 2009. Four-footed pharmacists: indications of self-medicating livestock in Karamoja, Uganda. *Economic Botany* 63(1): 29–42.

Grandin, T. 2008. *The way I see it: a personal look at autism and Asperger's.* Arlington, TX: Future Horizons Inc.

Grandin, T. and Deesing, M.J. 1998. *Genetics and the behavior of domestic animals.* San Diego: Academic Press.

Grandin, T. and Johnson, C. 2006. *Animals in translation: using the mysteries of autism to decode animal behavior.* New York: Harcourt.

Green, S. 1997. *Urban Amazons: lesbian feminism and beyond in the gender, sexuality and identity battles of London.* London: Macmillan.

Greene, E. and Meagher, T. 1998. Red squirrels, *Tamiasciurus hudsonicus*, produce predator-class specific alarm calls. *Animal Behaviour* 55(3): 511–518.

Griffin, D.R. 2001. *Animal minds: beyond cognition to consciousness.* London: University of Chicago Press.

Griffin, D.R. and Speck, G.B. 2004. New evidence of animal consciousness. *Animal Cognition* 7: 5–18.

Hansen, K.T. 2004. The world in dress: anthropological perspectives on clothing, fashion, and culture. *Annual Review of Anthropology* 33: 369–392.

Haraway, D. 1984. Primatology is politics by other means. *PSA: Proceedings of the Biennial Meeting of the Philosophy of Science Association* 2: 489–524.

Haraway, D.J. 1989. *Primate visions: gender, race, and nature in the world of modern science*. London: Routledge.

Haraway, D. 1991. *Simians, cyborgs, and women: the reinvention of nature*. New York: Routledge.

Haraway, D. 2000. A manifesto for cyborgs: science, technology, and socialist feminism in the 1980s. In: G. Kirkup, L. Janes, K. Woodward and F. Hovenden (eds) *The gendered cyborg: a reader*. London: Routledge/Open University.

Haraway, D. 2003. *The companion species manifesto: dogs, people, and significant otherness*. Chicago: Prickly Paradigm.

Haraway, D. 2008. *When species meet*. Minneapolis: University of Minnesota Press.

Hare, B. and Tomasello, M. 2005. Human-like social skills in dogs? *Trends in Cognitive Sciences* 9(9): 439–444.

Harris, M. 1966. The cultural ecology of India's sacred cattle. *Current Anthropology* 7: 51–66.

Harris, M. 1974. *Cows, pigs, women and witches: the riddles of culture*. London: Hutchinson.

Harris, M. 1979. *Cultural materialism: the struggle for a science of culture*. New York: Random House.

Hart, L.A. 2005. The elephant–mahout relationship in India and Nepal: a tourist attraction. In: J. Knight (ed.) *Animals in person: cultural perspectives on human–animal intimacies*, pp. 138–189. Oxford: Berg.

Hartog, F. 1988. *The mirror of Herodotus: the representation of the other in the writing of history*. Berkeley: University of California Press.

Hastrup, K. 1987. Fieldwork among friends: ethnographic exchange within the Northern civilization. In: A. Jackson (ed.) *Anthropology at home*. London: Routledge.

Hastrup, K. and Elsass, P. 1990. Anthropological advocacy: a contradiction in terms? *Current Anthropology* 31(3): 301–311.

Haynes, G. 2007. A review of some attacks on the overkill hypothesis, with special attention to misrepresentations and double talk. *Quaternary International* 169: 84–94.

Hayward, E. 2010. Fingereyes: impressions of cup corals. *Cultural Anthropology* 25(4): 577–599.

Hearne, V. 2007. *Adam's task: calling animals by name*. New York: Skyhorse Publishing Inc.

Heidegger, M. 1962. *Being and time*. London: SCM Press.

Hell, B. 1996. Enraged hunters: the domain of the wild in north-western Europe. In: P. Descola and G. Pálsson (eds) *Nature and society: anthropological perspectives*. London: Routledge.

Herdt, G.H. 2006. *The Sambia: ritual, sexuality, and change in Papua New Guinea*. Belmont, CA: Thomson/Wadsworth.

Herodotus. 2003. *The Histories*, trans. A. de Sélincourt and J. Marincola. London: Penguin.

Herzog, H. 2010. *Some we love, some we hate, some we eat: why it's so hard to think straight about animals*. London: HarperCollins.

High, C. 2010. Agency and anthropology: selected bibliography. *Ateliers du LESC* 34. Available at: http://ateliers.revues.org/8516

Hill, C.M. 2000. Conflict of interest between people and baboons: crop raiding in Uganda. *International Journal of Primatology* 21(2): 299–316.

Hillman, G.C., Hedges, R., Moore, A.M.T., Colledge, S. and Pettitt, P. 2001. New evidence of Late Glacial cereal cultivation at Abu Hureyra on the Euphrates. *The Holocene* 11: 383–393.

Hockings, K. and Humle, T. 2009. *Best practice guidelines for the prevention and mitigation of conflict between humans and great apes*. Gland, Switzerland: IUCN/ SSC Primate Specialist Group.

Hodder, I. 1985. Post-processual archaeology. In: Schiffer, M.B. (ed.) *Advances in archaeological method and theory*, vol. 8, pp. 1–26. New York: Academic Press.

Hodkinson, P. 2002. *Goth*. Oxford: Berg.

Hoinville, L.J. 1994. Decline in the incidence of BSE in cattle born after the introduction of the 'feed ban'. *Veterinary Record* 134(11): 274–275.

Holt, R. 1989. *Sport and the British: a modern history*. Oxford: Oxford University Press.

Holy, L. 1996. *Anthropological perspectives on kinship*. London: Pluto Press.

Hornborg, A. 2006. Animism, fetishism, and objectivism as strategies for knowing (or not knowing) the world. *Ethnos* 71(1): 21–32.

Horst, H.A. and Miller, D. 2006. *The cell phone: an anthropology of communication*. Oxford: Berg.

Huffman, M.A. 1997. Current evidence for self-medication in primates: a multidisciplinary perspective. *Yearbook of Physical Anthropology* 40: 171–200.

Huffman, M.A. 2003. Animal self-medication and ethno-medicine: exploration and exploitation of the medicinal properties of plants. *Proceedings of the Nutritional Society* 62(2): 371–381.

Huffman, M.A. and Quiatt, D. 1986. Stone handling by Japanese macaques (*Macaca fuscata*): implications for tool use of stone. *Primates* 27(4): 413–423.

Hufford, M. 1992. *Chaseworld: foxhunting and storytelling in New Jersey's Pine Barrens*. Philadelphia, PA: University of Philadelphia Press.

Hulsewé, K.W.E., Van Acker, B.A.C., Von Meyenfeldt, M.F. and Soeters, P.B. 1999. Nutritional depletion and dietary manipulation: effects on the immune response. *World Journal of Surgery* 23(6): 536–544.

Hume, D. 1826. *A Treatise on Human Nature*. In: *The Philosophical Works of David Hume*. London: A. Black & W. Tait.

Humle, T. and Matsuzawa, T. 2002. Ant-dipping among the chimpanzees of Bossou, Guinea, and some comparisons with other sites. *American Journal of Primatology* 58(3): 133–148.

Hurn, S. 2008a. What's love got to do with it? The interplay of sex and gender in the commercial breeding of Welsh cobs. *Society & Animals* 16(1): 23–44.

Hurn, S. 2008b. The 'Cardinauts' of the western coast of Wales: exchanging and exhibiting horses in the pursuit of fame. *Journal of Material Culture* 13(3): 335–355.

Hurn, S. 2009. Here be dragons? No, big cats! Predator symbolism in rural west Wales. *Anthropology Today* 25(1): 6–11.

Hurn, S. 2010. What's in a name? Anthrozoology, human–animal studies, animal studies or...? *Anthropology Today* 26(3): 27–28.

Hurn, S. 2011a. Dressing down: clothing animals, disguising animality. *Special Issue*: *Les apparences de l'homme. Civilisations* 59 (2): 123–138.

Hurn, S. 2011b. Like herding cats! Managing conflict over wildlife heritage on South Africa's Cape Peninsula. *Journal of Ecological and Environmental Anthropology* 6(1): 39–53.

Hurn, S. forthcoming. *The politics of the periphery: tradition, ritual and identity in rural Wales*. London: Ashgate.

Imanishi, K. 1952. Evolution of humanity. In: K. Imanishi (ed.) *Man*, pp. 36–94. Tokyo: Mainichi-Shinbun-sha.

Ingold, T. 1980. *Hunters, pastoralists and ranchers*. Cambridge: Cambridge University Press.

Ingold, T. 1987. *The appropriation of nature*. Iowa City: University of Iowa Press.

Ingold, T. (ed.) 1994a [1988]. *What is an animal?* London: Unwin Hyman.

Ingold, T. 1994b. From trust to domination: an alternative history of human–animal relations. In: A. Manning and J. Serpell (eds) *Animals and human society: changing perspectives* pp. 1–22. New York: Routledge.

Ingold, T. 2000. *The perception of the environment: essays in livelihood, dwelling and skill*. London: Routledge.

Ingold, T. 2007. The trouble with 'evolutionary biology'. *Anthropology Today* 23(2): 13–17.

Ingold, T. 2010. Anthropology comes to life. *General Anthropology* 17(1): 1–4.

Ingold, T. 2011a. Footprints through the weather-world: walking, breathing, knowing. In: T.H.J. Marchand (ed.) *Making knowledge: explorations of the indissoluble relation between mind, body and environment*. London: John Wiley and Sons.

Ingold, T. 2011b. *Being alive: essays on movement, knowledge and description*. London: Routledge.

Isack, H.A. and Reyer, H.U. 1989. Honeyguides and honey gatherers: interspecific communication in a symbiotic relationship. *Science* 243: 1343–1346.

Itani, J. and Nishimura, A. 1973. The study of infra-human culture in Japan. In: E.W. Menzel Jr (ed.) *Symposia of the Fourth International Congress of Primatology*, vol. 1, pp. 26–60. Basel: Karger.

Iwasaki-Goodman, M. and Freeman, M.M.R. (1996) Social and cultural significance of whaling in contemporary Japan: a case study of small-type coastal whaling. In: E.S. Burch Jr and L.J. Ellanna (eds) *Key issues in hunter-gatherer research*. Oxford: Berg.

Izar, P., Verderane, M.P., Visalberghi, E., Ottoni, E.B., Gomes de Oliveira, M., Shirley, J. et al. 2006. Cross-genus adoption of a marmoset (*Callithrix jacchus*) by wild capuchin monkeys (*Cebus libidinosus*): case report. *American Journal of Primatology* 68(7): 692–700.

Jackson, M. 1998. *Minima ethnographica: intersubjectivity and the anthropological project*. London: University of Chicago Press.

Janik, V.M., Sayigh, L.S. and Wells, R.S. 2006. Signature whistle shape conveys identity information to bottlenose dolphins. *PNAS* 103(21): 8293–8297.

Jha, D.N. 2002. *The myth of the holy cow*. London: Verso.

Jones, O. 2003. 'The restraint of beasts': rurality, animality, Actor Network Theory and dwelling. In: Cloke, P. (ed.) *Country visions*, pp. 283–303. Harlow: Pearson.

Josephides, L. 1985. *The production of inequality: gender and exchange among the Kewa*. London: Tavistock.

Joubert, D. and Joubert, B. 2009. *Eye of the leopard*. New York: Rizzoli.

Kalland, A. 2009. *Unveiling the whale: discourses on whales and whaling.* Studies in Environmental Anthropology and Ethnobiology Series. New York: Berghahn Books.

Kalof, L. and Fitzgerald, A. (eds) 2007. *The animals reader: the essential classic and contemporary writings.* Oxford: Berg.

Kant, I. 1930. *Lectures on ethics.* London: Methuen.

Katz, S.H. 1987. *Food and biocultural evolution: a model for the investigation of modern nutritional problems.* New York: A.R. Liss.

Kawai, M. 1965. On the newly acquired pre-cultural behavior of the natural troop of Japanese monkeys on Koshima Islet. *Primates* 6: 1–30.

Kean, H. 1998. *Animal rights. political and social change in Britain since 1800.* London: Reaktion.

Keesing, R.M. and Strathern, A. 1998. *Cultural anthropology: a contemporary perspective.* Fort Worth, TX: Harcourt Brace.

Keller, L. and Surette, M.G. 2006. Communication in bacteria: an ecological and evolutionary perspective. *Nature Reviews Microbiology* 4(4): 249–258.

Kellett, P. 2009. Advocacy in anthropology: active engagement or passive scholarship? *Durham Anthropology Journal* 16(1): 22–31.

Kennedy, J.S. 1992. *The new anthropomorphism.* Cambridge: Cambridge University Press.

Kinsey, A.C., Pomeroy, W.B. and Martin, C.E. 1998 [1948]. *Sexual behaviour in the human male.* Bloomington: Indiana University Press.

Kipling, R. 1899. *The white man's burden: a poem.* London: Doubleday.

Kirksey, E. and Helmreich, S. 2010a. The emergence of multispecies ethnography. *Cultural Anthropology* 25: 545–576.

Kirksey, E. and Helmreich, S. (eds) 2010b. *The emergence of multispecies ethnography – special issue. Cultural Anthropology* 25.

Kirtsoglou, E. 2005. *For the love of women.* London: Routledge.

Klein, N., Fröhlich, F. and Krief, S. 2008. Geophagy: soil consumption enhances the bioactivities of plants eaten by chimpanzees. *Naturwissenschaften* 95(4): 325–331.

Knight, J. (ed.) 2000a. *Natural enemies: people–wildlife conflicts in anthropological perspective.* London: Routledge.

Knight, J. 2000b. Culling demons: the problem of bears in Japan. In: J. Knight (ed.) *Natural enemies: people–wildlife conflicts in anthropological perspective*, pp. 145–169. London: Routledge.

Knight, J. 2005. Feeding Mr Monkey: cross-species food exchange in Japanese monkey parks. In J. Knight (ed.) *Animals in person: cultural perspectives on human–animal intimacies*, pp. 231–253. Oxford: Berg.

Knight, J. 2006. Monkey Mountain as a megazoo: analyzing the naturalistic claims of 'wild monkey parks' in Japan. *Society & Animals* 14(3): 245–264.

Knight, J. 2011. *Herding monkeys to paradise.* London: Brill.

Knight, S., Vrij, A., Cherryman, J. and Nunkoosing, K. 2004. Attitudes towards animal use and belief in animal mind. *Anthrozoös* 17(1): 42–62.

Köhler, W. 1925. *The mentality of apes.* London: Paul, Trench, Trubner & Co.

Köhler, W. 1928. *Gestalt psychology.* New York: H. Liveright.

Kohn, E. 2007. How dogs dream: Amazonian natures and the politics of trans-species engagement. *American Ethnologist* 34: 3–24.

Kramsch, C.J. 2008. *Language and culture.* Oxford: Oxford University Press.

Kroeber, A.L. 1948 [1923]. *Anthropology: race, language, culture, psychology, pre-history.* New York: Harcourt Brace.

Kruger, K.A., Trachtenberg, S.W. and Serpell, J.A. 2004. *Animals help humans heal? Animal-assisted interventions in adolescent mental health*. Center for the Interaction of Animals and Society, University of Pennsylvania School of Veterinary Medicine.

Krutzen, M., Mann, J., Heithaus, M.R., Connor, R.C., Bejder, L. and Sherwin, W.B. 2005. Cultural transmission of tool use in bottlenose dolphins. *PNAS* 102(25): 8939–8943.

Kruuk, H. 2002. *Hunter and hunted: relationships between carnivores and people*. Cambridge: Cambridge University Press.

Kuchler, S. and Miller, D. 2005. *Clothing as material culture*. Oxford: Berg.

Kuhl, G. 2011. Human–sled dog relations: what can we learn from the stories and experiences of mushers? *Society & Animals* 19(1): 22–37.

Kuper, A. 1999. *Culture: the anthropologist's account*. Cambridge, MA: Harvard University Press.

Kwon, H. 1998. The saddle and the sledge: hunting as comparative narrative in Siberia and beyond. *Journal of the Royal Anthropological Institute* 4(1): 115–127.

Laidlaw, J. 2002. For an anthropology of ethics and freedom. *Journal of the Royal Anthropological Institute* 8(2): 311–332.

Langford, D.J., Crager, S.E., Shehzad, Z., Smith, S.B., Sotocinal, S.G., Levenstadt, J.S. et al. 2006. Social modulation of pain as evidence for empathy in mice. *Science* 312(5782): 1967–1970.

Lansbury, C. 2007. The Brown Dog Riots of 1907. In: L. Kalof and A. Fitzgerald (eds) *The animals reader: the essential classic and contemporary writings*, pp. 307–321. Oxford: Berg.

Larrère, C. and Larrère, R. 2000. Animal rearing as a contract? *Journal of Agricultural and Environmental Ethics* 12(1): 51–55.

Laska, M., Bauer, V. and Salazar, L.T. 2007. Self-anointing behavior in free-ranging spider monkeys (*Ateles geoffroyi*) in Mexico. *Primates* 48(2):160–163.

Latimer, J. and Birke, L. 2009. Natural relations: horses, knowledge, technology. *Sociological Review* 57(1): 1–27.

Latour, B. 1997. On actor-network theory: a few clarifications. *Soziale Welt* 47(4): 369–381.

Latour, B. 1999. On recalling ANT. In: J. Law and J. Hassard (eds) *Actor Network Theory and after*. Oxford: Blackwell Publishers.

Laughlin, W.S. (1968). Hunting: An integrating biobehavior system and its evolutionary importance. In: R.B. Lee and I. Devore (eds) *Man the hunter*, pp. 304–320. Chicago: Aldine.

Laule, G., Bloomsmith, M.A. and Schapiro, S.J. 2003. The use of positive reinforcement training techniques to enhance the care, management, and welfare of primates in the laboratory. *Journal of Applied Animal Welfare Science* 6(3): 163–173.

Lawrence, E.A. 1993. The symbolic role of animals in the Plains Indian Sun Dance. *Society & Animals* 1(1): 17–37.

Layton, R. 1996. Advocacy is a personal commitment for anthropologists, not an institutional imperative for anthropology. In: P. Wade (ed.) *Advocacy in anthropology*. GDAT Debate No. 7. Manchester: Manchester University Press.

Leach, E.R. 1964. *Anthropological aspects of language: animal categories and verbal abuse*. Cambridge, MA: MIT Press.

Leach, H.M. 2003. Human domestication reconsidered. *Current Anthropology* 44(3): 349–368.

Leach, H.M. 2007. Selection and the unforeseen consequences of domestication. In: R. Cassidy and M. Mullin (eds) *Where the wild things are now: domestication reconsidered*, pp. 71–99. New York: Berg.

Leca, J.B., Gunst, N. and Huffman, M.A. 2007. Japanese macaque cultures: Inter- and intra-troop behavioural variability of stone handling patterns across 10 troops. *Behaviour* 144(3): 251–282.

Lee, P.C. 2010a. Sharing space: can ethnoprimatology contribute to the survival of nonhuman primates in human-dominated globalized landscapes? *American Journal of Primatology* 72: 925–931.

Lee, P.C. 2010b. Problem animals or problem people? Ethics, politics and practice or conflict between community perspectives and fieldwork on conservation. In: J. MacClancy and A. Fuentes (eds) *Centralizing fieldwork: critical perspectives from primatology, biological and social anthropology*. Oxford: Berghahn.

Lee, P.C. and Priston, N.E.C. 2005. Human attitudes to primates: perceptions of pests, conflict and consequences for primate conservation. In: J.D. Patterson and J. Wallace (eds) *Primate–human interaction and conservation*, pp. 1–20. Alberta: American Society of Primatologist Publications.

Lee, R.B. 1979. *The !Kung San: men, women, and work in a foraging society.* Cambridge: Cambridge University Press.

Lévi-Strauss, C. 1963. *Totemism.* Boston, MA: Beacon Press.

Lévi-Strauss, C. 1966 [1962]. *The savage mind.* London: Weidenfeld and Nicolson.

Lévi-Strauss, C. 1985 [1983]. *The view from afar*, trans. J. Neugroschel and P. Hoss. New York: Basic Books.

Lévy-Bruhl, L. 1923. *Primitive mentality.* London: George Allen & Unwin.

Liebenberg, L. 2006. Persistence hunting by modern hunter-gatherers. *Current Anthropology* 47: 1017–1026.

Lieberman, P. 1994. The origins and evolution of language. In: T. Ingold, (ed.) *Companion Encyclopedia of Anthropology*, pp. 108–132. London: Routledge.

Lindquist, G. 2000. The wolf, the Saami and the urban shaman: predator symbolism in Sweden. In: J. Knight (ed.) *Natural enemies: people–wildlife conflicts in anthropological perspective*, pp. 170–188. London: Routledge.

Lindquist, J. 2006. Deep pockets: notes on the Indonesian cockfight in a globalising world. *IIAS Newsletter* 42(7).

Lipovetsky, G. 1994. *The empire of fashion: dressing modern democracy.* Princeton, NJ: Princeton University Press.

Lizarralde, M. 2002. Ethnoecology of monkeys among the Bari of Venezuela: perception, use and conservation. In: A. Fuentes and L.D. Wolfe (eds) *Primates face to face: the conservation implications of human–nonhuman primate interconnections*, pp. 85–100. Cambridge: Cambridge University Press.

Lupton, D. (2006) *Risk.* London: Routledge.

Lycett, S.J., Collard, M. and McGrew, W.C. 2007. Phylogenetic analyses of behavior support existence of culture among wild chimpanzees. *PNAS* 104(45): 17588–17592.

Lyng, S. (ed.) (2005) *Edgework: the sociology of risk-taking.* Oxford: Berg.

MacClancy, J. 2010. Popularizing fieldwork: examples from primatology and biological anthropology. In: J. MacClancy and A. Fuentes (eds) *Centralizing fieldwork: critical perspectives from primatology, biological and social anthropology*. Oxford: Berghahn.

MacClancy, J. and Fuentes A. (eds) *Centralizing fieldwork: critical perspectives from primatology, biological and social anthropology*. Oxford: Berghahn.

MacCormack, C. and Strathern, M. 1980. *Nature, culture and gender.* Cambridge: Cambridge University Press.

Macdonald, S. 1997. *Inside European identities: ethnography in Western Europe.* Oxford: Berg.

Malik, K. 2002. *Do humans own culture?* Debate proceedings, Royal Society and British Academy, October.

Malinowski, B. 1922. *Argonauts of the Western Pacific.* London: Routledge.

Malinowski, B. 1967. *A diary in the strict sense of the term.* London: Routledge & Kegan Paul.

Malinowski, B. 1974. *Magic, science and religion.* London: Souvenir Press.

Mandel, R. 1989. Turkish headscarves and the 'foreigner problem': constructing difference through emblems of identity. *New German Critique* 16(1): 27–46.

Mandel, R. 1990. Shifting centres and emerging identities: Turkey and Germany in the lives of *Gastarbeiter.* In: D.F. Eickelman and J.P. Piscatori (eds) *Muslim travellers: pilgrimage, migration, and the religious imagination,* pp. 153–172. London: Routledge.

Mandel, R. 1994. Fortress Europe and the foreigners within: Germany's Turks. In: V. Goddard, J. Llobera and C. Shaw (eds) *The anthropology of Europe.* Oxford: Berg.

Manser, M.B. 2001. The acoustic structure of suricates' alarm calls varies with predator type and the level of response urgency. *Proceedings of the Royal Society of London B* 1483: 2315–2324.

Marchal, V. and Hill, C. 2009. Primate crop-raiding: a study of local perceptions in four villages in north Sumatra, Indonesia. *Primate Conservation* 24: 107–116.

Marcus, G.E. and Fischer, M.M.J. 1999. *Anthropology as cultural critique: an experimental moment in the human sciences.* Chicago: University of Chicago Press.

Marais, E. 1990. *The soul of the ape.* Harmondsworth: Penguin.

Marino, L., Connor, R.C., Fordyce, R.E., Herman, L.M., Hof, P.R., Lefebvre, L. et al. 2007. Cetaceans have complex brains for complex cognition. *PLoS Biology* 5(5): e139.

Marks, J. 2003. *What it means to be 98% chimpanzee: apes, people and their genes.* Berkeley: University of California Press.

Marler, P. and Evans, C. 1996. Bird calls: just emotional displays or something more? *Ibis* 138(1): 26–33.

Marshall-Thomas, E. 2010. *The hidden life of dogs.* New York: Mariner Books.

Martello, M.L. 2004. Negotiating global nature and local culture: the case of Makah whaling. In: S. Jassanoff and M.L. Martello (eds) *Earthly politics: local and global in environmental governance.* Cambridge, MA: MIT Press.

Martin, P.S. 2007. *Twilight of the mammoths: ice age extinctions and the rewilding of America.* Berkeley: University of California Press.

Marvin, G. 1984. The cockfight in Andalusia, Spain: images of the truly male. *Anthropological Quarterly* 57(2): 60–70.

Marvin, G. 1986. Honour, integrity and the problem of violence in the Spanish bullfight. In: D. Riches (ed.) *The anthropology of violence,* pp. 118–135. Oxford: Blackwell.

Marvin, G. 1988. *Bullfight.* Oxford: Blackwell.

Marvin, G. 2000. The problem of foxes: legitimate and illegitimate killing in the English countryside. In: J. Knight (ed.) *Natural enemies: people–wildlife conflicts in anthropological perspective,* pp. 189–212. London: Routledge.

Marvin, G. 2001. Cultured killers: creating and representing foxhounds. *Society & Animals* 9(3): 273–292.

Marvin, G. 2002. Unspeakability, inedibility and structure of pursuit in the English foxhunt. In: N. Rothfels (ed.) *Representing animals*. Bloomington: Indiana University Press.

Marvin, G. 2003. A passionate pursuit: foxhunting as performance. *Sociological Review* 52(2): 46–60.

Marvin, G. 2005a. Disciplined affection: the making of a pack of foxhounds. In J. Knight (ed.) *Animals in person: cultural perspectives on human–animal intimacies*, pp. 61–77. London: Berg.

Marvin, G. 2005b. Sensing nature: encountering the world in hunting. *Etnofoor* 18(1): 15–26.

Marvin, G. 2006. Wild killing: contesting the animal in hunting. In: Animal Studies Group, *Killing animals*, pp. 10–29. Chicago: University of Illinois Press.

Masson, J.M. 1998. *Dogs never lie about love*. New York: Three Rivers Press.

Mathias-Mundy, E. and McCorkle C.M. 1989. *Ethnoveterinary medicine: an annotated bibliography*. Bibliographies in Technology and Social Change. Technology and Social Change Program, Series No. 6, Iowa State University.

Matsuzawa, T. 1994. Field experiments on use of stone tools by chimpanzees in the wild. In: R.W. Wrangham, W.C. McGrew, F.B.M. de Waal and P. G. Heltne (eds) *Chimpanzee cultures*, pp. 351–370. Cambridge, MA: Harvard University Press.

Mauss, M. 2001 [1954]. *The gift: forms and functions of exchange in archaic societies*. London: Routledge.

McComb, K., Baker, L. and Moss, C. 2006. African elephants show high levels of interest in the skulls and ivory of their own species. *Biology Letters* 2(1): 26–28.

McConnell, P.B. and Bayliss, J.R. 1985. Interspecific communication in cooperative herding: acoustic and visual signals from human shepherds and herding dogs. *Zeitschrift für Tierpsychologie* 67(1–4): 302–328.

McCorkle, C.M. 1986. An introduction to ethnoveterinary research and development. *Journal of Ethnobiology* 6(1): 129–149.

McGrew, W.C. 1992. *Chimpanzee material culture: implications for human evolution*. Cambridge: Cambridge University Press.

McGrew, W.C. 1998. Culture in non-human primates? *Annual Review of Anthropology* 27: 301–328.

McGrew, W.C. 2007. New wine in new bottles: prospects and pitfalls of cultural primatology. *Journal of Anthropological Research* 63(2): 167–183.

McKay, R. 2006. BSE, hysteria and the representation of animal death: Deborah Levy's *Diary of a Steak*. In: Animal Studies Group, *Killing animals*. Chicago: University of Illinois Press.

McMahan, E.A. 1983. Bugs angle for termites. *Natural History* 92(5): 40–47.

McMichael A., Powles, J.W., Butler, C.D. and Uauy, R. 2007. Food, livestock production, energy, climate change, and health. *Lancet* 370: 1253–1263.

McNeill, W.H. 1998 [1976]. *Plagues and peoples*. New York: Anchor Books.

McNicholas, J., Gilbey, A., Rennie, A., Ahmedzai, S., Dono, J.-A. and Ormerod, E. 2005. Pet ownership and human health: a brief review of evidence and issues. *British Medical Journal* 7527: 1252–1253.

Mead, G.H. 1934. *Mind, self, and society: from the standpoint of a social behaviorist*. London: Chicago University Press.

Menache, S. 1997. Dogs: God's worst enemies? *Society & Animals* 5(1): 23–44.

Menache, S. 1998. Dogs and human beings: a story of friendship. *Society & Animals* 6(1): 67–86.

Mercader, J., Panger, M. and Boesch, C. 2002. Excavation of a chimpanzee stone tool site in the African rainforest. *Science* 5572: 1452–1455.

Merleau-Ponty, M. 1962. *Phenomenology of perception.* New York: Humanities Press.

Mesoudi, A., Whiten, A. and Laland, K.N. 2006. Towards a unified science of cultural evolution. *Behavioral and Brain Sciences* 29(4): 329–347.

Midgley, M. 1994a. Beasts, brutes and monsters. In: T. Ingold (ed.) *What is an animal?* London: Routledge.

Midgley, M. 1994b. Bridge-building at last. In: A. Manning and J. Serpell (eds) *Animals and human society: changing perspectives*, pp. 188–194. London: Routledge.

Miklósi, Á., Polgárdi, R., Topál, J. and Csányi, V. 2000. Intentional behaviour in dog–human communication: an experimental analysis of 'showing' behaviour in the dog. *Animal Cognition* 3(3): 159–166.

Miller, D. 1998. *A theory of shopping.* Cambridge: Polity Press.

Miller, D. 2001. *Car cultures.* Oxford: Berg.

Miller, D. 2008. *The comfort of things.* Cambridge: Polity Press.

Milton, K. 1993. Diet and primate evolution. *Scientific American* August: 86–93.

Milton, K. 1996. *Environmentalism and cultural theory: exploring the role of anthropology in environmental discourse.* New York: Routledge.

Milton, K. 2000. Ducks out of water: nature conservation as boundary maintenance. In: J. Knight (ed.) *Natural enemies: people–wildlife conflicts in anthropological perspective.* Oxford: Berg.

Milton, K. 2002. *Loving nature: towards an ecology of emotion.* London: Routledge.

Milton, K. 2003. Comment. *Anthropology Today* 19: 19–20.

Milton, K. 2005. Anthropomorphism or egomorphism? The perception of non-human persons by human ones. In J. Knight (ed.) *Animals in person: cultural perspectives on human–animal intimacies*, pp. 255–271. New York: Berg.

Milton, Kay 2009. Science and personhood on the farm: cattle in crisis in the UK. *Ethnologie Française* 39(1): 69–78.

Montgomery, H. 2008. *An introduction to childhood: anthropological perspectives on children's lives.* London: Wiley-Blackwell.

Moore, R.S. 1994. Metaphors of encroachment: hunting for wolves on a central Greek mountain. *Anthropological Quarterly* 67(2): 81–88.

Morales, E. 1995. *The guinea pig: healing, food, and ritual in the Andes.* Tucson: University of Arizona Press.

Morris, B. 1998. *The Power of Animals: an Ethnography.* Oxford: Berg.

Morris, B. 2000. Wildlife depredations in Malawi: the historical dimension. In: J. Knight (ed.) *Natural enemies: people–wildlife conflicts in anthropological perspective*, pp. 36–49. London: Routledge.

Moss, C.J. 1988. *Elephant memories.* New York: William Morrow.

Muehlenbein, M.P. and Ancrenaz, M. 2009. Minimizing pathogen transmission at primate ecotourism destinations: the need for input from travel medicine. *Journal of Travel Medicine Volume* 16(4): 229–232.

Muehlenbein, M.P., Martinez, L.A., Lemke, A.A., Ambu, L., Nathan, S., Alsisto, S. et al. 2010. Unhealthy travelers present challenges to sustainable primate ecotourism. *Travel Medicine and Infectious Disease* 8(3): 169–171.

Mullin, M.H. 1999. Mirrors and windows: sociocultural studies of human–animal relationships. *Annual Review of Anthropology* 28(1): 201–224.

Mullin, M.H. 2002. Animals and anthropology. *Society & Animals* 10(4): 387–394.

Nadasdy, P. 2003. *Hunters and bureaucrats: power, knowledge, and aboriginal–state relations in the southwest Yukon.* Vancouver: University of British Columbia Press.

Nadasdy, P. 2005. Transcending the debate over the ecologically noble Indian: indigenous peoples and environmentalism. *Ethnohistory* 52(2): 291–331.

Nadasdy, P. 2007. The gift in the animal: the ontology of hunting and human–animal sociality. *American Ethnologist* 34(1): 25–43.

Nader, L. 1972. Up the anthropologist – perspectives gained from studying up. In: D.H. Hymes (ed.) *Reinventing anthropology.* New York: Pantheon Books.

Nader, L. 2001. Anthropology! Distinguished lecture – 2000. *American Anthropologist* 103(3): 609–620.

Naderi, S., Miklósi, Á., Dóka, A. and Csányi, V. 2001. Co-operative interactions between blind persons and their dogs. *Applied Animal Behaviour Science* 74(1): 59–80.

Nahallage, C.A.D. and Huffman, M.A. 2007. Acquisition and development of stone handling behavior in infant Japanese macaques. *Behaviour* 144(10): 1193–1215.

Nast, H. 2006. Critical pet studies? *Antipode* 38(5): 894–906.

Needham, R. 1963. *Durkheim/Mauss: primitive classification.* Chicago: University of Chicago Press.

Newton, M. 2002. *Savage girls and wild boys: a history of feral children.* London: Faber & Faber.

Nihei, Y. and Higuchi, H. 2001. When and where did crows learn to use automobiles as nutcrackers? *Tohoku Psychologica Folia* 60: 93–97.

Norman, E.S. 2009. *Luna/Tsu-xiit the 'whale': governance across (political and cultural) borders.* Northwest Indian College. Available at: https://www.evergreen.edu/tribal/docs/normanluna.pdf

Norris, K.S. 1991. *Dolphin days: the life and times of the spinner dolphin.* New York: Avon Books.

Noser, R. and Byrne, R.W. 2007. Mental maps in chacma baboons (*Papio ursinus*): using inter-group encounters as a natural experiment. *Animal Cognition* 10(3): 331–340.

Noske, B. 1989. *Humans and other animals: beyond the boundaries of anthropology.* London: Pluto Press.

Noske, B. 1997. *Beyond boundaries: humans and animals.* London: Black Rose.

Noss, A.J. and Hewlett, B.S. 2001. The contexts of female hunting in Central Africa. *American Anthropologist* 103(4): 1024–1040.

Nyanganji, G., Fowler, A., McNamara, A. and Sommer, V. 2011. Monkeys and apes as animals and humans: ethno-primatology in Nigeria's Taraba region. *Primates of Gashaka: Developments in Primatology: Progress and Prospects* 35: 101–134.

Obeyesekere, G. 2005. *Cannibal talk: the man-eating myth and human sacrifice in the south seas.* Berkeley: University of California Press.

O'Connor, T.P. 1997. Working at relationships: another look at animal domestication. *Antiquity* 71(271): 149–156.

Ólafsson, H. 1989. The hunter and the animal. In: E.P. Durrenberger and G. Pálsson (eds) *The Anthropology of Iceland*, pp. 39–49. Iowa: University of Iowa Press.

Ortega y Gasset, J. 1972. *Meditations on hunting.* New York: Scribner.

Ouattara, K., Lemasson, A. and Zuberbühler K. 2009. Campbell's monkeys use affixation to alter call meaning. *PLoS One* 4(11): e7808.

Pagden, A. 1982. *The fall of natural man: the American Indian and the origins of comparative ethnology.* Cambridge: Cambridge University Press.

Palmer, C. 1997. The idea of the domesticated animal contract. *Environmental Values* 6(4): 411–426.

Palmer, C. 2006. Killing animals in animal shelters. In: Animal Studies Group (ed.) *Killing animals.* Urbana: University of Illinois Press.

Pálsson, G. 1996. Human–environmental relations. In: P. Descola and G. Pálsson (eds) *Nature and society: anthropological perspectives*, pp. 65–81. London: Routledge.

Papastavrou, V. 1996. Sustainable use of whales: whaling or whale watching? In: V. Taylor and N. Dunstone (eds) 1996. *The exploitation of mammal populations.* London: Chapman & Hall.

Pardo, I. and Prato, G. 2005. The fox-hunting debate in the United Kingdom: a puritan legacy? *Human Ecology Review* 12(2): 143–155.

Patronek, G. 2008. Hoarding of animals: an under-recognised public health problem in a difficult-to-study population. In C.P. Flynn (ed.) *Social creatures: a human and animal studies reader*, pp. 220–230. New York: Lantern Books.

Patterson, F.G. and Cohn, R.H. 1990. Language acquisition by a lowland gorilla: Koko's first ten years of vocabulary development. *Word* 41(3): 97–143.

Patton, P. 2003. Language, power and the training of horses. In: C. Wolfe (ed.) *Zootologies: the question of the animal*, pp. 83–100. Minneapolis: University of Minnesota Press.

Paul, E.S. and Serpell, J.A. 1993. Childhood pet keeping and humane attitudes in young adulthood. *Animal Welfare* 2(4): 321–337.

Pavelka, M.S. 2003. Resistance to the cross-species perspective in anthropology. In: A. Fuentes and L.D. Wolfe (eds) *Primates face to face: the conservation implications of human–nonhuman primate interconnections*, pp. 25–44. Cambridge: Cambridge University Press.

Peace, A. 2002. The cull of the wild: dingoes, development and death in an Australian tourist location. *Anthropology Today* 18(5): 14–19.

Peace, A. 2005. Loving Leviathan: the discourse of whale-watching in Australian ecotourism. In: J. Knight (ed.) *Animals in person: cultural perspectives on human–animal intimacy*, pp. 191–210. Oxford: Berg.

Peace, A. 2008. Meat in the genes. *Anthropology Today* 24(3): 5–10.

Peace, A. 2010. The whaling war: conflicting cultural perspectives. *Anthropology Today* 26: 5–9.

Pepperberg, I.M. 2002. *The Alex studies: cognitive and communicative abilities of grey parrots.* London: Harvard University Press.

Perry, S.E. 2006. What cultural primatology can tell anthropologists about the evolution of culture. *Annual Review of Anthropology* 35: 171–208.

Peterson, D. and Ammann, K. 2003. *Eating apes.* California Studies in Food and Culture). Berkeley: University of California Press.

Petto, A.J. and Russell, K.D. 1998. Practicing anthropology on the frontiers of humanity: interspecies applied anthropology. *Practicing Anthropology* 20(2): 26–29.

Pfungst, O. 1911. *Clever Hans (the horse of Mr. Von Osten): a contribution to experimental animal and human psychology.* New York: Holt, Rinehart & Winston.

Philo, C. and Wilbert, C. 2000. *Animal spaces, beastly places: new geographies of human–animal relations*. London: Routledge.

Pieterse, J.N. 1992. *White on black: images of Africa and blacks in Western popular culture*. London: Yale University Press.

Pink, S. 1996. Breasts in the bullring: female physiology, female bullfighters and competing femininities. *Body & Society* 2(1): 45–64.

Pink, S. 1997. *Women and bullfighting: gender, sex and the consumption of tradition*. Oxford: Berg.

Plutarch. 2004. *Essays and miscellanies: the complete works of Plutarch*, vol. 3. Whitefish, MT: Kessinger Publishing.

Poiani, A.F. and Dixson, A.F. 2010. *Animal homosexuality: a biosocial perspective*. Cambridge: Cambridge University Press.

Pongrácz, P., Molnar, C. and Miklósi, Á. 2006. Acoustic parameters of dog barks carry emotional information for humans. *Applied Animal Behaviour Science* 100(3): 228–240.

Pongrácz, P., Molnar, C., Miklósi, Á. and Csányi, V. 2005. Human listeners are able to classify dog (*Canis familiaris*) barks recorded in different situations. *Journal of Comparative Psychology* 119(2): 136–144.

Popovich, D.G., Jenkins, D.J.A., Kendall, C.W.C., Dierenfeld, E.S., Carroll, R.W., Tariq, N. et al. 1997. The western lowland gorilla diet has implications for the health of humans and other hominoids. *Journal of Nutrition* 127(10): 2000–2005.

Rabinow, P. 1986. Representations are social facts: modernity and post-modernity in anthropology. In: J. Clifford and G. Marcus (eds) *Writing culture: the poetics and politics of ethnography*. Berkeley: University of California Press.

Radcliffe-Brown, A.R. 1951. The comparative method in social anthropology. *Journal of the Royal Anthropological Institute* 81(1/2): 15–22.

Radcliffe-Brown, A.R. 1952. *Structure and function in primitive society, essays and addresses*. Glencoe, IL: Free Press.

Rappaport, R.A. 1967. Ritual regulation of environmental relations among a New Guinea people. *Ethnology* 6(1): 17–30.

Rappaport, R.A. 1968. *Pigs for the ancestors*. New Haven, CT: Yale University Press.

Rapport, N. 2002. *British subjects: an anthropology of Britain*. Oxford: Berg.

Rapport, N. 2007. An outline for cosmopolitan study, for reclaiming the human through introspection. *Current Anthropology* 48: 257–283.

Rapport, N. and Stade, R. 2007. A cosmopolitan turn – or return? *Social Anthropology* 15(2): 223–235.

Rees, A. 2007. Reflections on the field – primatology, popular science and the politics of personhood. *Social Studies of Science* 37: 881–907.

Reinhardt, V., Abney, D., Conlee, K., Cunneen, M., Down, N., Lang, T. et al. 2006. Human–animal relationship in the research lab: a discussion by the Laboratory Animal Refinement and Enrichment Forum. *Animal Technology and Welfare* 5(2): 95–98.

Richards, P. 1993. Natural symbols and natural history: chimpanzees, elephants and experiments in Mende thought. In: K. Milton (ed.) *Environmentalism: the view from anthropology*, ASA Monographs 32. London: Routledge.

Richards, P. 1995. Local understandings of primates and evolution: some Mende beliefs. In: T. Corbey and B. Theynissen (eds) *Ape, man, apeman: changing views since 1600*. Leiden: Dept of Prehistory, Leiden University.

Richards, P. 2000. Chimpanzees as political animals in Sierra Leone. In: J. Knight (ed.) *Natural enemies: people–wildlife conflicts in anthropological perspective*, pp. 78–103. London: Routledge.

Riley, E.P. 2006. Ethnoprimatology: toward reconciliation of biological and cultural anthropology. *Ecological and Environmental Anthropology* 2: 1–10.

Riley, E.P. 2010. The importance of human–macaque folklore for conservation in Lore Lindu National Park, Sulawesi, Indonesia. *Oryx* 44(2): 235–240.

Riley, E.P. and Priston, N.E.C. 2010. Macaques in farms and folklore: exploring the human–nonhuman primate interface in Sulawesi, Indonesia. *American Journal of Primatology* 72: 848–854.

Ritvo, H. 2004. Animal planet. *Environmental History* 9(2): 204–220.

Rivas, J. and Burghardt, G.M. 2002. Crotalomorphism: a metaphor for understanding anthropomorphism by omission. In: M. Bekoff, C. Allen and G.M. Burghardt (eds) *The cognitive animal: experimental and theoretical perspectives on animal cognition*, pp. 9–17. Cambridge, MA: MIT Press.

Roberts, M. 2008. *The man who listens to horses: the story of a real-life horse whisperer*. London: Random House.

Rogers, L.J. and Kaplan, G.T. 2004. *Comparative vertebrate cognition: are primates superior to non-primates?*Dordrecht: Kluwer Academic/Plenum.

Romanoff, S. 1983. Women as hunters among the matses of the Peruvian Amazon. *Human Ecology* 11(3): 339–343.

Rosaldo, M.Z. 1980. *Knowledge and passion: Ilongot notions of self and social life*. Cambridge: Cambridge University Press.

Rosaldo, R. 1989. Imperialist nostalgia. *Representations* 26: 107–122.

Rosaldo, R. 2004. Grief and a headhunter's rage. In: A.C.G.M. Robben (ed.) *Death, mourning, and burial: a cross-cultural reader*. Malden, MA: Wiley-Blackwell.

Rosengren, D. 2006. Transdimensional relations: on human–spirit interaction in the Amazon. *Journal of the Royal Anthropological Institute* 12(4): 803–816.

Rowlands, M. 2008. *The philosopher and the wolf*. London: Granta.

Rowlands, M. 2009. *Animal rights: moral theory and practice*. London: Palgrave Macmillan.

Ruffolo, D. 2009. *Post-queer politics*. Farnham: Ashgate.

Russell, C.L. 1995. The social construction of orangutans: an ecotourist experience. *Society & Animals* 3(2): 151–170.

Russell, C.L. and Ankenman, M.J. 1996. Orangutans as photographic collectibles: ecotourism and the commodification of nature. *Tourism Recreation Research* 21(1): 71–78.

Russell, N. 2007. The domestication of anthropology. In: R. Cassidy and M.H. Mullin (eds) *Where the wild things are now: domestication reconsidered*, pp. 27–48. Oxford: Berg.

Ryan, R.P. and Dow, J.M. 2008. Diffusible signals and interspecies communication in bacteria. *Microbiology* 154: 1845–1858.

Ryder, R.D. 2000. *Animal revolution: changing attitudes toward speciesism*. Oxford: Berg.

Sahlins, M.D. 1976. *Culture and practical reason*. Chicago: University of Chicago Press.

Sahlins, M.D. 2004 [1972]. *Stone age economics*. London: Routledge.

Said, E. 1978. *Orientalism*. New York: Vintage.

Sanders, C.R. 1993. Understanding dogs: caretakers' attributions of mindedness in canine/human relationships. *Journal of Contemporary Ethnography* 22(2): 205–226.

Sanders, C.R. 2003. Actions speak louder than words: close relationships between humans and nonhuman animals. *Symbolic Interaction* 26(3): 405–426.

Sanders, C.R. and Arluke, A. 1993. If lions could speak: investigating the animal–human relationship and the perspectives of nonhuman others. *Sociological Quarterly* 34(3): 377–390.

Sapolsky, R.M. 1992. *Stress, the aging brain, and the mechanisms of neuron death*. Cambridge, MA: MIT Press.

Sapolsky, R.M. 2002. *A primate's memoir: love, death and baboons in East Africa*. New York: Vintage.

Sapolsky, R.M. 2006. Social culture among non-human primates. *Current Anthropology* 47(4): 641–656.

Sartre, J.-P. 1966. *Words*. London: Hamilton.

Saunders, N.J. 1994. Tezcatlipoca: jaguar metaphors in the Aztec mirror of nature. In: R. Willis (ed.) *Signifying animals: human meaning in the natural world*. London: Unwin Hyman.

Savage-Rumbaugh, S. and Lewin, R. 1994. *Kanzi: the ape at the brink of the human mind*. New York: Wiley.

Savage-Rumbaugh, S., Wamba, K., Wamba, P. and Wamba, N. 2007. Welfare of apes in captive environments: comments on, and by, a specific group of apes. *Journal of Applied Animal Welfare Science* 10(1): 7–19.

Sax, B. 2003. *Crow*. London: Reaktion.

Schaller, G.B. 2007. *A naturalist and other beasts: Tales from a life in the field*. San Francisco: Sierra Club Books.

Schapiro, S.J., Bloomsmith, M.A. and Laule, G..E. 2003. Positive reinforcement training as a technique to alter nonhuman primate behavior: quantitative assessments of effectiveness. Journal of Applied Animal Welfare 6(3): 175–187.

Scheper-Hughes, N. 1995. The primacy of the ethical: propositions for a militant anthropology. *Current Anthropologist* 36(3): 409–440.

Schmidt, B. and Schröder, I. (eds) 2001. *Anthropology of violence and conflict*. London: Routledge.

Schmidt, R.H. 2007. Complexities of urban coyote management: reaching the unreachable, teaching the unteachable, and touching the untouchable. In: D.L. Nolte, W.M. Arjo and D.H. Stalman (eds) *Proceedings of the 12th Wildlife Damage Management Conference*. Lincoln, University of Nebraska.

Schutz, A. 1967. *The phenomenology of the social world*. Evanston, IL: Northwestern University Press.

Scruton, R. 2006. *Sexual desire: a philosophical investigation*. London: Continuum.

Seeger, A. 1981. *Nature and society in central Brazil: the Suya Indians of Mato Grosso*. Cambridge, MA: Harvard University Press.

Serpell, J.A. 1987. Pet-keeping in non-Western societies: some popular misconceptions. *Anthrozoös: A Multidisciplinary Journal of the Interactions of People and Animals* 1(3): 166–174.

Serpell, J.A. 1989. Humans, animals, and the limits of friendship. In: R.A. Porter and S. Tomaselli (eds) *The dialectics of friendship*, pp. 111–129. London: Routledge.

Serpell, J.A. 1991. Beneficial effects of pet ownership on some aspects of human health and behaviour. *Journal of the Royal Society of Medicine* 84(12): 717–720.

Serpell, J.A. 1995. *The domestic dog: its evolution, behaviour, and interactions with people*. Cambridge: Cambridge University Press.

Serpell, J.A. 1996 [1986]. *In the company of animals*. Cambridge: Cambridge University Press.

Serpell, J.A. 1999a. Working out the beast: an alternative history of Western humaneness. In: F. Ascione and P. Arkow (eds) *Child abuse, domestic violence and animal abuse: linking the circles of compassion for prevention and intervention*, pp. 38–49. West Lafayette, IN: Purdue University Press.

Serpell, J.A. 1999b. Sheep in wolves' clothing? Attitudes to animals among farmers and scientists. In: F.L. Dolins (ed.) *Attitudes to animals: views in animal welfare*, pp. 26–33. Cambridge: Cambridge University Press.

Serpell, J.A. 2000. Creatures of the unconscious: companion animals as mediators. In: A.L. Podberscek, E.S. Paul and J.A. Serpell (eds) *Companion animals and us: exploring the relationships between people and pets*. Cambridge: Cambridge University Press.

Serpell, J.A. 2002a. Guardian spirits or demonic pets: the concept of the witch's familiar in early modern England, 1530–1712. In: A.N.H. Creager and W.C. Jordan (eds) *The animal/human boundary: historical perspectives*, pp. 157–190. Rochester: University of Rochester Press.

Serpell, J.A. 2002b. Anthropomorphism and anthropomorphic selection – beyond the 'cute response'. *Society & Animals* 10(4): 427–454.

Serpell, J.A. and Paul, E.S. 1994. Pets and the development of positive attitudes to animals. In: A. Manning and J.A. Serpell (eds) *Animals and human society: changing perspectives*, pp. 127–144. London: Routledge.

Servais, V. 2005. Enchanting dolphins: an analysis of human–dolphin encounters. In: J. Knight (ed.) *Animals in person: cultural perspectives on human–animal intimacy*, pp. 211–230. Oxford: Berg.

Shanklin, E. 1985. Sustenance and symbol: anthropological studies of domesticated animals. *Annual Review of Anthropology* 14: 375–403.

Shapiro, K. 1993. Editor's introduction. *Society & Animals* 1(1): 1.

Shelley, P.B. 2008. *Poems of Shelley*. London: Read Books.

Silva, K. and de Sousa, L. 2011. 'Canis empathicus'? A proposal on dogs' capacity to empathize with humans. *Biology Letters* [e-publication ahead of print].

Simoons, F.J. 1994. *Eat not this flesh: food avoidances from prehistory to the present*. London: Madison.

Singer, P. 1975. *Animal liberation*. New York: Avon.

Singer, P. 2001. Heavy petting – review of Midas Dekkers, *Dearest pet: on bestiality*. *Nerve*. Available at: http://www.nerve.com/opinions/singer/heavypetting/main.asp

Singer, P. 2006. *In defense of animals: the second wave*. Oxford: Blackwell.

Singer, R.S., Hart, L.A. and Zasloff, R.L. 1995. Dilemmas associated with rehousing homeless people who have companion animals. *Psychological Reports* 77(3): 851–885.

Smith, J.A. 2003. Beyond dominance and affection: living with rabbits in post-humanist households. *Society & Animals* 11(2): 181–197.

Smith, J.Z. 1972. I am a parrot (red). *History of Religions* 11(4): 391–413.

Smuts, B. 1985. *Sex and friendship in baboons*. New York: Aldine.

Sommer, V. and Vasey, P.E. 2006. *Homosexual behaviour in animals: evolutionary perspectives*. Cambridge: Cambridge University Press.

Sorenson, J. 2009. *Ape*. London: Reaktion.

Sperber, D. 1996. Why are perfect animals, hybrids, and monsters food for symbolic thought? *Method and Theory in the Study of Religion* 8(2): 143–169.

Sponsel, L.E. 1997. The human niche in Amazonia: explorations in ethnoprimatology. In: W. Kinzet (ed.) *New world primates: ecology, evolution and behavior*, pp. 143–165. New York: Aldine de Gruyter.

Sponsel, L. 2009. Reflections on the possibility of a non-killing society and a non-killing anthropology. In: P. Evans (ed.) *Toward a nonkilling paradigm.* Honolulu: Center for Global Nonkilling.

Stamp Dawkins, M. 1998. *Through our eyes only? The search for animal consciousness.* Oxford: Oxford University Press.

Steinen, K. v. d. 1894. *Unter den naturvölkern Zentral-Brasiliens. Reiseschilderung und ergebnisse der zweiten Schingú-expedition, 1887–1888.* Berlin: Hoefer & Vohsen.

Stern, N. 2007 [2006]. *The economics of climate change: the Stern Review.* Cambridge: Cambridge University Press.

Storr, A. 1991. *Human destructiveness: the roots of genocide and human cruelty.* London: Routledge.

Strang, V. 2000a. Not so black and white: the effects of Aboriginal law on Australian legislation. In A. Abramson and D. Theodossopoulos (eds) *Land, law and environment: mythical land, legal boundaries.* London: Pluto Press.

Strang, V. 2000b. Showing and telling: Australian land rights and material moralities. *Journal of Material Culture* 5(3): 275–299.

Strang, V. 2003. An appropriate question? The propriety of anthropological analysis in the Australian political arena. In: P. Caplan (ed.) *The ethics of anthropology: debates and dilemmas.* London: Routledge.

Strathern, A. and Strathern, M. 1971. *Self-decoration in Mount Hagen.* Toronto: University of Toronto Press.

Strum, S.C. 1994. Prospects for management of primate pests. *Revue Ecologie (Terre Vie)* 49: 295–306.

Strum S.C. and Mitchell W. 1987. Baboon models and muddles. In: *The evolution of human behavior: primate models*, edited by W.G. Kinzey, pp. 87–104. Albany: State University of New York Press.

Sutton, D.E. 1997. The vegetarian anthropologist. *Anthropology Today* 13(1): 5–7.

Sutton, D. E. 2001. *Remembrance of repasts: an anthropology of food and memory.* Oxford: Berg.

Suzuki, Y. 2007. Putting the lion out at night: domestication and the taming of the wild. In: R. Cassidy and M. Mullin (eds) *Where the wild things are now: domestication reconsidered*, pp. 229–248. New York: Berg.

Swabe, J. 2005. Loved to death? Veterinary visions of pet-keeping in modern Dutch society. In: J. Knight (ed.) *Animals in person: cultural perspectives on human–animal intimacy*, pp. 101–118. Oxford: Berg.

Sykes, G.. and Matza, D. 1957. Techniques of neutralization: a theory of delinquency. *American Sociological Review* 22(6): 664–670.

Tambiah, S.J. 1969. Animals are good to think and good to prohibit. *Ethnology* 8: 423–459.

Tanner, A. 1979. *Bringing home animals: religious ideology and mode of production of the Mistassini Cree hunters.* New York: St Martin's Press.

Tapper, R. 1994. Animality, humanity, morality, society. In: T. Ingold (ed.) *What is an animal?* pp. 47–62. London: Unwin Hyman.

Tarantino, Q. 1994. *Pulp fiction.* DVD. USA: Miramax.

Taussig, M.T. 1980. *The devil and commodity fetishism in South America*. Chapel Hill: University of North Carolina Press.

Taylor, J.J. 2007. Celebrating San victory too soon? Reflections on the outcome of the Central Kalahari Game Reserve case. *Anthropology Today* 23(5): 3–5.

Taylor, M. 2004. The past and future of San land rights in Botswana. In: R. Hitchcock and D. Vinding (eds) *Indigenous people's rights in Southern Africa*, pp. 152–165. IWGIA Document No. 110. Copenhagen.

Taylor, N. 2007. Never an it: intersubjectivity and the creation of personhood in an animal shelter. *Qualitative Sociology Review* 3(1): 59–73.

Taylor, N. 2010. Animal shelter emotion management: a case of in situ hegemonic resistance? *Sociology* 44(1): 85–101.

Theodossopoulos, D. 2005a. *Troubles with turtles: cultural understandings of the environment on a Greek island*. Oxford: Berghahn Books.

Theodossopoulos, D. 2005b. Care, order and usefulness: the context of the human–animal relationship in a Greek island community. In: J. Knight (ed.) *Animals in person: cultural perspectives on human–animal intimacy*, pp. 15–36. Oxford: Berg.

Thomas, K. 1983. *Man and the natural world*. London: Pantheon.

Thrift, N. 2003. Still life in nearly present time: the object of nature. In: P. Cloke (ed.) *Country visions*, pp. 308–331. Harlow: Pearson.

Thu, K.M. and Durrenberger, E.P. 1998. *Pigs, profits, and rural communities*. Albany: State University of New York Press.

Tilley, C.Y. 1994. *A phenomenology of landscape: places, paths, and monuments*. Oxford: Berg.

Torr, S.J., Mangwiro, T.N.C. and Hall, D.R. (2011) Shoo fly, don't bother me! Efficacy of traditional methods of protecting cattle from tsetse. *Medical and Veterinary Entomology* 25: 192–201.

Tuan, Y. 1984. *Dominance and affection: the making of pets*. London: Yale University Press.

Turnbull, C.M. 1965. *The Mbuti Pygmies: an ethnographic survey*. New York: American Museum of Natural History.

Turner, T. 1992. Defiant images: the Kayapo appropriation of video. *Anthropology Today* 8(6): 5–16.

Turner, V. 1977. Variations on a theme of liminality. In: S. Faulk Moore and B. Myerhoff (eds) *Secular ritual*, pp. 37–52. Amsterdam: Van Gorcum.

Tyler, S. 1969. *Cognitive anthropology*. London: Holt, Rinehart & Winston.

Tylor, E.B. 1968 [1871]. *Primitive culture*. London: Harper.

Ulijaszek, S.J. 2000. Nutrition, infection and child growth in Papua New Guinea. *Collegium Antropologicum* 24(2): 423–430.

Underwood, P. 1994. *Who speaks for wolf? A Native American learning story*. Austin, TX: Tribe of Two Press.

Vale de Almeida, M. 1997. Gender, masculinity and power in southern Portugal. *Social Anthropology* 5(2): 141–158.

van Dooren, T. (2010) Pain of extinction: the death of a vulture. *Cultural Studies Review* 16(2): 271–289.

van Lawick-Goodall, J. 1975. *In the shadow of man*. London: Fontana/Collins.

Vigo, R. and Allen, C. 2005. How to reason without words: inference as categorization. *Cognitive Processing* 10(1): 77–88.

Virányi, Z., Gácsi, M., Kubinyi, E., Topál, J., Belényi, B., Ujfalussy, D et al. 2008. Comprehension of human pointing gestures in young human-reared wolves (*Canis lupus*) and dogs (*Canis familiaris*). *Animal cognition* 11(3): 373–387.

Vitebsky, P. 2005. *Reindeer people: living with animals and spirits in Siberia*. London: HarperCollins.

Voltaire. 2010 [1764]. *Voltaire's philosophical dictionary*. Fairford: Echo Library.

Wait, C. and Buchanan-Smith, H. 2002. The effects of caretaker–primate relationships on primates in the laboratory. *Journal of Applied Animal Welfare Science* 5(4): 309–319.

Wallis, J. and Lee, D.R. 1999. Primate conservation: the prevention of disease transmission. *International Journal of Primatology* 20(6): 803–826.

Warner, M. 1994. *Managing monsters: six myths of our time*. London: Vintage.

Warrier, M. 2009. The temple bull controversy at Skanda Vale and the construction of Hindu identity in Britain. *International Journal of Hindu Studies* 13(3): 261–278.

Washabaugh, W. and Washabaugh, C. 2000. *Deep trout: angling in popular culture*. Oxford: Berg.

Weber, B. and Vedder, A. 2002. *In the kingdom of gorillas: the quest to save Rwanda's Mountain Gorilla*. London: Aurum Press.

Weiner, A.B. 1988. *The Trobrianders of Papua New Guinea*. New York: Holt, Rinehart & Winston.

Werbner, P. 2008. *Anthropology and the new cosmopolitanism: rooted, feminist and vernacular perspectives*. Oxford: Berg.

Western, D. 1984. Cultural materialism: food for thought or bum steer? *Current Anthropology* 25(5): 639–653.

Weston, K. 1993. Lesbian/gay studies in the house of anthropology. *Annual Review of Anthropology* 22: 339–367.

Whatmore, S. and Thorne, L. 1998. Wild(er)ness: reconfiguring the geographies of wildlife. *Transactions* 23(4): 435–454.

Whatmore, S. and Thorne, L. 2000. Elephants on the move: spatial formations of wildlife exchange. *Environment & Planning D* 18(2): 185–204.

Wheatley, B.P. 1999. *The sacred monkeys of Bali*. Prospect Heights, IL: Waveland Press.

White, T.I. 2007. *In defense of dolphins: the new moral frontier*. Oxford: Blackwell.

Whiten, A., Horner, V. and Marshall-Pescini, S. 2003. Cultural panthropology. *Evolutionary Anthropology* 12: 92–105.

Whiten, A., Goodall, J., McGrew, W., Nishida, T., Reynolds, V., Sugiyama, Y. et al. 1999. Chimpanzee cultures. *Nature* 399: 682–685.

Willerslev, R. 2007. *Soul hunters: hunting, animism, and personhood among the Siberian Yukaghirs*. Berkeley: University of California Press.

Willis, R. (ed.) 1994. *Signifying animals: human meaning in the natural world*. London: Unwin Hyman.

Wilson, P.J. 2007. Agriculture or architecture? The beginnings of domestication. In: R. Cassidy and M.H. Mullin (eds) *Where the wild things are now: domestication reconsidered*, pp. 101–122. Oxford: Berg.

Wittgenstein, L. 1958. *Philosophical investigations*. Oxford: Basil Blackwell.

Wolfe, C. 2003. *Zoontologies: the question of the animal*. Minneapolis: University of Minnesota Press.

Wolfe, C. 2009. *What is posthumanism?* Minneapolis: University of Minnesota Press.

Wolfe, L.D. and Fuentes, A. 2007. Ethnoprimatology: contextualizing human/ primate interactions. In: C. Campbell, A. Fuentes, K. MacKinnon, M. Panger and S. Bearder (eds) *Primates in perspective*, pp. 691–701. Oxford: Oxford University Press.

Woodburn, J. 1982. Egalitarian societies. *Man* 15: 431–451.

Woods, M. 1998. Researching rural conflicts: hunting, local politics and actor-networks. *Journal of Rural Studies* 14(3): 321–340.

Wrangham, R.W. 2000. A view on the science: physical anthropology at the millennium. *American Journal of Physical Anthropology* 111: 445–449.

Wrangham, R.W. and Peterson, D. 1996. *Demonic males: apes and the origins of human violence.* London: Bloomsbury.

Yates, R. 2009. Rituals of dominionism in human–nonhuman relations: bullfighting to hunting, circuses to petting. *Journal for Critical Animal Studies* 2(1): 132–171.

Yates, R., Powell, C. and Bierne, P. 2001. Horse maiming in the English countryside: moral panic, human deviance, and the social construction of victimhood. *Society & Animals* 9(1): 1–23.

Zingg, R.M. 1940. Feral man and extreme cases of isolation. *American Journal of Psychology* 53(4): 487–517.

Zuberbühler, K. 2000. Interspecies semantic communication in two forest primates. *Proceedings of the Royal Society, London B* 267(1444): 713–718.

Index

AAA (American Anthropological Association) 211
abattoirs 156
Abrahamic faiths 41, 45, 65, 88, 89, 93
Christianity 20–2, 70; Islam *see* Muslim; Judaism *see* Jews
Abu-Lughod, L. 29, 39
abuse 18, 191; human victims of 25, 160, 191, 198; nonhuman victims of 100, 172, 193, 197, 198, 199, 211; terms of abuse 9, 14, 199 *see also* cruelty, violence
actants, *see* ANT
Actor Network Theory, *see* ANT
Adamson, J & G. 129
adaptive behaviours 47, 143, 145, 146, 199–200, 204 *see also* maladaptive behaviours
adoption 120–1
advocacy 165, 166, 203, 211–14
aesthetics 99, 180, 194–5
affixation, *see* language
Africa 22, 23, 24, 43, 45, 93, 115, 140, 174
east Africa 114; north Africa 190; Southern Africa 42
agency
definition of 133; denial of 4, 12, 45, 58, 103, 116, 132, 133, 134, 141; human agency 88, 91, 132, 133; in nonhumans 46, 52, 53, 56, 57, 64–6, 132, 133, 141, 198 *see also* ANT, intentionality, personhood
aggression
in animals 102, 106, 144, 155; in humans 125, 195 *see also* animals, violence
agriculture, *see* farming
Agta (Philippines) 43
Ahearn, L. M. 133
alarm calls, *see* communication
Alger, J. M. and Alger, S. F. 120
alienation 59, 191, 202, 213, 217
of animals from the products of their labour 59, 109–10; as part of post-domesticity 67, 104, 105, 187

allopathic medicine 159, 160
see also medicine
altruism 188
Altzheimer's disease 155
'Amazonian multinaturalist framework' 214 *see also* Kohn, perspectivism, ontology
Amazonian peoples 50, 93, 105, 137, 158 *see also specific peoples* e.g. Runa
Amerindian perspectivism, *see* perspectivism; de Castro
America
Euro-America 2, 4, 17, 25, 46, 86, 103, 178; North America 30, 41, 85, 158, 160, 171, 193; USA 20, 33 *see also* Latin America, South America *plus specific countries* e.g. Brazil
ancient Hebrews 88
Andalusia 186 *see also* Spain
androcentricity 2
angling 173, 177 *see also* fishing, killing animals
Animal Assisted Therapy (AAT) 102, 160–1, 185, 219
animal behaviour 100, 115–20, 209 *see also* ethology
animal experimentation, *see* laboratory experimentation
animal mirror, the 3, 4, 142
animal rights 148, 165, 166, 188, 189, 190–1, 193, 196, 206
animal shelters 104, 120, 151
animal studies 5–6
animal turn, the 202, 203, 206, 213, 219
see also bringing in the animal
animal welfare 23, 109, 156, 159, 162, 167, 193, 198, 199, 213
animality 3, 12–26, 108, 160, 189, 202
and colonial expansion 20, 24; definition of 14; as justification of harm 21, 26
animals
as active subjects/social actors 53, 109, 114, 120, 125, 127, 154, 197, 198,

202, 203, 211; attacking humans 52, 79, 102, 106, 146, 170, 196, 205, 213; as children 8, 100, 149; classification of 202, 218 *see also* classification; as clothing/accessories 7, 64, 104; as cultural beings, *see* culture; definition of 3–4; as friends 15, 85, 100, 109, 110; in medicine/ medical research 7, 143, 151–63; negative views of 14, 58, 93, 126, 131, 146, 170, 183, 192, 195 *see also* conflict, scapegoats; as objects/ property/resources 18, 84, 89, 136, 152, 165, 166, 168, 172, 205 *see also* objectification; as persons, *see* personhood; as photographic subjects 80, 149, 172; as psychic 118; as quasi-human/equals 85, 86, 94, 107, 109, 125, 171; as sexual partners 189–201 *see also* bestiality, zoophilia; as symbols 66, 68, 90, 101, 104, 125, 126, 127, 161, 169, 170, 183–7 *see also* symbolic representations
animism 31, 32, 43–50, 71, 73, 75, 76, 93, 136, 137, 154, 181
ANT 132–4, 136
    and anthropology 131, 132
anthelmintic resistance 160
    see also parasites, zoopharmacognosy, zoonotic disease/parasites
Anthrax 205
Anthropocene, the 165
anthropocentricity 1–3, 63, 76, 122, 153, 154, 170, 196, 202, 203, 206, 215, 218
anthropogenic activity 63, 142, 145, 146, 165, 191, 198, 205, 213
    habitat destruction/loss 78, 80, 81, 142, 143, 148
anthropologists
    biases of 28–9, 70, 112, 122, 135, 149, 176, 180, 203, 204, 206, 214, 218; criticisms of 29, 95, 204, 210; as mediators 136, 213 *see also* advocacy; prioritising etic perspective 70, 76–7, 82; reluctance to consider animals 1, 25, 122, 132, 202, 203; well positioned to think about animals 6, 7, 10, 12, 25, 79, 103, 129, 135, 136, 144, 145, 149, 167

anthropology *see also* ethnographic fieldwork
    aims of 151, 209; applied anthropology 166; biological/ physical anthropology 1, 36, 60, 139, 143, 144, 157, 193; disciplinary identity 1–3, 4, 125, 126, 139, 143, 202, 203, 207; focus on culture 27–8, 29, 39, 112, 122, 202, 206, 215, 218; as handmaiden of colonialism 25; as practice of theory 126, 128, 203; prioritising primates 1, 36–7, 139, 149; social anthropology 2, 70, 139, 143, 144, 145
'anthropology of life' 214 *see also* Kohn
Anthropology Today (journal) 207
anthropomorphism 76, 80, 85, 108, 109, 113, 117, 129, 130, 134, 144, 152–4, 159, 170, 171, 198, 210
anthropophagy, *see* cannibalism
anthropozoometricity 117, 122, 123, 166, 195, 206, 218
anthrozoology 4, 6, 7, 10, 123, 139, 143, 204
anti-inflammatory drugs 205
anti-vivisection 191 *see also* animal rights
Appadurai, A. 211
appeasement of animals/spirits, *see* propitiation
Aquinas, T. 18
Arab world, the 190
archaeological evidence
    for chimpanzee tool use 140; for domestication 56, 57, 61, 62, 64, 88; open to debate 56, 178–9; and human evolution 96, 113, 179
Arens, W. 199
Arhuacos (Colombia) 212
Aristotle 16–18, 20, 27, 38
    History of Animals 17; and natural slavery 17–18, 192; Nicomachean Ethics 109; The Politics 18
armchair anthropology/anthropologists 3, 75
art *see also* aesthetics; representations
    animals as art 103; cave paintings 61; art produced by animals 34
ASA (Association of Social Anthropologists of the UK and Commonwealth) 211